Prisoners from Nambu

Prisoners from Nambu

Reality and Make-Believe in Seventeenth-Century Japanese Diplomacy

Reinier H. Hesselink

University of Hawai'i Press
Honolulu

©2002 University of Hawai'i Press
All rights reserved
Printed in the United States of America
07 06 05   6 5 4 3 2

Library of Congress Cataloging-in-Publication Data

Hesselink, R. H.
  Prisoners from Nambu : reality and make-believe in 17th-century Japanese
diplomacy / Reinier H. Hesselink.
     p.   cm.
  ISBN 0-8248-2409-1 (cloth : alk. paper) —
  ISBN 0-8248-2463-6 (pbk. : alk. paper)
  1. Japan—Foreign relations—1600–1868. 2. East Asia—Foreign relations.
3. Japan—Foreign relations—Netherlands. 4. Netherlands—Foreign relations
—Japan. 5. Dutch—Japan—Nanbu-han. 6. Prisoners—Japan—Nanbu-han.
7. Nanbu-han (Japan)—History. I. Title.

DS871.7 .H47 2001
952'.1—dc21   2001023840

Designed by Cindy E. K. C. Chun

Printed by The Maple-Vail Manufacturing Group

To Madeleine and Saskia

Contents

Acknowledgments

It has taken twelve years from the time I conceived this project to execute it and see the results of my research into print. During this time I have incurred numerous debts that I will never be able to repay. Larry Rogers was instrumental in getting me back into Graduate School. I received financial assistance from the University of Hawai'i's history department in the form of a teaching assistant position and the John F. Kennedy Memorial Fellowship, administered by the department, for dissertation research. I received additional funding from the Japan Foundation (1991–1992), the Japan Society for the Promotion of Science (1993, 1994, 1999), Japan Airlines (1995, 1996, 1997), the Graduate Division of the University of Northern Iowa (1996), the Study Group Japanese-Dutch Relations (1996), the Kashima Foundation (1997), and the Heiwa Nakajima Foundation (2000).

I spent the summer of 1991 conducting research in Holland, where I was helped by Arend and Luz Hesselink-Lopez Ortega, Sebastiaan and Loes Hesselink-Raeven, Sander Hesselink, Trix van Hoof, and Ineke Sandbrink. In Japan, I studied for many years at the Historiographical Institute of the University of Tokyo, with the support of Asami Masakazu, Gonoi Takashi, Katō Ei'ichi, Kurokawa Noriko, Matsui Yōko, Miyachi Masato, and many others. In Yamada, Iwate Prefecture, I was helped by Kawabata Hiroyuki, Kimura Teirō, Kinoshita Zenzaburō, Barak Kushner, Satō Hitoshi, Satō Kōsaku, Shimizu Seishō and Noriko, and many others. In Morioka I depended on Nambu Toshiaki, Ōshima Kō'ichi, and Takahashi Kiyoaki.

The first to read and comment on this manuscript in the form of the dissertation, "The Prisoners from Nambu: The Breskens Affair in Historical and Historiographical Perspective" (University of Hawai'i at Mānoa, 1992), were my adviser, Prof. V. Dixon Morris, and the members of my committee: John Stephan, Brian McKnight, Michael Speidel, and Arthur Thornhill. Later versions of the manuscript were read and commented on by Jerry Bentley, Marius Jansen, Idus Newby, Herman Ooms, Burchard Pennink, Willem Remmelink, Kenneth Robinson, Isabel Tanaka-van Daalen, Geoffrey Tudor, and Paul Varley. At the University of Northern Iowa I want to thank my colleagues in the history department, especially Louis E. Fenech and his wife Christine, Chuck Holcombe, John Johnson, and Charlotte Wells, for their efforts on my behalf. Two anonymous readers for the University of Hawai'i Press also provided valuable suggestions.

A Note on Titles and Names

TITLES

On numerous occasions I have quoted directly from Dutch and Japanese sources. In the Dutch texts, the shogun is referred to as Japan's "emperor" *(keizer)*. This was not, as is often thought, because the Dutch were ignorant of the existence of the demi-god living in Kyoto (he is called *"dairi"* in the Dutch sources), but because they were translating from the Portuguese used by the interpreters. The latter used the term *"imperador"* (lit., "he who commands"), which accurately conveys the shogun's function in Japan. I have not changed this usage in my direct quotations, but refer in the main text only to the shogun.

Similarly I have distinguished between castles and the Castle in Japan. The latter designation (with a capital C) always refers to the shogun's abode, Chiyoda Castle in the center of Edo.

Japanese sources refer to the Dutch *opperhoofd* (chief factor) by the word *"kapitan,"* also derived from Portuguese. To preserve some of this flavor I have retained this spelling in my translations of Japanese sources, and even substituted this word in some of the translations of Dutch sources whenever I came upon a direct address by a Japanese official to the chief factor.

NAMES

As with the spelling of all words, names were not standardized in the seventeenth-century Dutch sources. Often, we find the record keepers of the Dutch East India Company using idiosyncratic spellings for their own names. For example, whereas we find the surname Bijlevelt in the Alkmaar Municipal Archive, the Junior Merchant of that name signed himself always as Wilhem Bijlvelt. Governor General Anthonie Van Diemen "iberialized" his given name to Antonio, as did the merchant Anthonie Van Brouckhorst. I have chosen to unify the spelling of all the Dutch names taking the person's autograph signature as my standard.

Introduction
The Prisoners from Nambu

On 29 July 1643, ten crew members of the Dutch yacht *Breskens* were lured ashore in Nambu, a domain in northern Japan, by an equal number of attractive Japanese women. The day before, during a voyage of discovery to Northeast Asia, their ship had anchored in an idyllic bay where the crew had also made a landfall a month and a half earlier. This time, however, as soon as the Dutchmen had been led out of sight of their ship, they were surrounded by a crowd of men from the neighborhood. Trussed up, they were then brought to Morioka, the castle town of the domain. There they waited until police officers came from Edo to take them to the shogun's capital, where they were interrogated for four months before finally being released on 8 December 1643.

Prisoners from Nambu is the story of what these men experienced and saw in Japan. Narrative history has many advantages that, because of neglect of the genre in recent times, have remained unexplored so far in Japanese history. Through its narrow focus, it can evoke in the reader a feeling for the reality of the past such as analytical history rarely achieves. This account aims to give the reader an idea of what it felt like to be an ordinary Westerner suddenly forced to participate in the world of the samurai. It is a story of cross-cultural contact, in which, for a change, Westerners were not in control, but at the mercy of Japanese warriors.

During their detention, the prisoners were in a position to make firsthand observations of the internal structure of the Japanese government and its decision-making process concerning such matters as the eradication of Christianity. In particular, the Dutchmen were confronted on several occasions with four Jesuit priests who had tried to come ashore by stealth in Kyushu, only one month before the men from the *Breskens* had been arrested. Their observations document the brainwashing process, recently perfected in Japan, by which the Jesuits were forced to apostatize and become allies of the Japanese government in its battle against Christianity.

In the end, the Dutchmen were able to convince the Japanese authorities that they had nothing to do with such matters as bringing Roman Catholic priests ashore. However, the clearer it became that the Dutchmen had been arrested by mistake, the more imperative it became for the Japanese government to find a suitable excuse for having detained its own allies. When the representative of the Dutch East India Company residing in Nagasaki came to Edo to obtain the release of the Dutch prisoners he was forced to accept a description of them as shipwrecked sailors saved by the Japanese.

This version of events created tension and difficulties for the Dutch trade with Japan in the subsequent years. For if the shogun had "saved" the lives of ten Dutchmen, he should be thanked for such magnanimity in an appropriate manner. In the eyes of the shogun himself, no manner would be more appropriate than having an official embassy from Holland prostrating themselves in gratitude at his feet. In Dutch eyes, however, this would be turning the world upside down. As the years went by, however, shogunal officials in both Nagasaki and Edo made it clear that the Dutch trade in Japan would come to a halt if such an embassy did not materialize.

The solution was found in the time-honored East Asian manner of sending a bogus ambassador. In 1649, to appease the Japanese shogun by thanking him for the release of the prisoners from Nambu, a splendid Dutch embassy was prepared, ostensibly coming from Amsterdam, but in reality put together on Java. A Dutch schoolmaster, recently arrived in Batavia from Holland, was made ambassador to Japan, although he was sick to the point of dying. This was, of course, exactly why he was the appropriate man. For if he died at sea before arriving in Japan, it would be impossible for the Japanese to investigate who had sent him.

Everything happened as foreseen. The ambassador died and was duly mummified at sea, so the fact of his existence could be verified by the Japanese officials on the arrival of the ship carrying the embassy. Of course, nobody in Japan was fooled, least of all the Japanese officials in Nagasaki and Edo. However, without clear evidence of duplicity, these same officials, having insisted for six years that the Dutch should send an embassy, were now hard put to refuse to receive this one, even though the ambassador was dead and obviously fake. In the end, just as the organizers of the embassy in Batavia had hoped, the Dutch were allowed to perform their charade and the Dutch trade with Japan was preserved.

By recreating, through the story of Dutch prisoners, a slice of the life and times of the power holders in Japan during the 1640s, we are able to see close up who the men were who had just issued, in the 1630s, the series of regulations that came to be known as the "seclusion laws" *(sakokurei)*. The story allows us to view the politics and diplomacy of the time in a fresh, new light. The incident and its aftermath reveal how the Japanese saw themselves and provide insight into the motives that drove Japanese diplomacy at the time. Through this narrative, finally, we will be able to scrutinize some of the notions about the concept of *sakoku,* or seclusion, that have become fashionable in recent years and assert that we should abandon the notion that Japan was isolated during the early modern era.

JAPAN AND THE IDEOLOGY OF THE CHINESE CENTER

International relations between the countries of East Asia in the seventeenth century were still dominated by the ideology of the Chinese center,[1] which had influenced the area since the Han dynasty (beginning in 206 BCE). According to this ideology, international relations were personal relations between the rulers of East Asia, rather than relations between the states themselves. Such personal relations were always hierarchical and centered on the emperor of China.

The Chinese emperor, in this context, was known as the Son of Heaven, who had been granted a Heavenly Mandate to rule the world because of his Great Virtue. He was held to be responsible for the balance between Heaven and Earth. Although according to the Chinese ideal he was in reality destined to rule All under Heaven, in practice he only ruled the center of the surface of the earth, the Middle Kingdom, a term the Chinese still use to indicate China. All rulers who were allowed to have diplomatic relations with the Chinese emperor had to consent in principle to behave as his vassals.

What is more, the Chinese intellectuals who pondered these problems categorized foreign rulers as either civilized or uncivilized. Civilized rulers included only those who recognized the Great Virtue of the Chinese emperor and his right to be the center of the world. They brought him tribute in the form of products from their native land to demonstrate their subservience. In exchange, they received counter-gifts, court titles, and sometimes a counter-embassy, which would confirm the foreign ruler in his status as a vassal of the Chinese emperor and constitute proof of his participation in Chinese civilization. Although there were exceptions, in principle trade relations were only permitted within the framework of this lord-vassal relationship and the concomitant recognition of China's centrality and superiority.

This Chinese ideology was, of course, advantageous and flattering to China, and as time went on, other Asian countries adopted similar strategies, replacing the Chinese emperor and his court with their own rulers and their courts. The ideology of the Chinese center, furthermore, was so closely interrelated with the Chinese writing system that, for the areas that had adopted this system (Vietnam, Manchuria, Korea, and Japan), there really seemed to be no other way to theorize about international relations.

The emergence of "world centers" other than China brought forth all kinds of contradictions. In the first place, China itself was far from able to constantly prove military superiority over its border areas, so the Chinese emperor (or at least the bureaucrats charged with his diplomacy) often had to mitigate his demands on powerful neighbors. In the second place, the competition between the different centers of the world encouraged such phenomena as envoys "losing" their letters of accreditation, emissaries carrying forged documents, and from time to time even fake ambassadors being sent out to preserve existing trade relations or to try and create new ones.

Japan had been engaged in the adoption of the accomplishments of Chinese culture and civilization since well before the seventh century. From the beginning of this cultural transmission, however, Japanese rulers had consciously tried to downplay the idea of China as the political center of the world. Was the Japanese imperial family not descended from the Sun Goddess Amaterasu herself? And had the first earthly ancestor of this family not come straight down from Heaven in order to rule the Japanese islands?

In China, possession of the Heavenly Mandate explained the rise and fall of the different dynasties of Chinese history. But in Japan, with her own ideology of an uninterrupted imperial line, this idea of the Heavenly Mandate was superfluous. In the eyes of Japanese intellectuals the durability of the native dynasty proved its superiority over the chaotic succession of dynasties that characterized Chinese history.

Even during Japan's medieval civil wars, which began in 1467 and lasted for more than a century, the idea of the divine descent of the Japanese imperial family continued to dominate power struggles among generals in the field. The Japanese emperor might have lost most of his political and economic power during this period, but he remained the only source of political legitimacy recognized throughout Japan.

When Japan's military and political unity was restored during the second half of the sixteenth century, the country's new military leaders again began to cherish ambitions of creating a Japanese Center of the World that could compete with (and ultimately outdo and replace) the eternal Chinese center. The first of the two generals to reestablish Japan's unity, Oda Nobunaga (1534–1582), for example, used the term *"tenka"*—the Japanese pronunciation of the Chinese characters for "All under Heaven" *(tianxia)*—for his domain on Honshu, which during his lifetime he steadily enlarged. By the use of this term, he clearly indicated his desire to conquer all of Japan and possibly even more territories beyond.

In 1591 the second general, Nobunaga's vassal and successor Toyotomi Hideyoshi (1537–1598), finally accomplished the goal of his murdered lord by subjugating all daimyo (military leaders) of Japan. During the process of political unification through military force and the astute use of argument, an important factor was Hideyoshi's plan to organize, after the unification of Japan, a grand campaign through Asia. The aim of this campaign was to realize the dream of every proud Japanese warrior: to replace China as the center of the world by conquering and occupying Beijing.

Hideyoshi sent two large expeditions to Korea in 1592 and 1597. Although neither succeeded in crossing the border of Korea and Manchuria, these were by far the largest military expeditions the Japanese had ever undertaken abroad. The grandiose scale of Hideyoshi's failure remained an important fact in Japanese foreign policy until the first half of the twentieth century. His legacy to the military rulers that followed him was an unfulfilled dream.

THE EUROPEANS IN ASIA

The arrival in Asia of the Portuguese, and later the Spanish, the English, and the Dutch, added a completely different element to inter-Asian relationships. The superiority of European ships at sea introduced, for the first time, the idea of the ocean as an avenue of regular communication with the peoples of Asia. Previously, in Japan for example, the ocean had always been considered a wall between the Here and the Hereafter. In the interior of India, Southeast Asia, China, and Japan, the old traditions remained intact for the moment, but along the coasts, things started to change.[2]

The Portuguese were the first to begin building trading posts in Africa, Arabia, Persia, India, Malaysia, Java, the Moluccas, and later even in China and Japan. These settlements or factories were of course dependent on the goodwill of the local rulers, but the Portuguese freedom to act tended to grow in direct proportion to the weakness of central authority in the area where a factory was located. In China, where the Portuguese reputation of being slave traders and robbers had preceded them, they were at first not welcome and were forced to trade with Chinese traders on the open sea.

In the course of such trade, in 1542, three Portuguese merchants who had boarded a Chinese junk were separated from their own ship by a bad storm off the Chinese coast; they and the junk were blown all the way to Japan. The treatment accorded to them there and the Japanese interest in the firearms they had brought differed so greatly from their experience with the Chinese thus far that Japan soon acquired among European traders the reputation of being a sort of Eldorado, a land of untold possibilities.

The enduring civil war had provided a great stimulus for the Japanese mining industry and the extraction of metals. As a result, when the Portuguese arrived Japan possessed a large surplus of silver. For that reason the price of silver in Japan was much lower than in China. In addition, the Portuguese traders soon understood that Chinese silk was in great demand in Japan. Because of the damage Japanese pirates had inflicted on the Chinese coast over many years, the relationship between China and Japan was at a very low point, and the Chinese emperor had proscribed all contact between his subjects and the Japanese. And as long as Japan refused to send tribute to China, this was not likely to change.

This meant a great opportunity for the Portuguese, who could now present themselves as middlemen between Chinese traders with silk for sale and an unquenchable thirst for Japanese silver, and Japanese traders with a clientele of big lords who all wanted to be supplied with Chinese silk and were prepared to pay in silver cash. Given the invulnerability of Portuguese galleons in Asian waters (because of their superior artillery and solid build), the Portuguese represented a good investment for both the Chinese and the Japanese.[3]

The situation provided the Portuguese with respectability in China and the cash to build a large settlement on the South China coast. Some assistance they rendered the Chinese emperor in suppressing piracy along the coast at last gave him sufficient grounds to overlook the restrictions on trading with the Portuguese that had been issued earlier and to give them permission, from 1555 onwards, to start a settlement at Macao. This settlement grew and flourished as the silk trade between China and Japan continued in Portuguese vessels. And as it happened, the Portuguese traders soon came to be accompanied by Jesuit missionaries.

The Spanish came to Asia via Mexico, for in 1494 with the Treaty of Tordesillas, the Pope had accorded to the Spanish crown the right to colonize the Western hemisphere. They founded their first settlements in the Philippines and visited Japan from there. The Spanish did not present a direct threat to the Portuguese trade with Japan. That came only with the arrival in the area of the Dutch, who in 1600 first landed in Japan in the ship *Liefde* (Charity). The *Liefde*'s first mate was an Englishman by the name of Will Adams, and out of the whole crew he was chosen by the leading general of Japan of the time, Tokugawa Ieyasu, to become his adviser on European matters. Inevitably, both the Dutch and the English would try to force the Portuguese from Japan.[4]

From the beginning of the seventeenth century, therefore, the Asian seas became the battlefield of a growing competition between the Portuguese and the Dutch, and to a lesser extent, the Spanish and English. Of all these European nations, only the Dutch, at first, profited from a new capitalist system. The Dutch traders could expand their trade by drawing on voluntary contributions from the population of the Low Countries in the form of private investment in the different trading companies that were fanning out all over the known and into the unknown world at the time. In 1602, the companies that had been trading in Asia were consolidated into one large company, which was called the Vereenigde Oost-Indische Compagnie

(VOC), or Dutch East India Company.[5] This company held a monopoly on Dutch investments in Asia for almost two hundred years. The Portuguese, the Spanish and the English crowns, with their more limited income from taxes and their larger domestic responsibilities, were at first hard pressed to compete with it.

As a result of these conditions the Dutch trading fleet expanded on an enormous scale, and it eventually succeeded in pushing most of the Portuguese out of Asia, first from the Moluccas and Java, but later also from Ceylon, India, Malaysia, Southeast Asia, and Japan. In Japan the competition between the Portuguese and the Dutch lasted exactly thirty years: from 1609 when the first Dutch factory was established until 1639 when the Portuguese were finally forbidden to come and trade in Japan any longer.

THE TOKUGAWA BAKUFU

In 1600, two years after the death of Toyotomi Hideyoshi, who had not succeeded in establishing a firm foundation for the continuation of his dynasty, centripetal forces in Japan were realigned, once more, on the battlefield. The battle of Sekigahara pitted the new men of Hideyoshi's fledgling bureaucracy, in league with the lords of western Japan, against Tokugawa Ieyasu and the forces of the warrior clans of eastern Japan. The battle was won conclusively by the eastern side and the alignment of forces later served as a blueprint for the power structure imposed on Japan by Ieyasu.

Hideyoshi's federal organization of the country into domains, a legacy of the civil war of the previous centuries, was left intact.[6] The victorious eastern army ended up as the uncontested rulers of Japan, with Ieyasu alone holding as much as 25 percent of the productive acreage of the country. The five main cities of Japan (Kyoto, Edo, Osaka, Sakai, and Nagasaki) as well as the country's richest mines also became part of the Tokugawa domain, monopolizing in this manner Japan's distribution system, its money markets, and much of its manufacturing capacity.[7]

The officer corps of Ieyasu's personal army at Sekigahara was largely enfeoffed with smallish fiefs located in strategic places around the country, ranging between 10,000 and 100,000 *koku* (a unit for measuring rice, equivalent to about 5 bushels). These officers were known as the *fudai daimyo,* the most trusted of all vassals and the only ones eligible for the high positions in the Tokugawa central bureaucracy, or bakufu.⁸ A cordon of *fudai daimyō* fiefs protected the city of Edo, which had grown up around Ieyasu's Castle and housed the bakufu. Ieyasu's soldiers, or *hatamoto,* who fought the battle of Sekigahara, became the administrators of the countryside of the Tokugawa domain itself with salaries up to 5,000 *koku.*

Family members of the Tokugawa, or *shinpan daimyō,* were given bigger fiefs up to 500,000 *koku.* These, too, were located in strategic places. The houses of Ki and Owari dominated the Tōkaidō road, the central artery between eastern and western Japan, and so served as buffers against a possible resurgence of the western coalition. The house of Mito protected the shogunal capital of Edo from a possible attack from the north. These three houses were known as the *gosanke,* the main houses among the *shinpan daimyō.* Although well provided for in the material sense, for reasons of dynastic stability, none of the *shinpan daimyo* were eligible for government office.

Most numerous and varied among the domainal lords, however, were the outer lords, or *tozama daimyō.* Their income ranged between 10,000 and 1,000,000 *koku,* and their domains tended to be located on the periphery of Japan. Originally, the *tozama daimyō* were defined as the allies of the Tokugawa at Sekigahara, such as, for example, the generals of the eastern domains who had joined Ieyasu's side. However, those on the western side who had turned coat and joined Ieyasu during the battle, or even those lords who had simply refrained from entering the fray, were also allowed to retain their domains after the battle and were reenfeoffed as *tozama daimyō.*

It was the *tozama* who were most feared by the Tokugawa as competitors for power. Swearing an oath of allegiance to the Tokugawa and furnishing their Tokugawa liege lord with military assistance were the basis of an uneasy relationship. Hideyoshi had previously required vanquished daimyo to build residences next to his castle, where principal wife and heir of each daimyo lived as the ruler's hostages. The hostage system now became a central pillar of the Tokugawa structure and eventually all daimyo kept main residences *(kami yashiki)* around the Tokugawa Castle in central Edo.

In 1635, it became the general rule for daimyo to spend every other year in the shogun's capital. This involved much back and forth travel throughout Japan, for a daimyo needed to travel with a retinue indicative of the size of his domain. The necessary financial outlay provided economic stimuli for the regions along the country's highways and kept the daimyo from accumulating treasure that could otherwise have been turned into funds for resisting the Tokugawa. This system became known as *sankin kōtai,* or alternate attendance. It assured that about half the daimyo would be in the shogun's capital at any one time to perform a biweekly attendance at the shogun's court.

The daily governance of the country was in the hands of the shogun and his *fudai* advisers, who as time went on came to have specific duties on the various committees and subdivisions of the bakufu. The most important of these advisory councils was the *rōjū,* or senior councilors in charge of relations with the imperial house and the nobility of Kyoto, the *tozama daimyō,* and foreign policy in short, with the minor centers of power encompassed within the larger center represented by the Tokugawa. Two important members of the *rōjū* council were the most senior retainer *(tairō),* and the elderman *(toshiyori),* whose voices would be the most likely to reach the ear of the shogun.

MEASURES AGAINST CHRISTIANITY

In the 1630s the shogun and his advisers adopted a number of measures that resulted in the diplomatic isolation of the country from China, Southeast Asia, and Europe for a period that lasted, roughly, from 1639 to 1854. This period is known as *sakoku* (closed country).[9] It is not correct to assume that it was the intention of the Japanese authorities to close their country off from the outside world. Rather they wanted complete control over the diplomatic relations of their recently reunited island empire in order to create a Japanese center on the Chinese model.

The most important factor in the decisions that led to the break with all European nations (except the Dutch Republic) was the experience of the Japanese authorities with the activities of the southern European Roman Catholic missionaries in Japan. Following in the wake of the Portuguese expansion in Asia and in tandem with the christianizing of the New World (the Caribbean, Mexico, Peru, and Brazil), the target of the missionaries was soon enlarged to include the Asian side of the globe. From the second half of the sixteenth century, the intrepid missionaries of the new Jesuit order were already coming to Japan on a regular basis.[10]

This was precisely the moment that the civil war in Japan was at its height. Almost forty years later, as soon as Hideyoshi reunited the islands, he issued orders to the Roman Catholic missionaries to leave the country. Persecutions of Christians, however, only began in earnest after the Dutch (in 1609) and the English (between 1613 and 1623) had provided Tokugawa Ieyasu, the new ruler of Japan, with a Protestant alternative to trading with the Portuguese and the Spanish.

It was the existence of a Roman Catholic "center of the world" in Rome that worried the Japanese military leaders. They feared that Japanese Christians could become untrustworthy subjects, a sort of fifth column, following moral precepts controlled by foreign lords. As soon as Ieyasu had suppressed all internal resistance against his regime with the conquest of the fortress Osaka in 1615, Japanese Christians were persecuted with ever increasing intensity. The third Tokugawa shogun, prominent in this book as Tokugawa Iemitsu (1604–1651), became so immersed in what he considered his war on Christianity that he did not hesitate to participate personally in the brainwashing of arrested Jesuits.

After his death, in 1616, Ieyasu had already been deified as the "Light Shining in the East" *(tōshō)*.[11] This deification was at once a declaration of war against Christianity, a challenge to the idea of the Chinese center, and a reference to the age-old Japanese tradition of sun worship—all of these concentrated in the founder of the Tokugawa dynasty.

It was obviously no coincidence that the measures taken by Iemitsu to rebuild and enlarge Ieyasu's shrine at Nikkō coincided with the orders meant to eradicate Christianity in Japan, which later became the foundation for Japan's policy of isolation. On 6 April 1633, the military authorities or bakufu issued a list of seventeen articles, which prohibited foreign travel by Japanese nationals on ships that did not have special permission from the authorities in Edo for that purpose. Japanese who had lived abroad for some time were forbidden to return to Japan. The same list of articles reiterated the prohibitions against Christianity and refined the rules that foreign ships had to obey while they were in Japan.[12]

These seventeen articles were promulgated once more on 23 June 1634. At the same time, three new articles were added, forbidding foreign missionaries from coming ashore in Japan, Japanese traders from exporting weapons from Japan, and all other Japanese from leaving Japan for any reason. The next year, on 12 July 1635, these orders were tightened once more. This time, all Japanese ships (even those that had previously obtained permission to trade overseas) were prohibited from leaving the country.

One year later, on 22 July 1636, the bakufu sent a list of nineteen new articles to the governors of Nagasaki. These raised the rewards for denouncing Japanese Christians, expelled from Japan the children of mixed marriages, and tightened the prohibition against contact with overseas family members. Even correspondence with such family members was no longer allowed.

THE DUTCH IN JAPAN

At the same time that the Portuguese were bringing their last silk cargoes to Japan, the Dutch were trying to convince the Japanese authorities that they did not need to depend on the Portuguese for their foreign trade. The Portuguese were used to selling their cargo every year all at once, for prices they had agreed on with the merchants of the Japanese silk guild, the so-called *pancado* prices. As a first step in the process of replacing the Portuguese, the Dutch now had to agree that the silk they brought to Japan would be sold under the same conditions the Portuguese had been used to.

In May of 1636, the Portuguese residents in Japan were interned on Deshima. This was a fan-shaped, artificial island that had just been built in the bay of Nagasaki, on Japan's southern island of Kyushu. It was only connected with the city by a bridge and was intended to separate the Roman Catholic Portuguese from the citizens of Nagasaki. The following year, in nearby Shimabara, a revolt broke out in which a large number of Christians participated. The bakufu held the Portuguese co-responsible for this insurrection, and because of this eventually decided to prohibit them from coming to Japan.

In March of 1638, after the suppression of the insurrection (during which the Dutch had been asked to put their artillery at the service of the bakufu),[13] the Dutch chief factor was asked during his visit to the Edo that year if he could supply Japan with the same textiles as the Portuguese had always brought to Japan. One year later, the Huguenot François Caron, Dutch chief factor, convinced the supreme ruling council or *rōjū* of Japan that, at sea, the Dutch had nothing to fear from the Portuguese. With the help of charts brought along especially for that purpose, Caron elucidated the extent of the Dutch power in Asia and guaranteed the Japanese authorities that the Dutch would be ready to supply the Japanese with everything they needed. Happily, he was able to point out that during the previous trading season of 1638, the volume of the wares brought to Japan by the Dutch had finally exceeded that of the Portuguese.

Eventually, on 9 August 1639, a new series of orders was issued. The main difference was that the preceding four had been the shogun's direct orders to the governors of Nagasaki. This time, however, the orders were read to all the daimyo in Edo at that moment. The domainal lords were ordered to organize a security system with outlook posts all along the Japanese coastline, so that the bakufu might be informed as soon as possible about the arrival of any foreign ships. A direct representative of the shogun left immediately for Nagasaki to announce to the Portuguese their expulsion in person.

That the shogun was serious, he proved the following year when an unarmed Portuguese delegation from Macao visited Japan once more to beg for a revision of the expulsion order. Iemitsu sent two personal aids to Nagasaki, who had 61 men of the delegation decapitated for transgressing against his expulsion order of the previous year.[14] The same autumn the Dutch factory at Hirado received a visit of the ōmetsuke (chief spy) Inoue Masashige, who in the name of the shogun ordered the immediate destruction of all the buildings of the Dutch factory.

Inoue's words are quoted in the factory diary or *Daghregister:*

His Imperial Majesty had heard that all of you are Christians, just like the Portuguese. You honor the Sunday, you write the date of Jesus' birth on the facades of the houses you build, visible for everyone in the country. You keep the Ten Commandments, and you pray the Lord's prayer, you believe in baptism, the sharing of bread, the Bible, the testament, Moses, the prophets, and the apostles. . . . The differences between your religion and that of the Portuguese we hold to be very small. We have long known that you were Christians as well, but we thought another Christ was meant.

For these reasons, His Majesty has ordered me to instruct you to take down all the buildings (without exception) with the [offending] date. . . . We will not allow that you publicly observe the Sunday, so that the name of that holiday may be forgotten here.* From now on, the kapitan [chief factor] will not be allowed to reside in Japan for longer than one year and will have to be replaced every year.[15]

---

*Ironically, the Dutch word *"zondag"* survives today in the Nagasaki dialect as *"dontaku"* (holiday).

Even if he regretted tearing down the expensive warehouses and other buildings of the factory at Hirado, Caron did not hesitate, for he understood that permission for the Dutch to keep on coming to Japan depended on his decision of that moment. All the buildings, therefore, were destroyed, one after the other, and the next year Caron himself left Japan after a sojourn of twenty years. The new Dutch factor was told, during his visit to the court that year, that from now on the Dutch were to bring their trade to Nagasaki. The little island of Deshima, which had been empty since the departure of the Portuguese, would serve as their place of residence.

A JAPANESE CENTER OF THE WORLD

The Japanese military government allowed Chinese and Southeast Asian traders to come and trade in Nagasaki, but in contrast with the Dutch the merchants from these nations could never obtain permission to visit Edo for an audience with the shogun. From the beginning of the seventeenth century, there were therefore only two Asian countries that sent "official" embassies to Japan: Korea and Ryukyu. The relationship of Japan with Korea was a delicate one, for the King of the Land of the Early Morning Calm was traditionally a vassal of the Chinese emperor. The weakness of the present Ming dynasty, however, predisposed the Korean court to forget about Hideyoshi's invasions, and under Ieyasu the relationship with Japan was normalized on the basis of falsified documents.[16]

The falsifiers were the Sō family and their retainers, residents of the island fief of Tsushima, situated in the straits between Japan and Korea. Already during the Japanese civil wars, the daimyo of these islands had been recognized by the Korean court as the sole possible intermediary for its contacts with the different military leaders of Japan. It was the prerogative of the Sō to issue passports for visits to Korea, and for this reason the Sō were able to change the credentials of both sides in such a manner that the Korean king did not have to betray his Chinese liege lord, while the Japanese shogun was not disturbed by expressions in the documents referring to China's centrality.

The very learned gentlemen bureaucrats of the Korean court were still deadly afraid of a repetition of the massive invasion attempts by Japan during the last decade of the sixteenth century. Therefore, everyone (including the King) was prepared to send embassies to Japan every time the etiquette of East Asian diplomacy required a vassal to do so. In this way, they could at least be sure that those proud and violent neighbors of theirs would not suddenly threaten their door-step again. Their Japanese counterparts in the bakufu, in their turn, had "proof" that Korea was a tributary nation of Japan.

The position of the Ryukyu Islands was, if possible, even stranger. This island chain had been conquered in 1609 by soldiers of the southern Kyushu fief of Satsuma. The economy of the archipelago, however, was completely dependent on trade with China. Because of the lack of diplomatic relations between China and Japan, it would have been impossible to continue this trade if its conquest by Japan had become officially known in China. So to preserve the trade and to profit from it behind the scenes, the daimyo of Satsuma (with the silent permission of the bakufu) allowed the court of the Ryukyuan king to continue to exist and maintain its relations with the Middle Kingdom.[17]

Behind the scenes Satsuma ruled the islands. Whether the Chinese were really fooled by this charade or whether the magistrates of Fujian and Zhejiang provinces, on the other side of the Chinese sea, closed their eyes to avoid damaging the trade, does not become clear from the documents.[18] The fact remains that the so-called king of Ryukyu continued to send fake ambassadors to the Chinese court until the nineteenth century, while every time a new Ryukyuan king ascended to his "throne" he was officially invested as such by an envoy from China.

In both the Korean and the Ryukyuan cases, the confirmation of Japan's centrality by embassies sent from these countries was more apparent than real. The various daimyo of Japan may individually have been impressed by the power of the bakufu, but it is less sure that the military government of Japan itself was as convinced of its own influence overseas. It is not surprising, therefore, that the shogun and his advisers remained on the lookout for opportunities to expand the number of their foreign "vassals."

The Dutch, who among Europeans had proved to be the most willing to do the shogun's bidding, were naturally the obvious candidates for such an expansion of Japan's formal influence over-seas. In 1643, shortly after the move from Hirado to Deshima, an event suddenly occurred which, in the eyes of Tokugawa Iemitsu himself, provided a good opportunity for a tributary mission to be sent by this European vassal to Japan. The only problem was to make the Dutch agree and see things the way the Japanese wanted them to.

After the men from the *Breskens* had been arrested, they had to leave behind on their ship their own way of understanding the world. When the ship itself left, their familiar physical universe was gone and the men had no choice but to accept the world on the terms of their captors. The world of the warrior *(bushi)* was a frightening one, even for those who were born into it. The strand that held it together, at least up to the seventeenth century, was raw power. The rise to pre-eminence of Japan's warrior class was itself a sign of the gradual secularization of Japanese society. Because of the profession he was born into (which by Tokugawa times had already become his lineage), the warrior dealt in death. Death was the instrument by which, during the medieval period, the warrior class gradually fashioned a new society from the ruins of the ancient Japanese state.

The warriors who imposed their rationality of power on Japan constituted no more than 5 or 6 percent of the country's population. During the Edo period (1600–1868), they lived mainly in castle towns of the country, and especially in the castle town "par excellence," Edo, where they formed the majority of the population. Inside the castle towns of Japan the warrior class had its own quarters, closely packed around the castle itself. Physically, then, and mentally as well, the *bushi* class was separated from the rest of the population to a remarkable degree. Their education as specialists of power did much to reinforce this separation.

When power is valued as the ultimate touchstone of social relations it must be made visible. Death was visible in Japan to a degree hard for us to imagine today. Execution grounds were located along the main roads leading into and out of the cities. The two sabers the *bushi* carried were, at the same time, the symbols and the instruments of their power. The expected response of the masses was instant and total submission. The Dutch group caught on very quickly. One of the things stressed by them in the report they left of their captivity was that they constantly "paid their respects in the proper manner." This rather euphemistic expression meant that the Dutchmen would go down on their knees, put their hands flat on the floor in front of them, and bow their heads down until their noses touched the ground. Their hesitance to clearly admit to this fact afterwards is connected with their awareness that such an act of submission would not be understood in a European context, where one knelt on one knee in front of a king, and on two only when praying to God.[19]

In Japan, however, the Dutch were used to conforming to this local custom, which even today is still practiced by Japanese in a wide variety of social situations. The Dutch merchants were very much aware that they would only be tolerated in Japan on Japanese terms.[20] In this, their experience during the 218 years of their exclusive trading rights differed fundamentally from that of most of the other European nations that maintained settlements in Asia. As long as there was money to be made, the Dutch did the bidding of the Japanese. The story of the prisoners from Nambu is, maybe, the best example of this unequal relationship.

Chapter 1
Flying Dutchmen

On the third day of the fifth month in the year of the Sheep, Kan'ei twenty,* the lower white study of Chiyoda Castle was filled to capacity. Here, at eleven o'clock in the morning in a relatively small space of twenty-four and a half tatami mats in the middle interior of the central donjon *(honmaru)*, were gathered the biggest local power holders of Japan. Thirty men sat on their knees in five rows facing the upper white study, which was four tatami mats larger than the lower study but remained empty during the proceedings. Most of these men were usually not allowed this far into the castle, for they were outer lords *(tozama daimyō)*, whose place—when received by the shogun—was in the grand and wide audience hall *(ōhiroma)* near the entrance of the *omote*, the only part of the castle open to outsiders.[1] Yet here they sat, and the significance of the occasion was lost on none of them. Lined up, two to a mat, as neatly as school boys, they were put face-to-face with the awesomeness of someone who did not deign to appear.

The order in which they sat was the grand result of centuries of warfare. Although the castle had ushers, powerful men of low birth, who performed their duties on larger ceremonial occasions, these thirty lords knew their respective and reciprocal places well enough to have no need for such upstarts telling them where to sit. No man who did not know his exact place could survive inside the castle. If perchance a man should forget himself so far as to make a mistake and he was well liked or lucky, a short snakelike hiss from somewhere

---

*Thursday, 18 June 1643.

would warn him and he might have a few precious seconds in which to correct himself. Failing this, it would not be long before the most offended man around him would plunge his dagger into his back. Such was the atmosphere of the castle, and such was the importance of the seating arrangements in the eyes of the participants in the game of power.

The shogun's close relatives, the Matsudaira of Echizen and Echigo, were the first, by virtue of their name, their rank, and the size of their holdings. They were followed by the shogun's adopted relatives, men who had sided with or never been defeated by the first Tokugawa shogun Ieyasu, such as the Maeda of the Kaga domain, the Date of the Sendai domain, and the Shimazu of the Satsuma domain. These families administered the largest fiefs in the country, the Kaga domain being valued at more than one million *koku* of rice.* They had been Tokugawa rivals once and were still under suspicion, but they had been appeased and granted the Matsudaira family name.[2] Twenty of these and other outer lords were followed by two more relatives of the shogun, *shinpan daimyō,* one of whom was Hoshina Masayuki, the second shogun's youngest son and brother of the present shogun Tokugawa Iemitsu. Masayuki had been adopted into the Hoshina family, and was now the future shogun Ietsuna's guardian. In ten years he would be the most powerful man in Japan, but at this moment he was still only number 24 among those called up. After him followed six *fudai daimyō,* once loyal followers of Ieyasu, but now excluded from bakufu affairs because they had accumulated too much wealth.[3]

When all these men were seated, seven other *fudai* made their appearance. They proceeded to sit in a row at the top of the room, near the partition to the Upper Study, facing the men who had been called up. First among them was Ii Naotaka, fifty-four years old, the senior counselor *(tairō)* to the present shogun, a largely ceremonial position. He was flanked by Doi Toshikatsu, the most powerful man in Japan during the reign of the previous shogun, Tokugawa Hidetada, but at this moment seventy-one years old. Half paralyzed, he had trouble sitting up straight. Third in line was Sakai Tadakatsu, at fifty-six years old Iemitsu's closest advisor and policy maker. Thirty-five-year-old Hotta Masamori sat next to him: he was Iemitsu's *mignon* and closest confidante. This line of the shogun's representatives was completed by Matsudaira Nobutsuna and the Abe cousins, Tada'aki and Shige-

---

*A little less than 5 million bushels.

tsugu—Iemitsu's workhorses, for the business of government was conducted mainly through them.

Out of the thirty-seven men present in the lower white study, the personal names of eleven of them started with the character for "loyalty" *(tada)*, which was the most popular character for such names at the time. As such it had replaced the character for "be victorious" *(katsu)*, which had enjoyed great popularity during Ieyasu's time. Six of the men in the room still had the latter character in their names, but only one of them was under thirty years old. Obviously, then, for the upper *bushi* or warrior class, proving one's loyalty (starting with the name one received at one's coming-of-age ceremony) had become more important than showing one's desire to emerge victorious in battle. Sakai Tadakatsu, the foremost power broker present, may have exemplified this trend. His name was the only one made up of both auspicious characters (but "loyalty" came first!). Another seven of the men present had the character "shining" *(mitsu)* in their names. All of them, except one, were under thirty, having come of age in the time when Iemitsu (from whose name they derive this character) had become shogun.

It was not a special ceremonial event. These *tozama, shinpan,* and *fudai daimyō* had been called up to hear a message from the shogun. But it was a message that could not wait until the fifteenth of the month when all the lords were due to appear again for their biweekly court attendance. On this occasion, Sakai Tadakatsu and Matsudaira Nobutsuna notified the lords of the attainder of Katō Akinari, who had been daimyo of the Aizu domain until the day before. For "reasons of illness," states the latter's official biography,[4] Akinari was reduced in income from 400,000 *koku* to the 10,000 *koku* his son received in the province of Iwami. The arbitrariness of the proceedings was the most frightening aspect. Two days before, on the first of the fifth month, Akinari would still have been sitting among his peers collected here. Now he had become forever out of their league. The man whose will was being done chose not to appear. The distance between the shogun and his vassals was thus clearly demonstrated.

The record states further: "Before the above mentioned gentlemen retired toward the Ōroka corridor, Izu no kami [Matsudaira Nobutsuna], Bungo no kami [Abe Tada'aki] and Tsushima no kami [Abe Shigetsugu] repeated the shogun's order not to be lax [in guarding the coast]. This order was issued just as the year before, because a *gareuta* [galliot] ship had been seen recently at Kinkazan and Iwaki Bay [off the coast] of Mutsu province."[5]

It is this latter part of the shogun's message that interests us here. News about the sighted ship must have been received in Edo earlier, for fishermen and low-ranking local officials had been exchanging fish for liquor with foreign sailors along the Pacific coast of Japan's main island of Honshu since the end of May.[6] This time, however, the information had come from Sendai via the official channel of the Date family and could no longer be kept from other daimyo. The ship was neither Spanish nor Portuguese, but Dutch. In fact, there had been two Dutch ships off the coast of Honshu since the end of May, although the Japanese were still unaware of this. Through the announcement to the holders of the largest fiefs in Japan the whole country was put on full alert. On returning to their private mansions in the city, these lords would command their men to send an express messenger back to their own castles in order to transmit the shogun's orders and intensify the defense of their coasts.

One man, Nambu Shigenao, the lord of the Nambu domain to the north of Sendai, we do not find among those called up on this occasion, although we know that he, too, was in Edo at the time. Eight days after this meeting he is recorded to have received permission to go back to his castle in Morioka.[7] Administering lands worth a mere 100,000 *koku*, he was out of his league compared with the other *tozama daimyo* gathered here, whose average assessed domain income (*kokudaka*) was 320,000 *koku*. Still, he was probably informed of the matter on the same day, for one copy of the *Kan'ei nikki* (Diary for the Kan'ei era, 1624–1644) records that he was among those appointed temporary caretakers of the Aizu domain, which had just been taken away from Katō Akinari.[8] When Lord Nambu returned to Morioka in the beginning of July, the news awaited him there that one of the ships in question had visited his domain on 10 June, eight days before the full alert was proclaimed in Edo. As we shall see, he immediately issued orders to tighten the coastal defense of Nambu.

In the fall of 1642, two expeditions of exploration were prepared at Batavia, the hub of the Dutch trading empire in Asia. One expedition was sent under Abel Tasman to explore the "Southland."[9] It was a successful voyage because Tasman discovered and named Tasmania and New Zealand, but Dutch trade in the East Indies was not in-creased by these discoveries. The other expedition was sent north to discover the "Unknown Coasts of Tartary, the Kingdom of Cathay, and the West Coast of America, as well as the Gold and Silver Islands."[10]

The latter islands had been the object of one previous Dutch expe-dition under Matthijs Quast and Tasman in 1639.[11] The man behind these voyages of exploration was the governor general of the Dutch East Indies, Anthonie Van Diemen—or Antonio, as he signed his name, mocking the Portuguese whom he admired even as he was replacing their power in Asia with that of Holland.

Van Diemen had been bankrupted by speculation in his younger years and had first left Holland for the East Indies under an assumed name in order to escape from his creditors. But unlike most such ad-venturers, he seems to have taken seriously the misfortune of losing his credit and reputation; his whole subsequent career in the service of the Dutch East India Company was marked by his desire to show that he was a dependable merchant. Oddly enough, in a time when most of the employees of the Dutch company do not seem to have adhered to strict moral and ethical standards of behavior, Van Diemen stands out as an incorruptible and hardworking (if somewhat dour) company man who climbed the ladder from common soldier until he became governor general in January of 1636. He died nine years later, in 1645, probably from overwork.[12]

By the end of the 1630s, even the parsimonious Dutch East India Company could well afford a few voyages of discovery. The decade had been the most profitable one since the establishment of the com-pany in 1602, and would turn out to be the second most profitable one in the whole subsequent history of the company until its demise in 1799.[13]

Proposals for different voyages had been made since the late 1620s, and among them the quest for the Gold and Silver Islands, begun by the Spanish in 1611, had figured prominently.[14] But the coasts of Tartary and Korea had also been on the agenda of the company since at least 1638. Quast had been ordered to sail there in case he was successful in finding the famous islands. After the failure of Quast's voyage, however, the managers of the company at Batavia had begun to realize that the Gold and Silver Islands east of Japan might be nothing more than a sailor's dream.[15] But the College of Gentlemen XVII, the supreme management council of the company in Amsterdam, was still excited about the prospect and wrote in 1640 to that effect.[16] They again referred to the matter in a letter dated 11 April 1642,[17] and later that year the Council of the Indies at Batavia decided to prepare another expedition to satisfy the demands of their superiors.

The *Instructions* for the new expedition were drawn up by Justus Schouten, Councilor of the Indies, in collaboration with the future commander of the expedition, Maerten Gerritsz Vries.[18] Information on the main goal of the voyage, the fabled trade of Cathay or Tartary, was mainly based on Marco Polo's account of China, and therefore dated from some three hundred and fifty years earlier. The planners do not even seem to have realized that China and Cathay were the same country.

Two ships, the fluyt *Castricom* and the yacht *Breskens*, were filled with a cargo of miscellaneous goods. As manpower had been a problem on Quast's expedition, this time 110 men were to sail on the two ships.[19] This number represented more than twice the manpower necessary for just sailing the ships, and included ten professional soldiers, five on each ship. Therefore, even if a third of the men were to die of illness or exposure, there would still be enough people left to enable the expedition to establish a trading post or factory in unknown but promising territory in case the opportunity presented itself.

The ships were to sail from Batavia to the Moluccas, east of Celebes, refresh at the port of Ternate, and then head due north over a presumably empty stretch of the Pacific Ocean east of the Philippines. This was a route to Japan that had never been taken before by any European ship. Obviously, the purpose was to see if the fabulous Gold and Silver Islands might not lie further south than had been thought previously.

The *Instructions* mapped out the progress of the projected expedition in amazing detail. Japan's main island of Honshu was to be reached between 20 and 25 May, and the two ships were to continue "north and northwest" until they found out how far north the island stretched and how it related to "the land called Jeso by the Japanese."[20] However, the fleet was not to waste time on this problem. The trading cities of Jangio and Brema, located somewhere near or at the mouth of a great river, were the true goal of this voyage. According to the *Instructions*, the ships should reach these cities between 15 and 20 June.

The duties en route were also spelled out. Both ships were to keep detailed logs and draw up maps featuring all the "islands, capes, gulfs, inlets, bays, rivers, shoals, sandbanks, reefs, cliffs, and rocks" they encountered.[21] The logs should record the latitude and longitude of the ships at noon each day, and describe the respective positions of all the visible landmarks. The voyage had been planned so that the ships would sail north while the weather was likely to be getting warmer and the days were still lengthening. In this way, the expedition was expected to continue sailing during the short summer nights so that more distance might be covered in a shorter time.

When going ashore, the crews were warned to anchor in a place that could be easily entered and left again, and to always be on their best behavior. They were told to ignore small provocations, such as theft by the natives, and to try and learn as much as possible about the places they were visiting or going to visit. "All of which you will observe sharply, copy well and describe perfectly, keeping a detailed and extensive journal for that purpose in which everything you experience will be noted down so that, upon your return, you will be able to report properly to us."[22] With such precise *Instructions,* it is small wonder that the subsequent logs were kept according to the highest standards.

After visiting and exploring Tartary for the possibilities of trade, the expedition was expected to leave the far north in the beginning of August and sail southeast again "until [you reach] the longitude of the eastern end of Japan, or until you come upon the west coast of America."[23] The two ships were allowed two or three weeks to explore this coast of America, which was obviously thought to approach Tartary very closely. After 25 August, however, the ships should spend some time looking for the Gold and Silver Islands. It is noteworthy that of the four goals of the expedition (Tartary, the Kingdom of Cathay, the west coast of America, and the Gold and Silver Islands) the legendary islands are ranked last, included only, it seems, to satisfy the demands of the Gentlemen XVII. We will see, however, that the sailors of the expedition themselves were eager to pursue the search for these islands, over and above the other goals of the voyage.

As voyages of exploration are wont to do, this one too took a different course from the one foreseen in the *Instructions.* On 19 May, one and a half months after leaving Ternate on 4 April, the two ships ran into a heavy storm off the island of Hachijōjima, south of Japan. We have an account of the storm written by the diarist of the *Castricom,*

from which it appears that the fluyt only barely escaped being thrown on the rocks at this time.[24] Because of this the keeper of the log christened the unknown island, "The Unfortunate Isle." After the storm had passed, the *Breskens* was no longer in sight.

In the event they became separated by stormy weather (a possibility that had been foreseen in the *Instructions*), the two ships had agreed to meet off the coast of Japan at 37.5 degrees northern latitude, where they would wait and make their presence known to each other by firing their cannon at regular intervals. The *Castricom* reached the Japanese coast first. On 22 May, her journal reports a morning visit of two Japanese fishing vessels, each with eight men on board. The Japanese brought so much fish that there was enough to feed the *Castricom*'s whole crew of fifty men. The Dutch reciprocated with rice and arak, a liquor distilled from molasses or rice in the Indies. The fishermen are recorded to have drunk a good deal, "as fishermen usually do."[25] The journal continues: "A little after noon, one of the fishermen came on board again and brought more fish. He was accompanied by another fishing boat that did not have any fish. They left in friendship after having been served liquor, and rowed back to shore."[26] As we shall see below, it is possible that this "fishing boat that did not have any fish" already contained a local Japanese official in disguise, coming to check on the Dutch vessel.

Further north near Cape Shioyasaki, on 24 May, more fishermen came on board and gestured that the Dutch should stop sailing north. In the late afternoon of the same day the *Castricom* had another, slightly mysterious, meeting at sea: "When it was getting dark, a Japanese boat sailed past and called out 'Toy, toy,' pointing toward the north. He indicated that, if we wanted, he could bring us to a harbor in the north. This was different from the other Japanese who had always told us not to sail north. When he saw that we took down our topsails, clewed up our [main] sail and foresail, and set course to the east with the mizzen sail, he pulled his own sail taut and called out that it was no good sailing east or seaward and set his course toward the north. In this boat there were four Japanese."[27]

It seems that this was neither a fishing nor a cargo boat, so the four men probably were local officials eager to lead the *Castricom* into a port where they would have a better chance at investigating her.

The next day, 25 May, the ship reached 37.5 degrees. There she cruised, waiting for the *Breskens*. "At night, the weather was nice and calm, with the wind coming from the west. When there was no moon, we always had two fires going, and from time to time we fired our cannon, so that if our companion were around she might hear and find us by the sound of the shots."[28] The ship had several other encounters with Japanese vessels, some of them warning the Dutchmen that they should not be sailing further north.

On 29 May, the *Castricom* had reached 38 degrees and was four Dutch sea miles, or about 22 kilometers, away from the shore of present-day Miyagi prefecture.* Two days later, the ship's council was convened in the commander's cabin. The council decided that the time to wait for the *Breskens* was up and that they had to continue the expedition on their own. Three days after this, on 3 June, the *Castricom* reached 39 degrees and sailed along the coast of the Nambu domain. Her journal reports: "Here many Japanese came on board and gave us thirty red sea bream and three cod in exchange for which we gave them some rice and poured them a drink of arak. Two or three Japanese then came on board and offered to bring us to a harbor which they called Nabo [Nambu?] and another place called Schay. When they saw we were not interested in visiting any harbors here, they left in friendship."[29] This was the *Castricom*'s last meeting with Japanese vessels.

Four important facts can be gleaned from these entries reporting on the contacts of the *Castricom* with the Japanese. First, Japanese fishermen were eager to disobey the orders of the Japanese military government, or bakufu, and come aboard the Dutch ship to fraternize with food and liquor. Second, the Dutch were warned time and again that their presence off the coast of northern Honshu was known to, and frowned on by, the Japanese authorities. Third, as the *Castricom* was, for reasons of storage space, carrying the greater part of the provisions of both Dutch vessels, she had a surplus of rice that could be exchanged for fresh fish. Finally, we see that Commander Vries was very careful not to enter any Japanese harbor or bay.

On 10 June, the *Castricom*'s position was estimated to be at 42 degrees, 29 minutes northern latitude, and 163 degrees, 19 minutes eastern longitude.† When, at noon that day, the proper calculations were made with the quadrant, it was found they were at 42 degrees, 37 minutes northern latitude, which put them east of Hokkaido.[30]

---

*One Dutch sea mile = 5555.6 meters.
†Counted from Tenerife on the Azores west of Africa.

The longitude, counted from the Azores, could only be estimated but not yet measured at this time.[31] For this same day we have news of the *Breskens,* which had been given up for lost in the storm near Hachijōjima by the crew of her sister ship, but is recorded to have been at 39 degrees, 27 minutes northern latitude.

The *Breskens*' rough measures were 108 feet long and 25 feet wide, and she carried seventeen pieces of artillery. The ship was of medium size for a yacht, for the dimensions of this type of ship ranged between 80 and 135 feet in length. She may have reached not quite eighty *last* of tonnage.* Yachts were square stern ships, generally with three masts and square sails. They looked like East Indiamen, only smaller, and they were particularly useful in shallow waters. Fast sailers with but little cargo space, they generally carried few pieces of artillery, so the *Breskens* was exceptionally well armed for its type. Her hull may have been between nine and ten feet deep, with room for no more than one deck below the *kuip* or "waist" of the ship.

The *Breskens,* as her name indicates, was built by the Kamer Van Zeeland (one of six "Chambers" making up the Dutch East India Company), most likely on its wharf at Middleburgh. She may have been brand new on 26 March 1642 when she left Zeeland from the Wielingen channel, just outside the Scheldt estuary, with forty-four sailors and fifteen soldiers on board. Her captain was Lieven Van Couwenburg at the time, also from Zeeland to judge by his name.[32] The *Breskens* arrived in Batavia on 21 December of the same year. The trip to the East Indies had taken almost nine months, not excessively long but no quick voyage by any means, for arrivals within four to six months were common.

The crew was allowed a little respite before being sent off to Tartary on 3 February 1643. Even if the trip from Holland to the Indies had taken a rather long time, there do not seem to have been any deaths on the way. So we may be fairly sure that when the ship finally reached Japan, the crew was, except for the officers and possibly the soldiers, still more or less the same as when she had departed Holland for Batavia the year before. This is important, for it indicates that most of the sailors were new to East Asia.

Captain Hendrick Cornelisz Schaep, who replaced Captain Lieven

---

*One *last* = 125 cubic feet.

van Couwenburg at Batavia, was the only one on board who we
know for sure had been to Japan on previous occasions.[33] Schaep's
experience with the route to Northeast Asia was one of the qualifica-
tions that had made him eligible to participate in this voyage of discovery. We cannot be certain, however, that the crew of the *Breskens*
was pleased to see Lieven van Couwenburg replaced, for anyone who
managed to sail to the Indies without losing a single sailor in nine
months would have shown a deep concern for the welfare of his men.
If the greater part of the sailors had been mustered in Zeeland, then
Schaep, whose wife was living in Amsterdam,[34] but who himself had
been born in the province of Utrecht, cannot have been popular with
his crew from the very beginning.

On 10 June 1643, the *Breskens* visited the Bay of Yamada on the
northeastern shore of Honshu. The ship entered from the south,
tacking along the coast, the easiest (if not the only) way to find the
narrow entrance to the bay, which cannot be seen from the open sea.
This rocky coast of present-day Iwate prefecture, the Rikuchū kaigan,
displays a great variety of granite formations. The sea has been eating
away at these giant rocks for millennia, exposing different layers of
various colors. Some are red, some black, green, or yellow. Some glis-
ten with water in the sun. Some form steep walls, and others consist
of little rocky islands or complete gateways with fir trees growing on
top. The local fishermen have named them all with imaginative names.

The men on the *Breskens,* however, had the Gold and Silver
Islands in mind, and it is small wonder that they decided to follow
the curving wall of rock, which changes color every five or ten minutes, and forms the southern loop into the bay. This is the north
coast of the Funakoshi peninsula. Takahashi Tōyō, a former *daikan*
(provincial officer) of Miyako, north of Yamada, and later a Confucian scholar at Morioka, wrote around 1765: "This bay is on all sides
surrounded by high mountain peaks [pointed] like hands [pressed
together] in prayer. The entrance toward the sea opens to the north
[and is so narrow that] it reminds one of a bag closed with a string.
For this reason, it is hard to see from ships at sea. [Once] inside, it
opens up wide into one giant lake, the shoreline of which is indented
like a crane's or a lapwing's foot. . . . In the middle of the bay are a
big and a small island, and multi-colored shells are plentiful."[35]

The Dutchmen on the *Breskens,* then, suddenly found themselves
in an idyllic bay, glittering in the afternoon sun. It was surrounded by
mountains as far as the eye could see—layer upon layer of mountains,

with different shades of grays, greens, and browns, under an expanse of blue sky. Sounding for depth, they were amazed to find the bottom deep and anchorage safe. A stream flowing into the bay near its entrance, at a little beach locally known as Okinosawa, or Offing's Marsh, was soon found. Captain Schaep sent out a boat with several armed men to go ashore and refill their water casks. The ship anchored nearby, probably just inside the bay, not far enough to notice the hamlet of Ōura just around the corner.

Ōura was a prosperous fishing community, which, lying on a peninsula connected with the mainland only by a thin marshy strip of land, was as isolated as if it had been on an island.[36] Its main mode of communication with the outside world was by rowboat or sailboat over the bay to the village of Yamada, the largest settlement along the bay on the north-south coastal road. Such remote settlements as those around the Bay of Yamada were set in their ways and had their own local traditions, dating back perhaps thousands of years to the Jōmon period, when fishermen were first known to inhabit the general area of Yamada and Ōzuchi, to the south.

It was not long before the "Big Ship" (as the *Breskens* is referred to in the local documents) was noticed by the people of Yamada. We do not have the log of the *Breskens* any longer, so we do not know the exact order of events. But just as in the case of the *Castricom,* people came on board to inspect the ship, exchange freshly caught fish for liquor, and drink together with the foreigners who had so miraculously appeared out of nowhere: truly a rare occurrence calling for celebrations.

Men, women, and children from Yamada, Ii'oka, Ōsawa, Orikasa, Funakoshi, and as far away as Tanohama and Koyadori on the other side of the Funakoshi peninsula came in little boats to see the ship.[37] Some of those who came brought things like tobacco pipes and "mountain knives" to exchange with the foreigners.[38] "It is hard to say how many things [were exchanged]," states the *Satōke monjo* or document kept in the Satō family of Yamada, guardians of the Kumano Daigongen shrine located on their property.

In accordance with their *Instructions,* the men from the *Breskens* behaved as exemplary hosts, pouring arak for the men and women, and going down into the hold to fetch some goods from the cargo to give in exchange for the gifts brought by the locals: a Dutch hatchet for a Japanese one, a sailor's pipe for a fisherman's. Some bars of Swedish steel were brought out and changed hands. Again we wish for the log of the *Breskens*. Junior Merchant Wilhem Bijlvelt would certainly have kept an exact record of what parts of the cargo were used and how many things were exchanged.

That night, there may have been music, a fire on the beach, and more eating and drinking. There was someone on the *Breskens* who could play the violin and another sailor played the flute.[39] Although the Dutch sources are silent about this night, the Japanese sources and later events indicate that the sailors of the *Breskens* must have had a very good time. There may have been local women who were not afraid to come close to the Dutchmen. What is clear is that the new laws against consorting with foreigners, proclaimed throughout Japan a few years before, had still not made an impression on the people living around the bay. Orders had been given, however, that all foreign ships entering Japanese had were to be reported.

A document preserved by the Minato family of Yamada mentions that it was one their forebears, Minato Yozaemon, who was charged with the duty of running to report the arrival of the Big Ship in Morioka.[40] It is said that he covered the distance between Yamada and Morioka in one day, clearly an impossible feat. He may have run to tell the news at Ōzuchi, fifteen to twenty kilometers away. This was the nearest government office of the Nambu fief, where the *daikan* of the Hei district resided. From there, relay messengers could have been sent to reach Morioka in twenty-four hours.

The following morning, by order of Captain Schaep, the *Breskens* weighed anchor and turned around in the bay. The ship left to continue her expedition with a fresh supply of water on board. Did her crew grumble about leaving paradise so soon? For the next month and a half, until 28 July, all we have on her adventures is the information provided by Nicolaas Witsen in his well-known book on Tartary. Witsen is the last man on record to have seen the log of the *Breskens*, for it disappeared after the publication of his book (1692).

Witsen seems to faithfully summarize the route taken by the *Breskens* after she left Yamada. He notes how the ship reached "Jesso," and met with Ainu men and women. He mentions that later, at 47 degrees 8 minutes northern latitude, they discovered land, covered in snow and very misty. Witsen guessed this might be the "west coast of America."[41] After noting how the *Breskens* missed the straits separating Ezo and Honshu, Witsen writes: "Later this yacht turned around and sailed back the way she had come, until 37 degrees latitude, at the easternmost cape of Japan. From there she sailed east in order to discover some islands or main land they had been ordered to find."[42] With these last two sentences we have already passed the important days of 28–31 July 1643. It seems, then, that Witsen was not interested in revealing the contents of the *Breskens'* log at this point, for he glosses exceedingly smoothly over these momentous events.

To understand what happened, we have to start at Morioka, where Lord Nambu Shigenao had returned to his castle at the beginning of July. The daimyo had spent the past year in Edo in attendance on the shogun. We may be certain that, before his departure from the shogun's capital, Shigenao had been informed of the mysterious ships, which had been appearing and disappearing off the coast of Honshu over the past two months.[43] It is likely that, when Shigenao reached Morioka, he was told of the visit of the *Breskens* to his territory by his police officer *(metsuke)* and sometime Confucian scholar, Urushido Kanzaemon Masashige.

Kanzaemon lived inside the compound of Shigenao's castle, near the northern inner moat, a few minutes' walk from the daimyo's private quarters.[44] He had been introduced to Shigenao in Edo and had followed him to Morioka after the latter had inherited his fief in 1632. He was part of a whole group of new men assembled by Shigenao in Edo to reorganize the fief of his forefathers on the new Tokugawa pattern. Kanzaemon had studied Confucianism with Ishikawa Jōzan in Kyoto,[45] and therefore he was wise in the ways of the world. Shigenao had recognized this ability and offered him employment at Morioka at half the stipend he was getting in Edo, but with better prospects for an increase in power and wealth.[46]

At this time, Kanzaemon was ordered by his lord to travel to Yamada in the company of Shigenao's senior retainer, Shichinohe Hayato Naotoki, who seems to have replaced his lord in Morioka while the latter was away in Edo. The two men were to follow the road through the interior, via Tōno, and reach the coast at the *daikan's* office in Ōzuchi.[47] There they could pick up reinforcements to accompany them to Yamada. On their arrival at the place where the foreign ship had anchored, they were to see to it that an example was set to impress upon all the inhabitants of the neighborhood the importance of the new shogunal orders concerning the treatment of foreign ships. They were to leave immediately for Yamada.

The next information we have puts the two representatives of the daimyo with a few hardened samurai warriors square in the middle of the village of Yamada. They seem to have commandeered the Ryū-shōji, a Zen temple built as a registration office in compliance with the country's new anti-Christian edicts.[48] There they collected testimony on the visit of the Big Ship, assembled the goods exchanged with the foreigners for closer inspection, and were preparing a grand tribunal to decide what was to be done with all those who had transgressed the shogun's new laws. As a preliminary measure, because the investigation seemed too weighty to be handled by anyone other than the shogun's own police officers, they had announced that all these people had to make ready to leave for Edo: "not only all those who had exchanged goods with the foreigners but also those who just had gone to see the ship," states a document kept in the Uezawa family of Yamada.[49]

There were few families around the bay without a relative who had gone to see the Big Ship, so the consternation after this announcement by the authorities of Nambu was great. Enough examples had been set recently with native Christians in the area for everyone to be quite clear as to what was going to happen to anyone found to have broken the anti-Christian laws. On this occasion, a fellow from Ōura called Bunshichi seems to have been summarily seized by the daimyo's men on suspicion of Christian sympathies, just because each of the two characters that made up his name had (with a little imagination) the shape of a cross.[50] He was sent ahead to Edo for questioning. For the villagers around the bay there seemed to be no way out. In their quiet despair, all they knew to do was to pray for the Big Ship to come back.

Three shrines are known to have been popular at this time—one in Orikasa dedicated to Kumano Daigongen, the Great Avatar of Kumano; one in the Suginoshita neighborhood of Yamada dedicated to Shinzan Daigongen, the Avatar of the Deep Mountains; and one in Ōsawa dedicated to Onibarai Daimyōjin, the Great God Expelling Demons. These were all domesticated mountain deities of varying degrees of fierceness. They were held in awe and dreaded at the same time. That, according to the local documents, all of them were invoked at this time testifies to the villagers' predicament. Prayers were held for the return of the Big Ship. If the ship would just come back once more, the reception could be redone and the past be wiped clear.

"Soon enough a wind started blowing from the west," tells the document of the Uezawa family. "However, the domain officials expressed their doubts. When they were asked [by the villagers] if they could go and pray again for a divine wind to blow in their direction, they gave permission, for it seemed the only thing left to do. Not long afterwards, the aforementioned Big Ship came sailing briskly back before the wind over the open sea and entered our bay for the second time."[51]

It was around ten o'clock in the morning.[52] Schaep and his men were, of course, unaware that a completely different situation awaited them at Yamada. All they had in mind was to go and rest once more in that idyllic bay in northern Japan, before sailing straight across the Pacific Ocean to search for the Gold and Silver Islands, the last remaining goal of their voyage.

The expedition had been a hard one for the *Breskens*. First they had lost most of their rice supply, which had been stored on the *Castricom*. Then, after leaving Yamada on 11 June, they had encountered nothing but cold and miserable weather north of Japan. They had discovered land, but were unsure if it belonged to a continent or if it was an island, for it had been hidden in mist and snow. Many of the crew were weak and starting to get sick with scurvy.

Even if Schaep had wanted to sail past the entrance to the Bay of Yamada, he might not have dared to do so, for fear of trouble from his men, desperate to go back to this sailors' paradise: safe anchorage, fresh water, secluded beaches, plentiful fish, fresh rice, vegetables, and willing women. Who could ask for more? Again we wish for the log of the *Breskens* to get at least a glimpse of the reasoning behind the return to Yamada. Was Schaep forced to give in to the demands of his crew? Was it his own idea? Or was it a combination of both, with Schaep's shaky position as an outsider on his own ship forcing his hand?

On the Japanese side, in any case, it is not surprising that the ship was received even more warmly that it had been the first time, on 10 June. The gods had heard the prayers of the villagers, and through their unfathomable magic powers, had brought the ship back into their hands. The danger to all those living around the bay had been averted. Only very happy faces looked up to the unsuspecting Dutch sailors hanging over the railing of their ship. Words did not seem necessary. "Come ashore! Come with us!" everyone seemed to be saying. "You're back. Let's celebrate!" To be the cause of so much happiness evident all around them must have been irresistible to the weakened crew. It is a miracle Schaep kept anyone on board at all.

Chapter 2

Ganji Garame

This time, the first to visit the ship was Kanzaemon. He was planning to set a trap and catch himself some Dutchmen, but first he needed to go and scout out the enemy. Afterwards he wrote a report:

> In the 6th month, on the 13th day, at the 4th hour, a Big Ship sailed into the Bay of Yamada of Hei district. It anchored about one and a half *ri** over the water away from Yamada. While I was thinking of a way to bring the foreigners ashore, it was clear that this could not be done without first observing the situation on board. Shichinohe Hayato and I agreed to board a fishing boat to go over to the Big Ship. When we had come alongside, they threw a net down from the ship and invited us up. Grabbing the net, we climbed aboard the Big Ship and then we were led by the hands and pulled into what seemed to be the captain's dwelling, which was about the size of five or six tatami mats.[1]

We have a description of Kanzaemon and Lord Naotoki (here called Shichinohe Hayato) from the Dutch side as well, but for reasons that will become clear below, this report starts one day later. For information on what happened on 28 July, therefore, we mainly have Japanese sources aside from those fragments of information we can distill from the debriefing report later written by the Dutch side.

Kanzaemon was "a nobleman" to the Dutch, by which they must have meant a sword-carrying samurai, a member of Japan's warrior class.[2] Although Kanzaemon reports that Lord Naotoki came along

---

*One *ri* = 654.5 meters.

on this first visit to the ship, the Dutch report written by Junior Merchant Wilhem Bijlvelt (with some additions by Captain Schaep) implies that Kanzaemon was alone on this occasion. This would seem logical, and Kanzaemon's inclusion of Lord Naotoki in his bravura was no more than the after-the-fact *omote* (i.e., surface) obligation of a subaltern toward his superior. This is a peculiarity of Japanese sources one has to watch out for.

Other Japanese sources (including the venerable *Tokugawa jikki,* or Veritable Record of the Tokugawa) have the two domain officials donning the disguise of fishermen to board the Dutch ship. However, the fact that Kanzaemon was recognized as "a nobleman" by the Dutch sailors indicates that it is very unlikely that he disguised himself on this occasion.[3] We have seen in the case of the *Castricom* that some officials along the coast probably did dress up as fishermen in order to avoid arousing suspicion among the Dutch sailors. As always with Japanese sources, then, there may be a kernel of truth in these reports about the disguise. It may also be indicative of the way those in Edo who compiled such reports thought a visit to a foreign ship *should* be handled.

For Kanzaemon this was probably the first time he had ever seen a well-armed European ship up close, and to climb aboard from his fishing dinghy, a height of about eight or nine feet, required a considerable amount of courage for a man of his intentions. After climbing over the railing, he was led to the captain's cabin in the aft castle. Kanzaemon's report continues: "They brought out liquor etc. and offered us drinks. After that Hayato went back [to shore] and I remained behind on the ship by myself. While somehow communicating with the foreigners, I thought I should go ashore together with them. When I had spun them some good yarns, they said they would come to shore with me, so five or six foreigners as well as myself got into the Big Ship's boat. Just at the moment that the boat was going to be [lowered] beside the ship, her guns boomed once."[4]

Unavoidably, perhaps, Kanzaemon not only edited but also somewhat abbreviated this account of his first visit to the Dutch ship. It seems, according to the Dutch report, that he saw some pistols lying on Captain Schaep's desk and was curious to see how they worked.[5] When shown, he asked if he could try and shoot one of them, which was permitted. He may have shot out of one of the cabin windows into the sea. What Kanzaemon also forgets to mention here is how he was given a tour of the whole ship.

Coming out of the captain's cabin, they passed the locked door to the gun room which Kanzaemon demanded to be opened. He took careful mental note of the contents: the twenty muskets hanging on the wall, the twenty cutlasses hanging from the ceiling, the bullets and gun powder stored in bags.[6] Then they went down to the lower deck, where the large artillery pieces stood, eight culverins in their carriages, four on each side of the ship.[7] The space between them was taken up by the chests of the sailors and their hammocks.

Although Dutch ships were clean by contemporary European standards, Kanzaemon must have winced at the smells and looks of these men, half starved and sick with scurvy. "All over the ship barbarians were lying in their hanging beds," he wrote later.[8] He must have been relieved when he came out on the upper deck again, and eager to go back to shore: "We went together to my place, and I brought out sake, etc. At that time they gave me a piece of red cotton and a piece of white cotton. Later Hayato also came to my place and served the foreigners in order to drink together, and then went home again. What we told the foreigners was that the spot where the ship was anchored now was dangerous and that it would be better if they moved her a little further into the bay. One of the two men who seemed to be chiefs went back to the ship to move it closer [to shore]."[9]

The ship was moved further into the bay. The Japanese sources do not agree on its anchorage.[10] The wide expanse of water between Ōsawa and Ōshima, the larger of the two islands in the bay, would obviously have been the first choice for the Dutch. But to the Japanese officials the ship must have seemed too far out of reach, so Kanzaemon's little ruse may have brought her closer to Cape Densaku, off the village of Orikasa.

Once more, we wish we had the log of the *Breskens* to tell us who were the two "chiefs" going ashore with Kanzaemon. Did Schaep remain on board himself? Did he send first mate Bruijn and merchant Bijlvelt? Until what time did these five men stay ashore? Did they come back to the ship after dark? Or is there any truth to the tantalizing fragment in the document preserved in the Minato family, that a party with attractive women was held that night: "Ten pretty women were made to board a pleasure boat and to sing songs with loud voices while they went to welcome the foreigners. The men from the Big Ship boarded [their own boat] and came to Yamada. That night staying at. . . ."[11]

Here the text breaks off. This document is the oldest local copy we have, dating from the first half of the eighteenth century. The sheet on which it was written was cut after the third line and then pasted onto the next sheet. From the size of the previous sheet, which is whole and counts thirteen lines, we may surmise that at least ten lines are missing. This, of course, is just enough for a juicy story, which some unknown patriot (from the Minato family?) thought better to omit from the history of early Dutch-Japanese intercourse. The document preserved in the Satō family has a similar story: "A mysterious thing happened! [The villagers] saw with their very own eyes the said Big Ship being blown back from Kawashiro.* Ten pretty women from here were made, as a ruse, to board a welcoming boat and rowed over [to the foreign ship]. The sailors of the said Big Ship also boarded a boat to meet them and came to the ridge of Iioka. That night a feast was prepared for them."12

Kanzaemon himself is vague: "During that time, I showed the other chief the sights around the neighborhood, and we went together to my house before he went back [to the ship]. Because the Big Ship had moved closer [to shore], I thought she would not be likely to leave that night. Fooling them meanwhile some way or other, when they told me they were going back to the said Big Ship, I boarded their boat together with them and went to the Big Ship where I stayed until the fourth hour that night [10 p.m.]. Employing all kinds of wiles, I returned to shore after having made them promise to come to my place the next day to go sightseeing etc."13

This time the Dutch report is explicit. When the men returned from their visit to the shore, they had been given some onions and leeks, and were accompanied by both Kanzaemon as well as Lord Naotoki.14 The Dutch took the latter for "the headman of the village," so that they had correctly assessed his superior status among the Japanese.15 If they came back to the *Breskens* before sunset, Lord Naotoki must also have been given the tour of the ship. Again drinks were served unstintingly to reciprocate the hospitality enjoyed ashore. When the officials left, a salute was given with the ship's cannon. The sound reverberated on all sides of the bay in a manner never heard before. The day ended with the Dutch convinced that they had made some new friends, while the Japanese officials must have been just as confident that no one on the *Breskens* suspected their true intentions toward the ship and its crew.

---

*Hamlet outside the Bay of Yamada, along the coast toward Miyako.

~

The next morning it was drizzling.[16] Around breakfast time, Kanzae-mon and some other samurai came on board again. The Dutch report states: "He presented us with a bag of rice and motioned further that we were free to come ashore as we pleased in order to buy what we needed. We thanked him profusely (bowing deeply), and invited him into the cabin, gave him arak, Spanish wine, and *vino tinto,* and pre-sented him, in exchange for the said bag of rice, with a pair of silk stockings, which he indicated to us to desire very much and for which he thanked us."[17]

Again, Kanzaemon wanted to have a tour of the ship. For his com-panion or for himself? There must have been places he had not dared visit on the day before when the smells of the Dutch ship may have chased him back on deck. The Dutch wrote his behavior off as "Japa-nese curiosity," and make no mention of it at this point in their report: "After having eaten, we went ashore together with the said nobleman in our small boat to see whether we could get some fresh vegetables for our crew (taking some Guinean linen and other fabrics of little value). We ordered our first mate and the other officers to take good care and keep an eye on us."[18]

Kanzaemon wrote: "From among the three men who seemed to be chiefs, two chiefs came, and one page, six rowers and one helmsman, in all ten foreigners boarded the Big Ship's boat and so did I."[19] This time, the two "chiefs" were thirty-two-year-old Captain Schaep and twenty-four-year-old Wilhem Bijlvelt, and their page was cabin boy Jacob De Pauw, fourteen years old. Among the six rowers was Siewert Jansz Mes, aka Buijsman, indicating he used to work on the Dutch herring fleet. At thirty-three, he was the oldest of the ten men, and probably had been forced to sail to the Indies because of a slump in the herring industry caused by the war with Spain.[20] He was the *Breskens'* steward or quartermaster, in charge of the ship's food sup-plies and liquor distribution, an important task which required a huge man. He had been wounded fighting the Portuguese at Ceylon the year before, so he must have been one of those who joined the crew with Schaep at Batavia. Schaep may have felt safe having a giant with him.

The others included the ship's cooper, twenty-six-year-old Pieter Gerritsz; her boatswain's mate, twenty-year-old Hans Slee; and artil-lerist Jurriaen Scholten, who may not have been Dutch but Swedish, for he is mentioned in the *Instructions* as someone who spoke Polish and Russian.[21] Then there were two common sailors: Abraham Pietersz Spelt, age twenty-two; and Hendrick Van Elsfort, twenty. Kanzaemon's "helmsman" was probably the fifteen-year old "boy" Aert Bastiaensz, aka Boerman, indicating his peasant background. The Dutch report continues: "Meanwhile, Japanese came to see the ship with their women and children, sailing to and fro in great numbers. When we landed, the said nobleman brought us to his house (which was near the beach), where we were regaled by him with Japanese wine and *seccanen,** etc. and were treated in a friendly manner. After we had sat there a while, we asked permission to go *kenbotsen* [Japanese *kenbotsu* or *kenbutsu*] or look around in the village (in order to buy what we needed and do the things we had come to shore for)."[22]

The Dutch report was written about half a year later, and its obvious purpose was to justify, to their superiors at Batavia and Amsterdam, the line of action taken by the officers of the *Breskens*. The main problem the writer(s) had to face was how to explain away the obvious: to have entered a bay and to have gone ashore unarmed in Japan, although not specifically forbidden in their *Instructions,* had been imprudent.

Their report stressed, therefore, the need for fresh water, vegetables, rice, and repairs (which may have been true enough), as well as the friendliness of the local authorities. Kanzaemon's "friendly" thoughts were the following: "We went ashore to my place. I thought that if I would tie them up in the vicinity of the Big Ship it might leave or even start shooting its guns. So we went together along the coastal road to a place called Orikasa at a distance between fifteen and twenty *chō*† from Yamada. But first we went together to Hayato's place."[23]

The Dutch report agrees with him on this last detail: "Our request was granted freely. The said nobleman even went with us personally and led us first to the house of the chief of the village (the one we had also received yesterday on board and had treated in a friendly fashion), where we drank another two or three cups of Japanese wine."[24]

After this they took their leave from Shichinohe Hayato, and went *"kenbotsen"* with Kanzaemon. The Dutch report uses this word (which means "sightseeing") repeatedly, and obviously it was a word

---

*From Japanese *sakana* ([dried] fish).
†One *chō* = 109.9 meters.

used over and over by Kanzaemon, in whose report it also appears in the same connection. Apart from being one of the first words they learned in Japan, I believe the reason why it was used in the debriefing report left by the Dutch sailors was because the Dutch group did not understand its precise meaning. Its meaning may have been taken to include "shopping" or "partying." This impression is made the stronger when we read that Kanzaemon, "seeing our sailors standing guard over the boat, pointed at them and said that they should come to *kembotsen* as well. And as we understood this to be a courtesy and a reward for the fact that he had been allowed to see our ship inside and out, as he had wished, yesterday and today, we ordered our men to follow us (not to seem ungrateful and to show all the more that we had come to this bay as friends in order to buy what we needed and to repair our ship, and also that we had come ashore in good faith and with the permission of the said nobleman himself)."[25]

They walked for about half an hour along the beach road, keeping the beach on their left side and farmland on their right. They saw some radish and cucumber but these were still small and of a kind they were not familiar with. Crossing the hill at Iioka, they disappeared from the sight of the ship and entered the "beautiful valley" of Orikasa with rice fields and grazing cows. There Kanzaemon led the party to a farmhouse, a stone's throw away from the road.

He gestured to the Dutch to sit down and rest a bit with him "until the greatest heat of the sun had passed." It must have been just after noon. While sitting there, and communicating with hand gestures and bodily motions as best they could, they learned the word *daikon,* which is "radish" in Japanese. They told Kanzaemon that the crew was sick and needed to eat radish and cucumbers and other vegetables. They offered to pay for everything with Guinean linen or anything else the farmers might want. With Confucian sophistication, Kanzaemon told them that he had already ordered everything to be brought and that the supplies would arrive shortly. His face remained as placid and friendly as always.

When they had spent more than an hour in the farmhouse, the Dutch started to get fidgety. No supplies had come yet, and they decided to take their leave from this nobleman and walk back to their ship. Kanzaemon gestured to them not to be in such a hurry, for he had ordered horses to be brought to take them back to their ship. Schaep politely refused, saying they preferred to walk, and making a last feeble attempt at a joke, showed him his legs. He laughed and said that they were "still young" and could walk very well. Kanzae-mon kept insisting, however, and when the Dutch group saw that the horses had come that very moment, they had to accept his courtesy and do as he wanted.

They mounted the horses, but were surprised to find that suddenly each of them was surrounded by five or six men holding on to them, pretending to do so for fear they might fall off. Motioning that this was not necessary and that they were sitting firmly in the saddle, the Dutch finally became suspicious when they saw that they were being led down the hill further into the valley instead of back toward the bay. Then they spotted a man riding a horse in great haste on the other side of the river and realized they knew him, for he had come to the ship in the company of Kanzaemon that morning. The man was carrying Schaep's cutlass, which he—on coming ashore—had asked to see and then had refused to give it back, pretending it was too heavy and that he would carry it for the captain until they got back to their boat.

> So we quickly dismounted, as we wanted to go back the same way we had come, but looking back we saw the road and the hillside so full of Japanese, as if the whole place were sprouting them and a whole army had (in that short a time) gathered there for the sole purpose of catching us. We then suddenly understood that we had been betrayed and caught. Some of us started to run toward the sea, trying to escape in Japanese boats, but each was pursued by at least twenty men who quickly brought them back. We were still consid-ering breaking through the crowd along the way back, as the Japa-nese hesitated greatly at first to lay hands on us (even though we had no guns with us), but when their leaders had them surround us, we were each seized by at least twelve men (most with unsheathed swords in their hands), lifted up between them and thrown roughly on the ground.[26]

Again the Japanese sources essentially corroborate the Dutch ver-sion of what happened. The document preserved in the Satō family reports: "[The next day,] they were called to Funakoshi with the in-tention to tie them up in that village. They were made to mount horses and accompanied there [by the domain officials]. What can they have been thinking at that moment? When they dismounted at Orikasa everyone [in the neighborhood] was there to meet them."[27] A fine ex-pression: "meet them"! Yes, indeed, while the ten Dutchmen had been waiting patiently in the farmhouse, Kanzaemon's men had positioned all the able-bodied men from the neighborhood to surround the Dutch party in the valley. Having no choice, the farmers and fishermen had obeyed, and scared though they may have been, made the best of this "meeting" with their old friends.

The Dutch report of the capture contains one very intriguing clause: "We were still considering breaking through the crowd along the way back, *as the Japanese hesitated greatly at first to lay hands on us* (even though we had no guns with us) . . . [emphasis added]." It seems that at one moment during their capture the Dutchmen thought that they still had a chance to get away because "the Japanese" were afraid to commit violence against them. To understand why this was so, we have to realize that at this very exciting moment, three worldviews were clashing together, even though the Dutch prisoners could only see two of these, their own and Kanzaemon's.

Both the Dutch understanding of the capture as well as Kanzaemon's were modern and rational, in that the event was essentially interpreted as a matter of relative power. The Dutch suddenly understood that Kanzaemon had been fooling them all along, and that his polite behavior had just been a cover to get them into his power. At this moment, then, the Dutch and Kanzaemon understood each other perfectly. What the Dutchmen did not know, however, was that Kanzaemon's power was not nearly as solid and massive as it seemed. When the Dutch wrote "looking back we saw the road and hillside so full of Japanese, as if the whole place were sprouting them and a whole army had (in that short a time) gathered there for the sole purpose of catching us," they did not know that the vast majority of these men who had been drummed up from the neighboring villages to surround them did not consider the Dutchmen ordinary men like themselves.[28] The villagers of Yamada, in other words, held a worldview very different from that of the Confucian-trained samurai Kanzaemon and his men.

Everything in the Dutch and Japanese sources indicates that, in the backwater of the Bay of Yamada, there still survived a very ancient interpretation of reality as suffused with supernatural powers. The Uezawa document quoted above contains an example of this. When the villagers wanted to invoke the help of the gods, the officials from the Nambu domain scoffed and only gave their permission because "the situation [of the ship being gone] had lasted so long already."[29] But the gods had helped, for they had blown the Big Ship right back into the Bay of Yamada! To the villagers this must have constituted clear proof that the Dutchmen were somehow connected to the gods of their shrines.

The fact that they were sailors only confirmed this, for ships were, in the early magical worldview of Japan, considered to be divine domain *(muen)*, that is, places where the usual human relations and obligations did not reach.[30] Because of this, the Japanese fishermen always felt free to ignore the shogun's laws while they were on the high seas, as we have seen in the case of their visits to the *Castricom.* The *Breskens,* moreover, was a ship of a superior kind, never before seen in the Bay of Yamada. The men who had made it obviously must have possessed supernatural knowledge.[31] To deal with such men, clearly, Japanese specialists of the divine were necessary.[32]

We find the story of the women of Yamada luring the Dutch ashore also in the *Ōzuchi shihairoku* (Record of the Ōzuchi Administration), compiled by the office of the Ōzuchi *daikan,* the administrative official of Hei district to which Yamada belonged.[33] According to this source, the episode with the women happened on the day of the capture, 29 July, instead of the day before as suggested in the documents preserved by the Minato and Satō families of Yamada. Although in the absence of the log of the *Breskens* the exact truth of this matter is difficult to determine, the following facts can be established.

All local Japanese sources agree that women were used to lure the Dutch, but both Kanzaemon and Bijlvelt, each for reasons of his own, chose to erase the episode from their written reports. So did someone from the Minato family, independently, a few hundred years later. Bijlvelt, when writing his report, must have known what the log of the *Breskens* contained up to the day of the capture. He could not write anything in his debriefing report that would contradict the log. If the log contained a reference to a party on shore on 28 July, that would be a good reason for starting his debriefing report on the 29th, instead of the more logical date of the day before when the *Breskens* had returned to the Bay of Yamada. I suspect, therefore, that the documents preserved in the Minato and Satō families are correct, and the Ōzuchi source mistaken, and that the party was held on the evening of 28 July.

There is another possibility. It may be that there was more than one party. For the Uezawa document has this statement: "At that time about eight or nine young ladies, nicely made-up, went together ashore on the little island in front of the Densaku promontory, and while the sailors of the Black Ship were engrossed with them, [the officials] boarded the Big Ship and arrested the captain, taking him to shore and sending him to Edo."[34] According to this document, then, the men on the ship were lulled into inaction. Having had the time of their lives on Koshima, they may have thought that the group going ashore was being similarly treated elsewhere. This would fit in with the evidence from the Dutch debriefing report, which makes one think that the men on the ship were not unduly worried about the disappearance of Schaep's party until the next day, when they received a note from the prisoners in Ōzuchi, twenty kilometers away.[35]

That sex was undoubtedly involved is proven by a lone (and so far overlooked) reference to this episode in the Dutch sources. The first letter written by Governor General Van Diemen after he had learnt of the capture of the men from the *Breskens* is dated 2 May 1644 and addressed to Johan (or Jan) Van Elserack, chief factor of the Dutch settlement in Nagasaki. It contains this commentary: "the ships *Castricom* and *Breskens* have not been able to reach Tartary, nor have they encountered Mr. Versteegen's Gold and Silver Islands; the results of this expedition are described for you in the enclosed summary. Captain Hendrick Cornelissen Schaep has gone ashore for some debauchery in a very imprudent manner and quite contrary to our orders, from which have resulted the present difficulties. May God protect us from more serious trouble. However, upon his arrival at Batavia after his release, he will have to account for his transgressions."[36] Obviously, by the time this letter was written, the log of the *Breskens* had arrived in Batavia, for that is the only way Van Diemen and his Council could have known of the "debauchery."

The document preserved in the Satō family, moreover, concludes with the following remark: "[The present document] was composed with the purpose of informing those who come after us. An account of the way money was spent in connection with this affair as well as the orders issued by the domain officials have been written down on a separate piece of paper and are put away together with this document so that they may be read by our children and grandchildren far into the future. Furthermore, the matter of the reward for the women who boarded the welcome boat on this occasion also has been recognized and recorded on the separate sheet."[37]

A cost accounting receipt for the "services" provided by the local women, then, existed once upon a time! The Satō document is a copy dating from the early nineteenth century, and unsurprisingly, the "separate sheet" is missing nowadays.[38] It may well be that it is missing for the very same reason the log of the *Breskens* was lost and the Minato document vandalized: Everything seems to indicate that the Dutch (from Schaep and Bijlvelt up to Witsen) were not proud to have fallen into such a simple trap, whereas the Japanese, starting with Kanzaemon himself, although originally proud to have fooled the Dutch, later became ashamed of their own methods.

Or was there something else involved? There is, I suspect, more to this episode with the women than first meets the eye. Again, we have to remember that the records quoted in this connection are the reflections of two worldviews, one prevalent among the Dutch at Batavia (debauchery), and the other held by the samurai of Nambu (a ruse). But these were local women; in the Ōzuchi source they are called "*yūjo*," a word written with the characters for "play" and "woman." Its translation "playgirl" is just as misleading as the Japanese term itself, for although the samurai view of these ladies was indeed condescending, the local view again differed considerably from that of the domain officials.

The villagers knew the ladies involved to be connected with the local shrines, although some may also have been wandering shamans *(miko)* or nuns *(bikuni)*, in the area more or less by accident. To the villagers these were not prostitutes or housewives earning extra income. These ladies were specialists of the divine. It is true they had intercourse with men, sometimes for money and sometimes for free, depending on the time and place.

Engelbert Kaempfer, who traveled through Japan some fifty years later, has described these ladies in detail. The order of the *bikuni* had a particular connection with the shrines at Kumano, he writes, "from whence they are call'd Khumano no Bikuni, or the Nuns from Khumano,"[39] and in exchange for a yearly payment to the shrines, they received the right to beg along the roads of Japan accosting travelers with their songs. They went about decently and neatly dressed as ordinary people, and wore gloves without fingers on their hands. They also wore a large hat to cover their faces, and they often used make-up. "Their voice, gestures, and apparent behavior are neither too bold and daring, not too much dejected and affected, but free, comely, and seemingly modest. . . . It must be observ'd, that they make nothing of laying their bosoms quite bare to the view of charitable travellers, all the while they keep them company, under pretence of its being customary in the country, and that for ought I know, they may be, tho' never so religiously shav'd, full as impudent and lascivious, as any whore in a publick bawdyhouse."[40]

We should recall that among the local documents quoted so far, there was one that was preserved by the hereditary priest of the local Kumano shrine, a subsidiary of the shrine complex of which Kaempfer speaks. Moreover, it was this same document that mentions the separate sheet of paper detailing the payments which were made by the office of the Ōzuchi *daikan* for the services of the women involved.

It seems possible, then, that *bikuni* like these were among the women who were called on to communicate with the sailors the first time the *Breskens* sailed into the bay on 10 June 1643. If this is true, then it is probable that the Dutch sailors were agreeably surprised to be able to "communicate" so easily in Japan. What is more, it becomes understandable why the *Breskens* came back to Yamada. The ship was, indeed, forced by the supernatural and divine powers of the shrine maidens at Yamada.

The Dutchmen were put flat on their stomachs with nooses around their necks and their hands tied behind their backs.[41] Japanese samurai were experts in tying people up. All prisoners were tied in exactly the same manner, with exactly the same number of knots and nooses, all at equal distances. There were loops around their breasts and necks. The elbows almost touched each other behind their backs, and the hands were firmly tied together.[42] This is what the Japanese call *"ganji garame"* (tied up like a goose), ready for the roasting.

While being bound, each one of the prisoners must have thought this was the last day of his life. After binding them, their captors washed their faces, and placed the men upright again. They were asked whether they would like to appear before the "emperor" (i.e., the shogun) and pay him their respects. Indignant and defiant, the Dutchmen told their captors that, indeed, they would like to do so, for "we were Hollanders and trusted that we would be freed by the emperor (when he understands the reason for our coming here), as our Captain who resides in Nagasaki for the affairs of the Company, pays his respects and presents gifts to His Majesty in Edo every year."[43]

Since all the men were still together at this moment, Schaep took advantage of the opportunity to warn his men to be silent about everything concerning "the expedition and papistry." He encouraged them to be patient, to bear their present captivity with endurance, and to pray to God that He might grant His blessing, either in this life or the next.

~

What are the facts of the capture of the men from the *Breskens?* We know from the Dutch debriefing report that the *Breskens* sailed into the Bay of Yamada for the second time on the morning of 28 July 1643. We also know that ten of her crew were detained on shore against their will a little more than twenty-four hours later. Everything described above that occurred in between, however, is educated guesswork. And even if we look at these two facts only, a host of questions remain.

Without the log kept on the *Breskens,* it is not possible to determine exactly why the yacht returned to Yamada, where she had taken water on 10 June of that year. Along the northern coast of Honshu there are a number of other bays that have more accessible anchorage than Yamada. The reason the prisoners themselves would later give —that the ship needed fresh supplies and repairs—is clearly insufficient to explain why Schaep and his men waited to go ashore until they arrived at Yamada's latitude.

Seen from the perspective of the villagers around the bay, the return of the *Breskens* to Yamada takes on a completely different aspect. From the local sources it is clear that, in the eyes of the villagers, the foreigners had been brought back by "a divine wind." What needs to be stressed here is that this concept of the "divine wind" was, in the framework of the local worldview, as much of an "undeniable fact" as the date of the return of the *Breskens* is in our framework, and it should be admitted that ultimately both frameworks are nothing but man-made conventions.

The same is even more true of the arrest of the Dutchmen. As we will see later in this study, to the outside world the Japanese authorities always denied that an arrest had taken place. On the contrary, in their view, shipwrecked sailors had been saved in Japan. To deny such a "fact" would have been extremely dangerous at the time, and it is not surprising that what started as an expedient explanation of an embarrassing situation took on a life of its own and has continued to the present day.[44]

The detained Dutchmen, however, never referred to themselves other than as "prisoners from Nambu," an expression implying that an arrest had taken place. However, if we look at the same event through the eyes of the villagers, this fact, again, fits into a completely different context. It is clear that the villagers around the bay were forced, on this occasion, to make a choice of whom to fear most: their own gods or the authorities of the Nambu domain. Not surprisingly, they chose the certain over the uncertain. Although to commit violence against the Dutchmen might anger their gods, to disobey the order of Lord Nambu's samurai was certain to entail the immediate destruction of all the villages around the bay.

From the evidence available it is clear that the villagers did their utmost to appease their gods in the eventuality they were contemplating sending any more disasters. This, I think, explains why two of the three shrines mentioned in the local documents are still said to preserve relics *(shintai)* from the *Breskens*. These are the shrines dedicated to Kumano Daigongen and Shinzan Daimyōjin. So far, only the former has allowed inspection of its treasure, a bar of iron hammered into a gourd-shaped object, the metal of which has been determined to be of European origin. From the continuing existence of such relics, which have been kept with religious care for more than 350 years, we may infer that the arrest of the men from the *Breskens* had considerable impact on the religious life of the people around the bay.

Chapter 3
Incompatible Jailbirds

On 27 June 1643, Ichinokai Jinbei set out to bring in his oxen, which he had left tied up near the shore of Kachime Ōshima. This was an island off the coast of Chikuzen (Fukuoka), where Jinbei had lived all his life. Approaching the spot, he was surprised to see a boat in the water and people on the beach. They were dressed as Japanese, carried swords, and had done up their hair in samurai fashion. Some of them were of such large size and had such long noses, however, that it made Jinbei suspicious and hesitant to go near them.[1]

Then, one of the strangers called out to him and began to ask questions in Japanese about the neighborhood, and in particular about the purpose of the building on top of the mountain. Jinbei told him it was a lookout, guarded by men of the daimyo to watch out for foreign ships, especially those of *kirishitan* (Christians), Spanish or Portuguese, "in case they came by stealth to spread the Evil Religion."[2] That seemed to frighten the strangers. They offered Jinbei two pieces of silver if he would wait on the beach until they had climbed back into their boat and sailed off and their sail had disappeared. Jinbei took the money, stayed for a while where he was, and then ran back home to see Ichinokai Jirōzaemon, his older brother, who was the guardian of the island's shrine.[3]

Together they went to warn Murai Jin'emon Muneyuki, the *bugyō* (highest official, usually translated as "governor") of the island, who happened to be at the mountain lookout. Someone was sent up to fetch him. When Murai came down and heard what had happened, he immediately ordered a boat to be made ready for pursuit. He commanded the strongest of the villagers to board it with him, even though the strangers were already so far off it seemed impossible to overtake them. But the wind turned, so the sail of the foreign boat was of no use to its fleeing crew. At Jinoshima, off Ashiya-ura, the villagers caught up with the boat of the strangers and Jin'emon shot a warning arrow over their heads. After that the strangers let down their sail to indicate that they were giving up their attempt to escape and waited for the villagers' boat to come alongside.

Jin'emon jumped into their boat, and tied up all the foreigners. Then he towed the boat back to Ōshima. There were ten prisoners in all, and Jin'emon reported this to his lord in Fukuoka. Word came back that he was to bring the prisoners to the castle town so that the daimyo, Kuroda Tadayuki, could have a look at them. Among the prisoners, there were four foreign priests *(bateren)*, one of whom was sixty-eight years old, and one lay brother *(iruman)* originally from Nagasaki. Of the five other *kirishitan*, three were Japanese. All of this was immediately reported to Nagasaki and Edo, and after their confessions had been written down, the group of foreigners was sent from Fukuoka to Nagasaki in carrying baskets. Kuroda Genzaemon and three captains of the domain's rifle brigade, two doctors, and more than three hundred men accompanied them there.[4]

Even though the *kirishitan* had more than two hundred pieces of gold, three *kamme* of silver,* and other valuable utensils on board, the Kuroda turned everything over to Lord Yamazaki Gonpachirō, the highest shogunal official in Nagasaki.[5] The news of the capture reached Edo on 12 July 1643,[6] and on that same a day a shogunal missive *(hōsho)* was sent back to Kuroda Tadayuki, praising him for governing his fief correctly, and expressing the shogun's satisfaction that he had arrested the followers of the Evil Sect so quickly.[7] Two days later, similar missives were sent to the daimyo of Ōmura and Saga, two Kyushu lords not in attendance in Edo at the time, urging them to be as vigilant as the Kuroda had been in guarding their fiefs from foreign intrusions.[8] The valuables of gold and silver that had been in the boat were ordered divided among the people of Ōshima.[9]

～

This group of missionaries is known as the second Rubino group.[10] *Visitator* Antonio Rubino, convinced the infamous Jesuit renegade

---

*One *kamme* = 3.75 kg.

Christovão Ferreira was "predestined to be saved,"[11] had organized two groups of men willing to join him in this enterprise to rescue Ferreira. The object of their effort was known in Japan as the spy *(mea-kashi)*, Sawano Chū'an.[12] Apprehended in 1633, the one-time Vice Provincial of the Jesuit mission in Japan had foregone his chance to become a martyr for his faith and apostatized after torture. Since that time, having undergone a complete brainwashing and loss of his former self, he had assisted the Japanese authorities at Nagasaki in their efforts to eradicate Christianity. For a small stipend, he wrote anti-Christian pamphlets,[13] and interpreted at the interrogations of Christians caught in the area. By the 1640s he had become the Society of Jesus' main nemesis in Japan. The Dutch traders met him frequently in Nagasaki, where he sometimes interpreted for them and sometimes came to visit the factory doctor to learn about "Dutch" medicine. Their verdict of him was: "Chū'an, who looks so mean and black in the face, reflecting his mind, as ever a papist can be."[14]

The first group of nine men, which included Father Rubino himself, arrived in the summer of 1642 off the coast of Satsuma, where they were arrested several days later and brought to Nagasaki on 22 August. The case was allowed to be handled at Nagasaki, and the men were tortured with water every other day to induce their apostasy. They held out until March of 1643. On the seventeenth of that month, the Dutch factor at Nagasaki noted in his journal that "The papists and their servants, nine men in all, who have been imprisoned here since 22 August [last year], have been led on scraggly horses through the whole town at the orders of the authorities. Callers, who called out who they were, what crime they had committed against the emperor's orders and how they were to die, went ahead."[15]

They died by the unspeakable *anatsurushi* method, or "hanging in the pits." Only one of the servants apostatized, but he died anyway, on the same day that he was let down from his gallows. The corpses of the other eight were "immediately hacked into small pieces and burned to ashes, which were later carefully collected and thrown out into the ocean far from the shore."[16]

～

The so-called second Rubino group (with which we are dealing here) arrived in Japan just three months after the first had been destroyed in the thorough manner described above. The leader of the second group was the Jesuit Pedro Marquez (1575–1657), born at Mouram, in the archbishopric of Evora, Portugal.[17] After his training and admission into the Society of Jesus at the age of seventeen, we find him in 1627 in Tonkin and in 1632 on the island of Hainan. In 1636, he was in Macao, where he cosigned the order expelling Ferreira from the Society for his apostasy. At the time of Marquez' capture, he was sixty-eight years old and had just received his appointment as Provincial, or head of the Roman Catholic Church in Japan.[18]

His three European companions were: Alonzo de Arroyo (1592–1644), fifty-one years old, from Malaga in Andalusia, doctor of philosophy and former priest of the Spanish settlement of Cavite in the Philippines, where he had arrived in 1621; Francisco Cassola (1603–1644), forty years old, a mathematician and astronomer who had been in Manila in 1636 with Mastrilli, later to become famous as a martyr in Japan; and Giuseppe Chiara (1603–1685), an Italian, also forty years old and recently coming from Manila as well. These four Jesuits were accompanied by six Asian converts: one lay brother *(iruman)* and five supporters *(dōjuku)*. The lay brother was Andreas Vieyra (1601–1678), forty-two years old, who had been born in Mogi and brought up in Nagasaki. He was later named Nampō, and had been educated in Macao and Manila. The supporters included two Japanese men: one from Imabashi Itchōme in Osaka, known to the Europeans as Julius and to the Japanese as Shirō'emon, fifty-one years old; and one from Mototsuchimikado machi in Kamikyō of Kyoto, known as Kassian and Mata'emon, also fifty-one years old.[19] These three men had left Japan in the early 1620s and were coming home, pathetically, to certain torture and death.

Then there was Lorenzo Pinto, thirty-two years old, whose father was Chinese and whose mother was of mixed Japanese and Portuguese descent. Even though his parents lived in Macao, Pinto had many friends and connections in Nagasaki.[20] The last two supporters were a twenty-year-old Chinese man from Canton, called Juan and later Saburōzaemon, and a seventeen-year-old Vietnamese man from Tonkin, known as Donatus or Nikan. These men were the last of the group to die, in 1697 and 1700 respectively.

The captives freely confessed they had come to Japan to preach Christianity, or as the Japanese put it: "to spread the Evil Doctrine in order to snatch away [authority in] the country of Japan."[21] They had disguised themselves as Japanese because the shogun had forbidden foreign priests to proselytize. Nevertheless, they were put to the water torture to make sure they were holding nothing back.[22] Professor Boxer has described two kinds of water torture from a Portuguese source:

> In the first kind, they hang the martyr upside down with his legs apart, placing his head in a bucket of water whose level is above his nostrils. After the chord attached to his feet is drawn tight, they let the body revolve slowly in the air. This is a very painful torture through the efforts the sufferer makes to breathe. In the second kind, they tie the martyr down on a board, leaving his left hand free so that he can place it on his breast if he wishes to give a sign that he will recant. His head is left hanging down a little, and the torturers do not stop pouring great quantities of water on his face (usually covered with a thin piece of cloth). The victims makes such frantic efforts to breathe that they usually burst a blood vessel.[23]

When the results of their interrogations at Nagasaki had been reported to Edo, word was received to send the prisoners there. They were to be accompanied by two professional interpreters of Portuguese, Namura Hachizaemon and Nishi Kichibei, who usually served the Nagasaki *bugyō* in his dealings with the Dutch at Deshima. The ubiquitous Sawano Chū'an (Ferreira) was to come along as well.[24]

In August of 1643, then, two separate trains of Japanese officials transporting foreign prisoners were moving toward the shogun's capital at the same time. It was inevitable that they should meet.[25]

After an exhausting trip through the interior of the Nambu domain, the men from the *Breskens* arrived in the domain capital of Morioka on 1 August. There they waited for two weeks before they were put on horses again and brought to Edo.[26] They arrived in the afternoon of 25 August and were lodged in the Nagasakiya, the inn where the Dutch factor stayed when he came to Edo on his yearly visit. In 1643, the Nagasakiya was already located at Kokuchō Sanchōme and was run by the son of its founder, Nagasakiya Gen'emon, the name also used by all his descendants down to the nineteenth century. The Dutch group was only too glad to be quartered here, for although prison-like it certainly was no prison. After almost one month in Japan, the Dutchmen were fully aware of the fact that criminals were treated in Japan in quite a different manner.

In contrast to the treatment of the other group of prisoners who were still on their way from Kyushu, the Dutchmen (who considered themselves the shogun's prisoners) were not jailed. From this we may already conclude that the bakufu realized, from the very time of their arrival in Edo, that the Dutch group would probably have to be released eventually. As foreigners who had entered Japan at an unusual place (Nambu), they were under suspicion (e.g., of being in league with the Portuguese), but being Dutch they were not automatically guilty of a crime.

Gen'emon's inn had two stories connected by an outside staircase.[27] The innkeeper, his family, and employees all lived there, so that the Nagasakiya must have had three or more separate apartments: one upstairs for the Dutch factor and at least two downstairs. Schaep's men were lodged downstairs rather than upstairs. If the innkeeper's own quarters were located in front, and those of the Dutch factor upstairs, the kitchen must have been in the middle before one reached the apartment of the Dutch captives in the back.

The whole inn was probably narrow in width, but fairly long, that is, twenty *ken*,* for that was the standard depth of all houses in the merchant quarter of Edo. This regulation left in the middle of each block an open space of about twenty *ken* square, closed off from the four streets the block faced, and shared by the inhabitants of four different block organizations.[28] In the case of Kokuchō Sanchōme, this common space was occupied by a large bell tower, in which hung an enormous bell. One wonders why the Dutch accounts never mention this bell, which was Edo's earliest timepiece. As a poetaster had it: "Kokuchō no / kane wa kōmō / made kikoe [Kokuchō's bell / is even heard by / the Red Hairs]."[29] The bell had been cast for use inside the shogun's Castle, but it was removed from there to the rice merchants' quarter in Hidetada's time (when it was replaced inside the Castle by the more martial and less obnoxious sound of a large drum). A man by the name of Tsuji Genshichi (as were all his descendants) was appointed to strike the bell every two hours. It must have been raised quite a few feet off the ground, for it is said that the executions in the Kodenmachō jail, five blocks to the east, were timed by the sound of the bell from Kokuchō Sanchōme.

When the Dutch group had been in the Nagasakiya for about half an hour, Kanzaemon appeared. The men were startled to see him. They

---

*One *ken* = 1.81 meters.

thought he had gone back to Yamada after he had brought them to Morioka, the castle town of the Nambu domain. His appearance brought back old fears of having a price on their heads. He acted friendly enough, but it was impossible for the Dutchmen to trust or like him. They imagined now that he had "a shifty look of false appearances on his face,"[30] thought that he was very disappointed to see them lodged where they were and not in jail, and suspected him of having instituted "judicial proceedings" against them.[31]

That same afternoon, Captain Schaep, Junior Merchant Wilhem Bijlvelt, and cabin boy Jacob De Pauw were summoned to the residence of "Sicungodonne," as the Dutch transcribed the Japanese court title Chikugo dono. The man so called was the Commissioner of Foreigners (and police official), Inoue Masashige. According to his official biography, Inoue Seibei Masashige (1585–1661) was born the fourth son of Inoue Han'emon Kiyohide in the province of Tōtōmi. In 1608, he came to serve the second shogun Hidetada as a castle guard, and in 1615, on the occasion of the siege of Osaka castle, Masashige managed to take his first enemy head. In 1616, he was placed close to the future shogun, Tokugawa Iemitsu, and in 1625 he advanced to *metsuke* (spy). The next year, he accompanied Iemitsu on his visit to the emperor in Kyoto, and on 27 April 1627 he was given the junior fifth rank lower grade as well as the title Chikugo no kami. On 26 January 1633, he was appointed *ōmetsuke* (grand spy), by which time the size of his fief had increased to more than 4,000 *koku*.[32]

Clearly, Inoue made his career as a protégé of the third shogun himself, who must have recognized Inoue's diverse talents. That Iemitsu recognized Inoue's abilities as a trouble shooter becomes especially clear from the time of Inoue's appointment as *ōmetsuke* onward: In 1636, he was sent to Okazaki in connection with the arrival of the Korean ambassador. At the time of the Shimabara rebellion, in 1637, he was sent to Kyushu as shogunal envoy. On 30 July 1639, he was granted an additional 6,000 *koku* and received orders to travel west to Nagasaki "in connection with the foreign trade and the interdiction of Christianity."[33]

In his official biography, Inoue's connection with the persecution of Christians in Japan is mentioned only once, despite that fact that it was the major preoccupation of the second half of his career in the shogunal administration. According to the Dutch factory journal, Inoue himself had been a Christian until he was forty, that is, around

1625.[34] Because of his earlier religious beliefs, perhaps, the compilers
of his biography did not stress this later aspect of Inoue's career. On
8 July 1643, however, Inoue's pay was raised another 3000 *koku*,
probably as a reward for his success in effecting the apostasy of several native and foreign Jesuit priests.[35] One of the last entries in his
biography is: "On 9 January 1651, because he had served on a falcon
hunt and bore the severe cold in spite of his advanced age, he was
praised for his continuous service and received from the shogun's own
hands his *haori* [jacket] to put on."[36] This incident proves that, up to
the very year of Iemitsu's death, Inoue succeeded in preserving the
shogun's faith in him, although sometimes, as we shall see, he skirted
the limits of Iemitsu's limited forbearance.

The Japanese sources do not give any details of Inoue's life before
his twenty-third year. But as he is one of the most prominent Japanese officials appearing in the journals of the Dutch chief factors,
more details can be added from this source. A revealing entry is the
following:

> Gen'emon, interpreter for Chikugo no kami, came tonight to
> request, in the name of his master, medicine for the same Gemba
> Sama (mentioned above . . . [as Inoue's son-in-law]) who was bleed-
> ing from the anus profusely, as he did periodically, in an unnatural
> manner. Gen'emon related very freely, shamelessly and without any
> prevaricating, that Gemba had incurred this in his youth through
> sodomy or acting like a woman for Chikugo no kami whose cata-
> mite he had been: having done this, he had been raised—oh horror!
> —to become the confidant of his master and had acquired high
> status (for he was of but very low origins himself). Our surgeon sus-
> pected that some hemorrhoid veins must have been ruptured in the
> anus and turned into abscesses. He supplied the necessary medi-
> cines for this ailment in accordance with the details he was supplied
> with in this case of a forty-five year old man who had continually
> been suffering from this.[37]

That Gemba was not the only one who rose to unknown heights
in this manner is clearly proven by many other cases in Iemitsu's own
vicinity, including Gemba's benefactor, the *ōmetsuke* himself, as the
following entry shows:

> On his return, the interpreter Hachizaemon (who often talks very
> freely) said that . . . (maybe he was not ashamed for his compa-
> triots' predilection for this vice or possibly he despised them for it,
> I don't know) this was very common among the great lords, who

usually care more for such bugger boys than for their own women, for which reason it often happens that they have few offspring. And when the shameful objects [of such desires] reach manhood (he said) they usually are raised above all other faithful retainers and loved by their lords. . . . The councilor Hotta Kaga no kami . . . . and also Inoue Chikugo and many others (who all surrendered their bodies to the former shogun) were promoted for these same reasons to such high positions.[38]

In 1643, Inoue had reached the apogee of his power and was living just outside the inner Castle moat at Hitotsubashi on the spot where now the Public University for Women is located.[39] This is about twenty or twenty-five minutes walk from Kokuchō Sanchōme.

On the warm summer evening of 25 August 1643, the three Dutchmen walked this distance for the first time. They were allowed to go without any guards other than their landlord Gen'emon and two of his servants.[40] On their arrival at Inoue's mansion, they entered through the gate, crossed the courtyard, and after passing through the hallway (genkan), were told to wait in Inoue's decorated antechamber. Shortly thereafter, Inoue appeared on the spacious verandah outside the antechamber, in the company of the Nagasaki bugyō residing in Edo, the veteran soldier in the shogun's army (hatamoto), Baba Saburōzaemon Toshishige.[41]

Baba's official biography does not give us the year of his birth.[42] It only tells us that he was born as a son of Baba Masatsugu and that he first served Tokugawa Ieyasu in 1600, so he probably was only a few years older than Inoue. It was also in 1600 that he followed his father into the battle of Sekigahara, which established the Tokugawa dynasty. Later he served the second shogun as Castle guard (goshoinban). He became metsuke (spy) in 1632, and he had accumulated fief lands worth 2600 koku by 1636. In that year he received orders to travel to Nagasaki to reorganize the city's political structure. When the Shimabara rebellion occurred in 1637, even though there were no incidents in nearby Nagasaki, Baba was ordered to go there just in case.

Later that year, he took part in the attack on Hara castle, the center of the rebellion, and after its fall he returned to Nagasaki. On 15 December 1637, he was appointed the city's bugyō, an office he held until he retired on 8 March 1652. He died five years later. It is clear that Baba did not have the same "connections" as Inoue did, but he was a self-made man who had seen battle on more than one occasion.

In Baba's case as well, the Dutch sources are able to add a new dimension to the flat hagiography of his Japanese biography. Chief Factor Jan Van Elserack wrote about Baba in the following manner: "Since before we were moved to Nagasaki, he had never reported anything good about the Dutch, but [on the contrary] he has always concentrated [in his communications with the bakufu] on all evil and calumny which were brought to his attention by his toadies (enemies of the Company) in Nagasaki, without investigating their allegations. In private, His Excellency despises us and tries to take his revenge in all possible ways."[43]

Inoue and Baba often appear in the Dutch journals of the 1640s and 1650s, and dominate the journal during the time the Dutch factors spent in Edo. If, as loyal servants of Iemitsu, these men can be said to have had any partiality toward the foreigners remaining in Nagasaki after the expulsion edicts of the 1630s, Baba may have favored the Chinese (who showered him with gifts), while Inoue may have preferred the Dutch for he had an interest in Dutch medicine (we have seen why) and instrument making.[44]

Officially, Inoue did not accept gifts, but the Dutch knew him better than that and "sold" him quantities of binoculars, maps, mirrors, ointments, pills, pistols, and various other goods at prices far below cost. Each year, the orders (eisch) from the Japanese included a list of things for Inoue, so that we are justified in suspecting this samurai of running a little sideline trading in Dutch articles. It is not surprising, then, that generally the Dutch sources of the 1640s are slanted in Inoue's favor, for he was their "protector" who had his own stake in the continued presence of the Dutch in Japan.[45] Inoue walked a fine line between favoring the Dutch and being favored by Iemitsu. The latter supposedly excluded the former, but Inoue was a consummate artist who never fell from grace.

Both men smiled when they saw the Dutch captives for the first time and said the magic word of mutual understanding: "Oranda! [Holland!]"[46] A Spanish apostate called Dōku, who had traveled with the shogunal police officers to bring the Dutch group from Morioka to Edo, was also present on this occasion.[47] He was ordered to translate the questions the Dutchmen had already been asked several times before: where had they come from, where did they want to go, why had they come so far north, and why had they entered the Bay of Yamada? The Dutchmen took care to answer these questions as they had before. The Japanese officials then produced a Portuguese map and had the Dutch explain their story using it. When Captain Schaep had finished, there was no comment. Sake was served, and each of the three Dutchmen was poured two cups before they were amiably given leave to return to their lodgings.

The next morning, 26 August 1643, all ten Dutchmen were again summoned to Inoue's residence. This time, the antechamber was full of people requesting an audience with the *ōmetsuke*. While they were waiting, two Japanese men, who spoke fluent Portuguese, came up to them. They said that they were merchants from Nagasaki and knew the Dutch factors there very well. They asked the captain if anyone of the Dutch group spoke any Portuguese or Spanish. Schaep denied they spoke anything other than Dutch.

Two hours later, they were interrogated and asked the same questions as the day before. Each of the sailors was given some sake and asked, just for the sake of becoming acquainted, if they were Portuguese. They all denied this: "No, Hollanders!" When they were leaving to return to the Nagasakiya, they noticed a commotion: "Coming out of the building, we saw in the yard three or four plain and tightly shut palanquins and a couple of people tied and trussed up. We were told these people were Japanese Christians who had been caught, and also that those who were sitting in the carrying baskets were four Portuguese papists. Our men told us that they had seen (while they were being interrogated) two baskets with several Portuguese frocks, coats, books, and manuscripts, and [several sets of] iron handcuffs being brought in (which frightened them a lot, because they thought they were going to be manacled)."[48]

Half an hour after the Dutchmen had returned to their lodgings, they were again summoned to Inoue's residence. The sudden recall frightened them, and when they asked the meaning of it, they were told that some great lords wanted to see them. Returning to the *ōmetsuke*'s mansion, they saw the same prisoners they had observed that morning. The priests were handcuffed in the presence of the Dutch group, which frightened them, for again they thought they were going to be treated in the same manner.

The Dutchmen noticed that, in the one- or two-hour interval

since they had walked to the Nagasakiya and back again to Inoue's, the tops of the Jesuits' heads had been shaved bald. In contrast, the first time the Dutch group had caught a glimpse of the priests, they had remarked that the men were still in their disguise with their hair done in the Japanese style.

After a short wait, Inoue and Baba appeared on the verandah. They were accompanied by another lord, who remains unidentified in the Dutch debriefing report, but who must have outranked Inoue considerably to be able to reverse his orders and have the Dutch come back to the mansion at Hitotsubashi at his request. He was probably someone from Edo's Castle with direct access to the shogun, and with orders to report to him immediately on the two groups of newly caught foreigners. He may have been someone like the personal attendants *(gosoba)* Makino Chikashige or Kuze Hiroyuki.

The Dutchmen were forthwith brought before this gentleman and again sharply interrogated about their voyage and their arrival in Nambu. They were also asked if they had brought any "papists" to Nambu. This the Hollanders vehemently denied, adding that

> [we were] willing to forfeit our lives if their Excellencies were ever informed of the contrary. They further told us that they had just caught the aforementioned papists (Jesuits they are); and also asked us if we were papists of the same sect and religion as well, and if we wished to be alone with them some time.
>
> We answered (showing our loathing of them, spitting at them and kicking them with our feet) that we did not belong to their sect or share their beliefs, indicating that we were ready to kill them if given permission to do so. Meanwhile, the steward Siewert Jansz Mes showed the injury (which had not yet completely healed) he had received (before Ceylon) from the Portuguese, telling them he would like to take his revenge (if permitted) on these papists (by taking their heads), which gave the said gentlemen plenty to think about and about which they showed us their satisfaction. We were then given our leave and walked (happy to be allowed to go so freely) back to our lodgings.[49]

This scene with the Dutchmen trying to ingratiate themselves with their Japanese captors obviously does not show the Dutch in the most heroic light.[50] That night, the apostate Dōku visited the Dutch in the Nagasakiya and took down their names and ages. He was accompanied by the two Japanese "merchants" they had met that morning at Inoue's. This time, they told Captain Schaep that they were, in reality, interpreters for the Dutch East India Company, and were called Kichibei and Hachizaemon. They had come to Edo with the captured Jesuits and were staying with another apostate "Siuan" (Ferreira), in the upstairs apartment of the same inn as the Dutch. Three government spies, then, had been lodged right over the heads of the Dutch captives.

~

Ten days later, on the morning of 5 September 1643, all the guests of the Nagasakiya, that is, the ten Dutchmen, the two Japanese interpreters Kichibei and Hachizaemon, and the apostate Sawano Chū'an, were brought with a large train of guards outside the city of Edo. The Dutch were extremely frightened again, for they feared they were being brought to an execution ground. They went along Kokuchō Street to its eastern end at the Asakusa Gate and the bridge over the Castle's outer moat. From there, they followed the Ōshūdō, or main highway leading to the northeast, along which they had entered the city ten days earlier.

On their right stretched, block after block, the shogun's warehouses, conveniently located along the mouth of the Sumida river. On their left, much of the land was still used to cultivate rice, although these fields would disappear to make room for commoner housing in the following decade. After an hour's walk, the train halted at "a large manor, about the size of a large village or a small town in Holland."[51] This "village" included the country mansion belonging to the Hotta family, and was located near the oldest temple in the Kanto plain, the Sensōji or Asakusadera, dating from the eighth century.

There exists a map of Edo, dating from the Shōhō period (1644–1647), and drawn up between 1644 and 1645. The interesting feature of this map, which comes uncannily close to representing the actual situation at the time of our focus here, is the large number of Buddhist establishments completely surrounding the Hotta property. It is not surprising that the Dutch report does not mention any of these temples for, architecturally, they would have been indistinguishable from the Hotta mansion. To the Dutchmen, the whole block looked like one village.

Although this spot, overlooking the Sumida river, was famous for its beauty,[52] the Dutch were convinced they were not on a picnic. The fearful tension that pervades their whole report comes to a climax here. On entering the "village," the Dutch were led through several alleys, gates, and corridors until they were first "put into a dark and ugly hole (in which we found the said captured papists and Japanese Christians), and later on the [bare] cobblestones under a covered shed in a large yard (with many small gibbets and large tubs filled with water, resembling a torture chamber, and with countless courtiers, secretaries, servants, executioners, etc. walking to and fro)."[53]

The Bluebeard of this place was Iemitsu's favorite councilor, Hotta Masamori. Masamori's is one of the more remarkable careers in Japanese history. Not only did he rise from obscure origins to one of the most powerful positions in the country, but by doing so at the right time when the social fabric seemed to be coalescing (later ossifying and at last petrifying) into immobile patterns, he assured the continued existence of his descendants on a similar elevated plane, a situation that has continued to this very day.[54] The question, of course, becomes: how did he do it?

"By being a wise councilor, much appreciated by the sage shogun Iemitsu," is the traditional answer in Japan. My own answer, based on an examination of the facts provided by both the Japanese and Dutch sources, would be: "By an uncanny ability to cater to, share, and appease Iemitsu's phobias." Masamori was the only person during Iemitsu's reign who might be called a "friend" of the shogun.

It all began when Masamori became Iemitsu's page in 1621. He was thirteen, and the future shogun, who had been born in 1604 on Tanabata or the seventh day of the seventh lunar month, was three and a half years older. Masamori must have been a handsome youth, for he was immediately noticed by the future shogun, whose sexual interest was exclusively for his own sex.[55] The *Tokugawa jikki* provides some interesting details of this relationship in the obituary for Sakai Shigezumi, another of Iemitsu's favorites:

> From his youth he served close to the shogun. Together with Hotta Kaga no kami Masamori he formed a pair of the shogun's lovers. The shogun took good care of him. In office and stipend, Shigezumi was not inferior to Masamori, and Masamori was not superior to Shigezumi. Whenever the shogun favored Masamori, he would invariably do the same for Shigezumi. When Masamori's fief was increased to 30,000 *koku*, Shigezumi's was also increased to 30,000 *koku* in Sekiyado in the province of Shimōsa. Afterwards, for some reason, when a year had passed in which [Shigezumi] had stayed at home because of what he called an illness, he was suddenly accused

of a crime and sent away to the province of Bingo, where he was
put under house arrest by Mizuno Hyūga no kami Katsunari. This
was because while staying so-called sick at home he had fathered
many children with his wife and concubines.[56]

Of the shogun's two favorites, then, it was Masamori who won
out, being appointed captain of the Castle guard *(bangashira)* in
1626, becoming a member of the *rokuninshū* advisory council in
1633, receiving the junior fourth rank lower grade in 1634, and
being given a whopping increase of 65,000 *koku* to a total of 100,000
koku as daimyo of the Matsumoto domain on 21 April 1638. Poor
Shigezumi, who had not been as obedient to the shogun's wishes as
Masamori, finally committed suicide in October 1642 out of jealousy
of Masamori, whose income had just been raised to 110,000 *koku* as
daimyo of the Sakura domain in August of that year.

There are several facts which recur time and again in Masamori's
biography: how Masamori often received game shot by the shogun
himself, how he and Iemitsu prepared each other tea, and how they
exchanged swords and tea utensils. All of these ritual exchanges were
more or less public and so signified Masamori's special position in a
world where all political power derived from one's relationship to the
shogun. The two men's giving and counter-giving of valuable swords
by famous sword smiths may have had, apart from their obvious
significance as symbols of warrior culture, a deeper Freudian meaning as well. Most significant in their relationship, however, is the
fact that the shogun visited Masamori's city and country mansions
on numerous occasions over a period of fourteen years, from 1637
until the shogun's death in 1651—this at a time when it was considered a great honor for a senior retainer to receive the shogun even once.
For example, Iemitsu visited the hard-working and loyal Matsudaira
Nobutsuna, who had been the shogun's personal attendant since the
latter's birth, only once.[57]

Iemitsu's visits to Masamori's residences, then, give us important
clues to the shogun's preoccupations, some of which have already
been mentioned: the hunt, the tea ceremony, and the martial arts.
However, from the Dutch account with its short but grim description
of the torture instruments present at Hotta's country mansion, we
may now add —to put it mildly—an interest in human endurance as
well. The following entries from Masamori's official biography should
make this even more clear:

On the 21st day of the 4th month of Kan'ei 20 [7 June 1643], the shogun came to his country mansion in order to correct the mistaken opinions of the adherents of the Evil Law with Inoue Chikugo no kami Masashige . . . .

On the 22nd day of the 7th month [5 September 1643], when the shogun visited him there was a severe interrogation of the barbarian prisoners and Christians caught in the territories of Nambu Yamashiro no kami Shigenao and Matsudaira Uemon no suke Tadayuki, altogether twenty people who were made to sit in the garden. Inoue Chikugo no kami appeared before the shogun.

On the 13th day of the 8th month [25 September 1643], the shogun came again and had Inoue Masashige again examine [the Jesuits] . . . .

On the 1st day of the 4th month of Shōhō 1 [18 May 1644], the shogun heard again the Christians being examined by Inoue Masashige at the Asakusa mansion.[58]

The editors of this biography included just a sampling of these ominous visits in Masamori's biography. This is proven by the Mito manuscript *Sokkyōhen,* which was analyzed in the 1930s by Professor Anesaki.[59] From his research we may add seven other occasions.* So, in the space of one year, the shogun visited Hotta's mansion in connection with the torture of Christians eleven times. In the same year, on several occasions, he went also to the country mansion of Sakai Tadakatsu at Ushigome for the same purpose, so these visits of the shogun connected with the torture of Christians averaged more than once a month.

That the Dutchmen were forced to sample the "dark and ugly hole" where the captured Jesuits were being kept while at Hotta's mansion was, of course, to impress on them the difference in treatment accorded them as nationals of a friendly nation. We do not know what passed between these incompatible jailbirds at the time, whether the Jesuits were again abused by their Dutch cell mates, or even how much time they spent together. The Dutch report is silent on these points, but it was probably not longer than an hour, for otherwise we would have some complaint from them. We will see that their presence in Hotta's mansion may also have been meant to show them the gradual

---

*22 October 1643, 18 December 1643, 21 January 1644, 16 March 1644, 7 May 1644, 27 May 1644, 3 June 1644.

deterioration of the Jesuits' humanity at the hands of their Japanese tormentors.

For the time being, the men from the *Breskens* were told to wait until the Jesuits had been interrogated, and then they would be called by "Owijsamma."[60] The latter is the way Bijlvelt wrote down "Ōi Sama," that is, Doi Toshikatsu (1573–1644), who had been brought up with the second shogun of the Tokugawa line, Hidetada, and had remained his lifelong confidant. He had been entrusted with the guardianship of Iemitsu together with Sakai Tadayo (1572–1636) and Aoyama Tadatoshi (1578–1643). Of the three, Doi was the only one left in Iemitsu's inner circle, albeit chiefly in a ceremonial position. On the surface it seems he was the highest official present at this time, for the shogun himself was there incognito. However, in view of Toshikatsu's debilitating illness, it is unlikely that he really made the trip to Asakusa for such a trifling matter as showing the Dutchmen to the shogun. From a later entry in the debriefing report,[61] it is also possible to speculate that Iemitsu himself hid behind Toshikatsu's title on this occasion.

Professor Anesaki has translated the relevant entry in the *Sokkyōhen* for this day: "Graciously went down to Hotta's villa a little before noon and stayed until dusk. The four Namban sent up from Chikuzen were examined, besides four or five Japanese *baterens* were present. The Dutchmen from Nambu, among whom two captains, were called; these men with red hair and silver eyes were also examined. Ichizaemon and Shōhaku, as well as two interpreters, were present."[62]

According to the Dutch report, the Dutchmen waited "all day," and so the interrogation of the Jesuits must have lasted most of the afternoon. We see that the apostates Shikimi Ichizaemon (1576–1647), a former Japanese Jesuit, and Shōhaku, formerly the Jesuit Juan Baptista Porro, were present to encourage the men of the second Rubino group to apostatize. After succumbing to the *anatsurushi* torture, both men must have looked exceedingly pitiful.[63] We know from the Dutch report that Chū'an was at Hotta's mansion as well, although he may not have been called to assist at the interrogation of the second Rubino group this time.

The Dutchmen were, not surprisingly in these surroundings, continually afraid. They attracted a great deal of attention from those around them, and they were given some sweet bread to eat. Finally, they were led through "a low gate" into "an attractive garden" and ordered to kneel outside on some plain mats in front of a wooden verandah. On its other side, in "an elegant room" they saw Inoue Chikugo no kami "with several great Japanese lords," among whom as we now know must have been Masamori, Toshikatsu, and Iemitsu himself, while Sakai Tadakatsu probably was present as well.

Although the *Tokugawa jikki* reports that Matsudaira Nobutsuna was sent by Iemitsu to Tenkai, the head priest of the Kan'eiji temple complex at Ueno (who was on his deathbed at this time), Nobutsuna must have been present by now, even if he had not been in time to attend the interrogation of the Jesuit priests.[64] The interpreters from Nagasaki, Kichibei and Hachizaemon, were there to translate, probably sitting on the verandah. The seating arrangements were again of the essence: the interpreters sat in between the Dutchmen in the garden and the "great lords" inside.[65] The Dutch debriefing report notes the course of the interrogation in a question and answer manner:

> QUESTION: Were we not Christians also (even if not papists) and did we not want to spend some time together with the aforementioned Jesuit padres?
>
> ANSWER: We were Christians . . . , but not papists, and we would not be overcome by the said papists (if the said gentlemen would kindly give us permission to kill them), which made the said gentlemen laugh.
>
> . . . .
>
> QUESTION: Did we have a chaplain on board?
>
> ANSWER: (even though this was an untruth, but in consideration [of the time and place where we were]) No, we did not have a chaplain on board.[66]

In fact, this was not a real interrogation at all. It was nothing but an opportunity for the shogun to meet the Dutch, for the ruler of Japan could neither receive prisoners inside the Castle, nor could he possibly go and see them at Inoue's, let alone in the Nagasakiya. The solution for Iemitsu's desire to see them was, of course, the usual one: to visit Masamori's country mansion which was equipped with all the necessary accouterments for making prisoners talk.

The Jesuits, too, had been shown to the shogun on this day. Since coming to power in 1623, Tokugawa Iemitsu had made the struggle against Christianity his private war and he kept a close tab on all arrests of priests throughout Japan. This time, he insisted on following the case of the freshly caught European priests with his own eyes. It is not clear where the group was kept the first ten days of their stay in Edo. They may have been held at Inoue's city mansion at Hitotsubashi, until it was decided—on this day and in the presence of the shogun himself—to put their faith to the test of the *anatsurushi*.

This torture involved hanging the victim upside down inside a closed pit, and would have been administered by Inoue's experts inside the Kodenmachō jail, ten minutes walk from the Nagasakiya. This jail was one of the most hellish places available on earth at the time. Here is the testimony of a Spanish observer:

> The cell was divided into two parts by a stout beam which ran from end to end; in both of these divisions there were three rows of [naked] men arranged in the following way. Two rows of men were seated along the two sides of the division, facing each other sole to sole, while the third row was seated in the middle between them. The third row was in the worst position of all because when the men sitting in the two outer rows grew tired of squatting, they stretched their legs over the others. And thus they suffocated the sick and the weak, because when those of the outer rows sat, their feet met in the middle and even then they could not fully stretch their legs. So great was the lack of room that if a man wanted to rest or sleep, he had to lean against his neighbor; and whenever the latter wanted to sleep, the man would have to support him with the same molestation. Often they did not reach accord and would dispute over time and space, which they duly measured, with one man declaring, My place is up to here, and the other replying, No, it isn't; this is my place. And because of this, or perhaps because one would lean too heavily against the other, they would fall to kicks and blows . . . .
>
> The winter was the worst time, although we did not feel the cold because of the great heat within the cell. The number of vermin increased in this season, and as we had so many it was impossible to kill them off; and as there was no light to kill them by, they grew and multiplied beyond count. The stench was unbearable, because there were usually sick men who could not stir and so performed all their natural functions where they sat; it was truly horrible as there was nobody to clean or wash them. And their neighbors not only had to bear the stench, but they were also fouled by the excrement. Thus driven to desperation, they would kill the sick man by striking him four or six times in order to free themselves from such torment. And those who could not bring themselves to kill the sick would do away with themselves, reckoning it better to die than to suffer in such fashion. When the prisoners quarreled and shouted, the

guards would climb up on top of the cell and pour urine and other filth over us all in order to silence them, and thus we were left in a truly miserable state. The pagans would hurl abuse at the guards, who would then in their anger deprive us of water for two or three days as a punishment, and thus we suffered greatly, all of us paying for what only some had done. But what inspired most horror and anguish was the fact that corpses were not taken away without written permission from the governor, and as this was difficult to obtain, the bodies remained there inside stinking for seven or eight days before being removed. And what with the great heat and fire which came from the multitude of living prisoners, a dead body would corrupt within seven hours and become so swollen and hideous that the very sight of it caused horror.[67]

But worse than being kept in such a cell, it was to be hung in the pits:

The most bitter of all tortures was the hanging by the legs from a gallows with the head inside a pit. The gallows was mounted over the pit, and in the middle of its crossbeam a pulley was fastened which held the rope tied to the victim's legs. By these means the latter was lowered down into the pit, so that only the feet extended through its cover. A sentry sat next to the gallows, who was relieved from a nearby guardhouse. In the head of the hanged man several cross-cuts had been made in order that the blood might slowly drip out, and the heart would not be overburdened. Some stayed alive like this for five, six, or more days before expiring. Francis Caron tells the story how he had talked to some who had already hung for three days, but in the end abjured their Roman religion because they could no longer stand a torture incomparably worse than fire or other imaginable cruelty; the intestines resting on the diaphragm seemed to squeeze the other organs of the body out of the throat, while blood was dripping from the eyes, mouth, nose, and ears.[68]

The first news of the apostasy of the second Rubino group we find in the debriefing report of the Dutch prisoners. The Dutch group had been staying quietly in the Nagasakiya between 6 and 22 September. On the evening of the 23rd, they were told by the "head servant" of the Nagasakiya that the innkeeper Gen'emon had gone to Inoue's to request permission to furnish the captives with Japanese clothing, for the weather was growing colder. The ōmetsuke had answered he would furnish them with Japanese kimono himself. The debriefing report says: "We were also informed (by sign language) that all the aforementioned Japanese Christians and some of the white papists had apostatized and become 'Japanese' (because of the dreadful tortures they had suffered)."[69]

We have seen that Iemitsu went to Hotta Masamori's country mansion on 25 September. The shogun would not have bothered to go, of course, within three weeks after his last inspection of the Jesuits on 5 September, unless the fathers had abandoned their faith in the meantime. So Inoue must have effected their apostasies during the two and a half weeks between 6 and 22 September 1643.

Chapter 4

A Strict Investigation

On the little fan-shaped island of Deshima, the two Dutch factors, Johan Van Elserack and Pieter Anthonisz Overtwater, and their subordinates were busy with the cargo brought by five Dutch ships from Batavia via Siam, Tonkin, and Taiwan. Elserack had arrived in Nagasaki from Batavia on 31 July to relieve his understudy Overtwater, who had run the Dutch trading post since the fall of the previous year. According to the new rules, the Dutch chief factor had to be replaced every year. Elserack was a man of experience, who had started out as an "assistant" and had now reached the rank of "president," earning 130 guilders a month. The eight years he had spent in Japan had been the most profitable as well as the most difficult years for the Dutch East India Company there.[1] Appointed chief factor in 1641, Elserack had made the first court journey to Edo under the new restrictive regulations, after the factory had been moved from Hirado to Nagasaki the year before.

Overtwater had been hired by the company in 1640. He immediately began at the rank of senior merchant with a salary of 90 guilders a month, as a result of a company policy to upgrade its management level personnel.[2] Since he had no previous trading experience, he must have had good connections inside the company. We know that he had been vice-principal of the Latin Grammar school at Hoorn, a town with a long maritime tradition, which looked out over Holland's Inland Sea. The town was one of the principal investors in the Dutch East India Company, making up one of its six Chambers.

The two chief factors seem to have gotten along well, for on his return home Elserack wrote to his superiors, the Gentlemen XVII at Amsterdam, that Overtwater was a "sensible man with an even temper."[3] From this we may conclude that the educated Overtwater had taken care to flatter self-made Elserack by listening quietly to his superior's lectures on the Dutch trade in Japan and the customs of the country. We will see later that the ex-schoolmaster was not nearly as sensible as Elserack had made him out to be.

Two hours before sunset on 10 September 1643, the *bugyō* (governor) of Nagasaki, Yamazaki Gompachirō, sent some interpreters to announce to Elserack that he had "at that very moment" received news from Edo "that a Dutch ship had anchored in the kingdom of Ockio or Massamone before the city of Nambo (which is at the furthest boundary of Japan)."[4] This, the interpreters reported, had caused "consternation" among the inhabitants, who were unfamiliar with European nations and had taken the men to be "Castilians, Portuguese, or suchlike Christians." Therefore, they had tried to bring all the men ashore to take them to Edo as prisoners, but the captain and merchant of the ship had negotiated so that, by surrendering themselves and eight other men to the authorities, the latter had agreed "to leave the ship and the rest of the crew in peace." The ten hostages had then been brought all the way to Edo, "a long journey of at least ten days travel or about one hundred miles."*

The "Ockio" of this entry in the *Daghregister,* or chief factor's journal, must be a miswriting for Ōshū, the province of the Deep North, and "Massamone" is the given name of Date Masamune (1567–1636), the well-known father of the present daimyo of the Sendai domain, a fief to the south of Nambu. The Dutch on Deshima, then, were given extremely vague geographical indications by the Nagasaki authorities about the spot where the *Breskens* had anchored. This impression is reinforced by the expression "city of Nambo," which strictly speaking did not even exist, for Nambu is a family name also used for the domain where the Nambu family had ruled since the twelfth century. That the captain and merchant would have agreed to become hostages for the rest of the crew and the ship was the Japanese way of explaining why only ten men had been caught, a solution that implied great flexibility and reasonableness on the part of the local authorities. Never mind that it bore only the faintest resemblance to the truth!

---

*That is, Dutch nautical miles, or 555 km.

The bulk price *(pancado)* for the raw silk imported that year had just been decided that same morning. The news, therefore, may have been four days old already, for on 5 September the governor of Nagasaki had still been inclined to let the Japanese silk merchants play their yearly procrastination game. The longer it took to agree on a price, the more pressed for time the Dutch became (because the date of their departure was fixed by the shogunal authorities on the twentieth day of the ninth lunar month), and the cheaper the Japanese were able to buy. On 7 September, however, suddenly decisive action had been taken by the municipal authorities of Nagasaki to have their merchants agree quickly on a price with the Dutch.[5] The letter from Edo, therefore, may have been received on the day before, 6 September. If it had been sent from Edo on the arrival of the Dutch prisoners there, that is, on 25 August 1643, the letter had taken twelve days to reach Nagasaki. Its contents clearly must have implied that the Dutch factor would be involved in the affair. Its reception, therefore, signaled to the Nagasaki *bugyō* that haste should be made with the trade that year.

The *bugyō* asked Elserack, through the interpreters, if he knew of the ship mentioned, and if he was acquainted with the men who had been arrested. The governor wanted to know what had been their intentions, and where they had been heading. Elserack truthfully told everything he knew about the expedition, noting in his journal that he knew "full well that the authorities had already heard everything from the mouths of the prisoners themselves," even though in reality this was not the case. He said that he was familiar with the ship and its crew, and told the *bugyō* of the plan to expand the company's trade to Tartary. The Dutch had heard that there existed a large city over there where "daily great quantities of Chinese silk were traded."[6] The ships had been sent so "that we will be better able to supply Japan from there than from Taiwan." Taking care, in this way, to suggest that the expedition might also be of advantage to Japan, Elserack concluded his answer to the *bugyō* with a request to be permitted to write a note to the prisoners. The governor, satisfied with Elserack's explanation, allowed the chief factor to write a note "but short, and to have a copy prepared in Japanese."[7]

After he had written the letter, Elserack was handed another note, written from Edo by the interpreter Kichibei, who informed him that the men from the *Breskens* were staying with him and Hachizaemon in the Nagasakiya, and that the ship had left the Bay of Yamada two days after the arrest. Having read this note, Elserack hastily added a postscript to his own letter, addressed to the men from the *Breskens*. In his journal, he later noted how lucky it was that two of the company's interpreters had happened to arrive in Edo at the same time and had been able to testify that the men were Dutch. He also registered his surprise, when he was told by the Japanese that none of the men spoke Portuguese or Spanish, writing in an aside: "(which is untrue for I know that the said Bijlvelt is fluent in the Castilian language. For what reason they pretend this, I have no idea yet.)"[8]

In fact, early in their captivity the Dutch had decided to pretend not to understand either Spanish or Portuguese, the two European languages with which a few Japanese were acquainted at the time. They hoped in this way to gain time to try and see what was safe to say and what not, before committing themselves to statements they might regret later. The burden of this pretense must have fallen on Wilhem Bijlvelt. It is likely, moreover, that cabin boy Jacob De Pauw also spoke either Spanish or Portuguese, for from the very first interrogations he was always taken along when his superiors were questioned. What is more, he was the only one of the crew who ever was interrogated by Inoue by himself.[9]

There was some merit to this kind of reasoning on the part of the prisoners. They correctly predicted that because of their pretended ignorance a Dutch-speaking interpreter would be found. However, in the end, that fact that they were dissimulating did not escape their interrogator, and therefore it is hard to say whether it did them any good at all. Also, I think there is more to this decision than first meets the eye. On closer examination, it may give us a glimpse into the characters of both Captain Schaep and Merchant Bijlvelt. It was clearly Schaep who was not familiar with either of the two Iberian languages. He had come to the Indies five years earlier, in 1638, at the age of twenty-seven, without the benefit of the upper-class education his companion Bijlvelt had enjoyed. The decision to pretend, therefore, must have been Schaep's. Quite possibly he thought he might lose control over the answers given during the interrogations, had he allowed Bijlvelt to use his knowledge. Bijlvelt does not seem to have protested. He may not have been a forceful personality, then, but someone quickly resigned to playing second fiddle. Schaep, on the other hand, we get to know here as someone reluctant to be out-smarted by his inferiors.

~

Elserack's note reached the prisoners on 27 September 1643. A letter from the Nagasaki *bugyō* to the Commissioner of Foreigners, Inoue, must have accompanied it. Now that it was known, through Elserack's explanation, that the true goal of the voyage had been Tartary (something the prisoners had concealed so far), a reaction from the *ōmetsuke* was to be expected. Indeed, on the afternoon of 28 September, the interpreters Kichibei and Hachizaemon as well as Chū'an, the apostate, visited the captives in their apartment. They explained what the chief factor had written, and asked the captain if it was true. Schaep, who must have been anticipating this, changed his story on the spot and answered that, indeed, it was true, but that they had abandoned the project after having lost their companion ship in a big storm before reaching Japan.[10]

On their admission that the true goal of their voyage had been Tartary, Chū'an pulled out a little map, drawn on Japanese paper, with a flat projection of the globe on a very small scale. This matter of the expedition's destination concerned Barbarian Knowledge, and therefore it was the apostate's turn to mix in the interrogation. The map showed "Japan, Korea, the coast of China, Tartary, Taiwan, Java, Ambon, the Moluccas, Manila, the Pacific Ocean as well as other countries and seas."[11] The Tsugaru Strait separating Honshu from Hokkaido had, however, been deleted from it.

Chū'an peered on this map and pointed at Tartary, which was shown to lie far inland, and asked how it was possible that they had been headed for a place so far away from the sea. Schaep answered that there seemed to be a great river, the Polisange, which "stretches more than eighty to a hundred miles inland and reaches the sea on the east coast of Tartary at 56 degrees northern latitude."[12] He explained that they would tell all the details of their story as soon as the Dutch interpreters arrived in Edo. Because of their ignorance of Portuguese, Spanish, or Japanese they had not been able to do so thus far. On being told this, the three men said good-bye and left.

The Dutchmen decided then and there to stick to the story they had just told the interpreters: that because of insufficient food supplies, they had decided after the storm of 19 May to return to Nagasaki, Taiwan, or Batavia, but that they had been unable to do so because of strong southwesterly winds and the many storms they had encountered, which had blown them constantly towards the northeast. They agreed to remain silent about the Gold and Silver Islands as well as the fact that they had been further north than 40 degrees latitude. If they were asked where they had been between 11 June and 28 July, they would answer that they had sailed due east for about two hundred sea miles.

On the evening of 30 September, the Dutch had more visitors. The interpreters from Hirado, Hideshima Tōzaemon and Shizuki Magobei, had arrived in Edo and obtained permission to call on the captives. Although neither of these two men is mentioned in the Dutch sources from the Hirado period (when, for example, Namura Hachizaemon appears as "interpreter" in the chief factor's journals of 1639 and 1640),[13] they may have been unofficial go-betweens for the Dutch and the local population, men of the level later called *naitsūji* (private interpreters) in Nagasaki.[14] In such a capacity, they would have done odd jobs relating to private trading and possibly procured women for the men of the Dutch factory or for visiting sailors. They would have been taking a cut from the Japanese side for such transactions, which may explain their absence from the Dutch payrolls. In any case, they were commoners, for the contrast between them and a man such as Hachizaemon is great. The latter served as an official go-between for the daimyo of Hirado and the Dutch traders, and was a sword-carrying samurai himself. His specialty, however, was the Portuguese language.

By the first of October 1643, the Japanese authorities were ready to begin their investigation of the Dutch prisoners from Nambu in earnest. On the afternoon of that day, the trio of the captain, the merchant, and cabin boy Jacob De Pauw were summoned to Hitotsubashi for a preliminary interrogation by Inoue Masashige, assisted by the newly arrived interpreters.

Again, the men had to answer the questions about their departure, their fleet, their destination, and the purposes of their expedition, as well as the reasons for their protracted sojourn along the Japanese coast and their entrance into the Bay of Yamada. Inoue also asked why the men had never mentioned before that they had been heading for Tartary. There was only one possible answer to this veiled accusation. Schaep told the *ōmetsuke* that they had been unable to do so for lack of an interpreter.

Then Inoue asked why they had been shooting at several places along the coast of Japan, "as if you were spies up to no good"? The men answered that they had agreed to do so with the officers of the other ship in case the two ships were separated. The *Breskens*, however, had not done so more than once, and then only "to call back our dinghy which had been sent to a Japanese vessel to ask after the fluyt *Castricom*."[15] In the Bay of Yamada, they admitted, they had fired several blanks "out of respect for and acting upon a request by the high officials who had come to visit our ship."[16]

The matter of the shooting was to become the main excuse used by the Japanese side as a reasonable and legal explanation for the seizure of the Dutchmen from the *Breskens*. The question about the shooting was put in the plural, and from this it is clear that the Japanese must have had more than one report of ships along the coast of Honshu. We have seen that the *Castricom* had been firing her guns on the night of 25 May off the coast of present-day Fukushima prefecture. The villages along that part of the coast were not as far from Edo as Yamada, so the news of the shooting ship or ships may have been received soon after reports of the fishermen from the Bōsō Peninsula had come in.

To have a series of reports from Chiba, Fukushima, Sendai, and Nambu about foreign ships of unknown identity and purpose must have agitated the shogun's guilty conscience about the fate of the unarmed Portuguese delegation from Macao, which he had ordered executed at Nagasaki in 1640. Sixty-one men had come to Japan the year after the Portuguese had been expelled, to try and change the shogun's mind about halting the trade on which the existence of the city of Macao depended. Iemitsu's fears of a Portuguese revenge for his summary dispatch of this embassy to the netherworld were among the principal reasons for his order to the daimyo to hermetically seal off the coast of Japan.

On the morning of 9 October, in the pouring rain, the interpreters again led the Dutch group to Masamori's country mansion at Asakusa. This time they were taken to a completely different area of the house to await the arrival of the shogun and his advisers. The change worried them anew, and all the more because the *kachimetsuke* (ambulatory spy), Fuji'i Zen'emon (who was one of the two shogunal police officers sent to Morioka to bring the Dutch group to Edo), separated the captain and merchant from the rest of the group. Zen'emon brought the two Dutchmen to the same spot in the garden from where they had been interrogated on 5 September, when they had shared a cell with the Jesuits for a while. On this spot they were first made to wait in the rain for half an hour, "because the councilors were having a meal."[17] Next, wet and miserable, the *metsuke* brought them into a hallway and from there into "an elegant room," where he was "just about" to pour them some hot sake when a message came that the council was seated for the interrogation. Schaep and Bijlvelt stood up in a hurry and were taken to the "audience hall" by the interpreter Tōzaemon. They were ordered to kneel down on the wooden floor of the hallway running along the room where the representatives of the shogun were sitting in the company of Inoue Masashige.

The debriefing report left by the Dutch does not specify who was present on this occasion. It only speaks of "great lords," who were sitting behind the *ōmetsuke* and could not be seen very well by the Dutchmen. These seating arrangements had likely been designed to give the Dutch as few clues as possible about the men with whom they were dealing. But because this was going to be their most important interrogation, we may surmise that the full council of elders or *rōjū* were present. The *Tokugawa jikki* helps out, for it records a visit of Iemitsu to Masamori's mansion on this day.[18] The Dutch factor's journal records that the shogun had attended "hidden behind sliding doors."[19] If Iemitsu, Masamori, Nobutsuna, and the Abe cousins were all present, it is likely that the great elder *(tairō)* Ii Naotaka and the senior councilor *(toshiyori)* Sakai Tadakatsu were also there. As before, I suspect that Doi Toshikatsu did not make the trip.

Inoue began the interrogation with the same questions about the expedition and their arrival in Yamada that the men had answered many times before. Then, by order of the *rōjū*, for whom it was impossible to talk directly to the prisoners, he asked them when and where they had first reached the Japanese coast, why they had tacked between the coast and the open sea, and why they had fired their guns so many times, which was considered an extremely serious offense? The men answered these questions in the same way they had before at Inoue's mansion in Hitotsubashi, explaining how they had first reached Japan at 37.5 degrees on 29 May, and had sailed back and forth for several days to look and wait for the *Castricom*. About the shooting they repeated they had done so only once and they added that they had not known that this was an offense.

The questions had been tendentious, and, as we have seen, rooted in a certain amount of uneasiness about a possible Portuguese revenge, but the next questions were even more biased, accusing the Dutchmen of having concealed their nationality to the fishermen who had come alongside the ship to exchange fish for rice. Because Iemitsu himself was present on this occasion, we must assume that the tone and direction of the questions reflected his wishes. Inoue continued implacably:

> As you knew very well that the Emperor of Japan has ordered lookouts to be organized on all extremities and mountaintops to watch for Portuguese who still continue to try and bring papists ashore in Japan, why didn't you, when tacking back and forth before the Japanese coast, send some of your officers in your small boat ashore to present yourselves to the authorities there, and explain that you were *Hollanders* passing by the coast; also why did you, by neglecting to do so, give [the people who lived there] cause for suspicion, which the Emperor and the Imperial Councilors of Japan take very seriously (in addition to the shooting which you deny but which has been reported to be true with sufficient testimony), for which reason you are guilty of a punishable offense.[20]

Both these questions were posed, not to receive an answer but, as attack is the best defense, to escape from the obvious but awkward situation of having arrested allies of Japan. This was done by the simple expedient of accusing the Dutch of not having identified themselves—a preposterous contention, of course, but the Dutchmen were in no position to sneer. All they could do was to profess ignorance of the strict coast guard and of the requirement that they should have come to shore to identify themselves. For the third time, they denied having fired their guns more than once along the coast of Japan, and suggested that it was probably the *Castricom* to which the Japanese police reports referred. Then they asked forgiveness for their ignorance of the Japanese laws.

"Did the Hon. Governor General order you to head for the coast of Japan and sail back and forth there, or did you do so on your own without his knowledge or orders?" In fact, the ships had been instructed by the governor general and his council "to sail along the Japanese coast and to head, after leaving the same, for the northwest (or in whatever direction we would be forced by the coast line) and steer for the coast of Tartary at 45 degrees."[21] But the interpreter Tōzaemon told the Dutch to answer, for reasons of expediency, that they had not been ordered to head for the coast of Japan nor that they should avoid it. They had merely been directed to agree on a place where they would be able to find each other again in case they were separated. This they had done, they said, at a session of the fleet's council before leaving Ternate, deciding "on the east coast of Japan (being the best place on our route for this, as the natives were our allies), consequently this was mainly done on our own initiative."[22]

This answer left the Japanese authorities a way out. For if it was admitted that the ships had been ordered to sail for the Japanese coast by the authorities in Batavia, it would have been more difficult to overlook what the Japanese clearly considered an intrusion into their territorial waters. Now that responsibility seemed to lie with the fleet's council, Inoue followed up with a factual question about the lines of command on both ships and the identity of the members of the fleet's council.

Iemitsu's fears about a possible European alliance against Japan had been reinforced by the arrest of two groups of Europeans at either end of Japan within one month of each other. Even if the Dutch and Portuguese were fierce competitors in Asia, was it not possible that they would team up as fellow Christians against a Japanese anti-Christ? From the directness of the phrasing itself, it is possible to speculate that the following question came straight from the shogun himself, who is certain to have been made suspicious by the truce concluded between the Dutch and the Portuguese in 1641:[23] "How is the emperor to know or make sure, now that you have concluded a truce with the Portuguese (who have been your enemies for so long), that you haven't brought papists to Japan, who are causing so much trouble in this country (instead of being headed for Tartary, as you pretend)?"[24]

The Dutchmen answered their interrogators that, in spite of the truce, the governor general would never agree to transport "any papists (who remain our deadly enemies)."[25] They were prepared, they said, to die "the most painful death which His Majesty might want to order" if he were ever informed of the contrary. Later during the interrogation, the questions came back to the same problem: "Were we not Christians, believing in one God (like the Portuguese), what were our holidays, and did we celebrate the day of the cross [Easter], and also were there no papists in Holland, and what was the difference between our religion and that of the Portuguese?"[26]

The men admitted that they were Christians, but denied that "papists" were tolerated in Holland (even though a major part of the Republic's population was still Roman Catholic). They contended that "the papists insult us, saying we are unbelieving heretics (and think we are less than dogs), so that their sect and religion is very different from ours," even though they professed to be unable to explain the differences properly, "not being learned in those matters."[27]

Both Schaep and Bijlvelt, of course, knew the differences between Roman Catholics and Protestants very well, for these differences formed the very core of the newly born Dutch national identity in the seventeenth century. They were wise, however, not to let themselves be dragged into a religious argument. Playing dumb was the best policy here.

The Dutchmen were asked in detail about Tartary, the goal of the expedition. How could they find a place without having a map of how to get there? Captain Schaep patiently explained that there were no maps of Tartary because no one who knew how to make maps had ever gone there by sea. That the country existed they had learned from "dependable books and manuscripts," and one of the purposes of going there was to make a map of the route thither. But, countered his interrogator, "How was it possible there were no maps of Tartary when there are maps of the whole world?" The Dutch sailors knew better than that and repeated laconically: "There can be maps of all the places which have been visited, but not of those where no one has been yet."[28]

It seemed hard to believe that anyone would attempt to travel to a place no one else had ever been: "Might the commander on the fluyt *Castricom* have any maps without your knowledge?" the Dutch were asked. They answered that they knew very well that their commander did not have any, and that if maps had been available, they would not have left without them. Still, their interrogator did not give up. "If we should send for maps from Nagasaki," he challenged the prisoners, "what would the captain and merchant say then?" The men shrugged: "Those might be terrestrial maps, but not nautical ones, and we don't believe there are any nautical maps of Tartary in Europe (as we have never heard of any ships having sailed there)."[29] Again, they repeated their willingness to submit to "the severest punishment, which His Imperial Majesty and the Imperial Councilors of Japan might want to inflict," if they could show them such nautical maps.

The interrogation seems to have gotten stuck here on the issue of the maps. It is difficult to say why. Possibly Iemitsu was slow in grasping the point that there were still unmapped places left in the world, and no one present dared explain this to him. Later on, it was given out that there had been a mistake in the translation of the interpreter

Tōzaemon, who had supposedly translated Schaep as saying the *Breskens* carried no maps at all, rather than simply no maps of Tartary.[30] Clearly, Tōzaemon served, in this case, as the scapegoat for somebody's denseness. Later he was given the status of soldier in the shogun's army *(hatamoto)* as a reward,[31] something that would have been unlikely had he really made serious mistakes.

In any case, war was on the mind of our warrior shogun: "What was the mission of the ships which the governor general sends every year to cruise around Cape Espiritu Santo and Manila?"[32] Those ships were cruising there, the Dutchmen answered, to try and spot the Spanish silver galleon that comes to Manila every year across the South Sea from Mexico, and to take it if possible. "Had the silver ship ever been taken?" The men had to deny this, but once, they said, a couple of years ago, it had been sunk.

There existed a plan in Edo for a joint Dutch-Japanese attack on Manila. It was Inoue's (and therefore probably Iemitsu's) own hobbyhorse. The *ōmetsuke* was in the possession of large, detailed maps of the city and its fortifications which he had had drawn up by the apostate fathers. Later he would show them to Elserack, who then asked for copies, which were promised but never materialized.[33] If the attack was ever carried out, Dutch ships might be employed to transport Japanese troops. "How does one fight with ships at sea?" the shogun wanted to know. "Do you come board to board immediately, or do you try to first render the other impotent with your cannon, and how is this done?"

Unaware that he was lecturing the shogun himself, Schaep pontificated: "When two ships of equal firepower meet, both will first try, if possible, to take the wind out of the other's sails, and then attack, while sailing, with their cannon." The ship that has been maneuvered to the lee side is then hindered by her own as well as her adversary's smoke, and is "often shot into the bottom of the sea, or waylaid, boarded and overpowered."[34]

"How many shots can a ship take before it sinks?" It all depends on where she's hit, answered the captain; "some ships can take between 1 and 200 shots, others are shot into the sea with one or two." "Can a small ship take a big one?" the shogun wanted to know, "and how is this done?" Sometimes a small ship can take a large one, but it is difficult, answered the captain. In such a case, the smaller ship had better hoist all her sails and be filled with men, sailing at dusk or by dark weather, without flying any flags or streamers to make herself inconspicuous. She would go right for the big ship, cling to her side and then, when least expected, overpower her by the sheer number of the attacking crew.

"Do you have bulletproof gunwales or redoubts on your ships to protect your men, and what purpose serves the armor and iron weapons that have been seen on Dutch ships?" The shogun's questions were getting more and more detailed. Schaep answered that they did not have any gunwales or redoubts on their ships, and that the bigger bullets flew right through the ship. The captain was getting fired up himself: "Consequently, our bodies are the redoubts, those who perish being thrown overboard (without the battle letting up any, but continuing as fiercely as before)." He denied using armor and iron weapons at sea; they served only when fighting on land.

"How did you Hollanders take the town of Quelang [Chilung]? Did it have any artillery, and who was living there (at that time)?" As neither of the men had been on Taiwan when the Dutch fought the Spanish there two years earlier, they had to admit ignorance of any details, but they had heard that "our men had first taken the lower fort of Quelang (which had some artillery pieces, but we don't know how many) with the force of our guns. After that the upper fort had not offered much resistance and had soon opened its gates to surrender, the residents being Castilians."

Sturdy guns had won the Dutch battles at sea and on land—guns that were mostly cast in Swedish foundries, where Dutch merchants had made such extensive investments in the iron industry that it was almost completely in Dutch hands.[35] Many Swedes, also, found employment with the Dutch East India Company, and as indicated in chapter 2 a Swede may have been sitting among the rest of the group from the *Breskens* not far from the spot where Schaep and Bijlvelt were being questioned.

At last Inoue said severely: "The reason why we interrogate you so harshly is because we want to know the truth from you; you will be called before the High Authorities once more, at which moment we order you unequivocally to speak the truth." If you do not, he continued threateningly, "the same is in store for you as [what happened to] the Portuguese papists who confessed through torture [the things] they did not want to confess at first of their own free will." The ōmetsuke warned the Dutchmen: "Look well ahead and [be aware] that it does not behoove you to lie in front of the High Authorities." Humbly, the two Dutchmen answered him that they "would heed his words, and truthfully answer all questions, which it would please their Excellencies to ask," and once more they repeated that they were willing to "submit to the heaviest punishment imaginable," if they were ever found guilty of a falsehood. We must acknowledge that they had caught on quickly how to get by in Japan.

This interrogation having lasted the best part of the afternoon, Schaep and Bijlvelt were taken back to their men, who had been waiting anxiously for them. The next afternoon, the two men were again summoned to Hitotsubashi for more questioning by Inoue Masashige. The ōmetsuke must have had precise instructions from the shogun on how to proceed, for he did not seem to tire of asking them the same questions as he had before. Again the Dutchmen had to explain all about their voyage and arrival in the Bay of Yamada. It was as if they had never been interrogated before, Bijlvelt noted.

First Inoue brought up the problem of the maps again, saying that the shogun and his councilors could not believe that the Dutch would attempt to sail to a place for which they had no maps, when all ships coming to Nagasaki carried maps. "How can you navigate without maps or compasses, as if you were totally blind?" he exclaimed. The men repeated what they had said before: that they did not have any map of Tartary because no European had ever been there to make one. Of course, they knew that all ships visiting Nagasaki carried maps, for this was a place they often visited. Yes, they said, they had several compasses on their ship, for without this instrument they could not navigate. "When we leave any place the position of which is known to us," they added, "we can always find it again, even without a map, by measuring the height of the sun."[36]

"How would you have been able to find Tartary then without a map?" Inoue insisted. Schaep explained that when they would have reached the end of their map, which extended to about 38 or 39 degrees, and left the northern extremity of Japan behind them, they would have sailed by their globes. Each ship carried one. Heading for the coast of Tartary on a northwesterly course, they would have sighted it at 45 degrees, he said, all the while making their own maps based on what they saw. If the commissioner had a globe, he said, he was willing to show him this, and where Tartary, the river Polisange, and the rich trading towns along it lay, which were their destination.

"Why did you not say so yesterday that you would have sailed by your globe for lack of a map?" Inoue wanted to know. "We have answered all of your Excellencies' questions, but this has not been asked," Schaep replied. Thereupon, Inoue had a Dutch globe brought in, which had been given to him by Jan Van Elserack two years before. After studying it for a while, but without showing it to the Dutchmen, he returned to the issue of the violence committed by the Dutchmen off the Japanese coast with their cannon, muskets, and locks. Again, the Dutchmen professed they were unjustly accused of this because they had fired their cannon only once.

They admitted: "In the bay of Nambu we have fired several shots (out of respect for and upon request by some Japanese officials, who came to visit our ship); also that some Japanese, who came into the cabin of our ship, saw our pistols and firelocks lying in their usual places and fired them several times with their own hands (out of curiosity, because they saw them go off without fire and thought it was a miracle)."[37]

"How many shots did you fire in the bay of Nambu?" Inoue asked. "Around twelve to fourteen shots," the men guessed. The matter of the shooting was hard to check. To the prisoners' minds, it was their word against that of Urushido Kanzaemon. They did not realize that the truth of the matter was not really what Inoue was interested in, but which facts to choose from among the myriad making up the whole truth, so that they could be used to bolster his case against the Dutch. It was the Japanese side that was embarrassed, and not the Dutch.

Next to the prisoners sat a Japanese man, who looked like a secretary or minor official. He seemed to be pleading against them and to be feeding the commissioner all the questions he was asking them. I have not been able to identify this man, who could order Inoue what to ask of the Dutch, but he must have been one of Iemitsu's favorites, representing the shogun on this occasion. Or, if we take seriously the words of the interpreter Tōzaemon, who said later that the shogun "almost does not trust anyone and is usually present at all meetings when prisoners are being interrogated,"[38] we could reach the outrageous conclusion that it was Iemitsu himself sitting there disguised as a minor official. If, indeed, the shogun had let himself go so far as to personally interrogate the Dutch, he must have flouted the advice of his most trusted councilors.

"What kind of gun was it then that you let the Japanese officials fire?" asked the ōmetsuke again. "Pistols and flintlocks, which go off with a flint hitting a steel pin or wheel, and such like."[39] Tōzaemon had seen such guns many times on the Dutch ships at Hirado and said so.

Inoue had a small handgun brought in,[40] which also had been given or sold to him by the Dutch. Studying this, he asked Tōzaemon if this was the kind of gun meant. The interpreter answered yes, indicating that it was somewhat bigger and longer. "We have been told that you have fired your guns yourselves," the ōmetsuke continued. "How is it possible that you could teach, without knowing any Japanese, people who do know how to handle guns, as they have never seen any before, how to fire them?"[41] Schaep said that they had fired their pistols and flintlocks themselves, and that the Japanese officials had done so as well, from curiosity and by their own desire. "We showed them how with our hands and fingers, as there really is very little to understand. We hope we did not, unknowingly, commit an offense this way," he added contritely.

All in all, to be sure, the Dutch had done nothing that had not been common practice at Hirado, such as shooting the ship's cannon to honor distinguished guests and pleasing visitors to the ship by letting them try to shoot a handgun. Important to remember here is that the Japanese side desperately needed a reason for having arrested the Dutch, and firing guns was deemed the most appropriate excuse. But Inoue tried out the viability of other reasons as well: "Why did you act defensively when you were captured, and pulled you cutlasses against the Japanese?" Schaep denied this vehemently: "We have never done this and are accused falsely, for we have let ourselves be captured like lambs, without offering any resistance, trusting we would be treated well and receive complete freedom from the Emperor whose allies we are." This, indeed, was the crux of the problem Inoue was wrestling with: the Japanese had arrested their own allies. It was an awkward situation calling urgently for a face-saving solution.

For the moment Inoue made the Dutch sign a paper, the closest possible to a confession of guilt: "Are you willing to sign a document which will commit you to come back to Japan at any time the Emperor desires you to do so, in case he is later informed that you have brought papists to Japan or have committed another crime against this empire?" he asked sternly. "Yes," Schaep answered, "we are prepared to do so because we are confident no trouble will result from this, and our captain at Nagasaki will surely commit himself for us."

One wonders who was fooled by this pedantic paper business with its mockery of reality and legality. Maybe it was just to appease Inoue who was in the habit of extracting written pledges from his prisoners.[42] Inoue moved away to the far end of the verandah to draft

the document. In the meantime, the Dutch were told to help the interpreter Tōzaemon translate Elserack's note to them from Nagasaki.
Of the "little official" we hear no more. He may have disappeared
discreetly during the last couple of questions. After a while, the Dutchmen were told to copy Tōzaemon's translation of the document Inoue
had drawn up, without adding or deleting anything:

> Document or Contract to Come Back to Japan at Any Time the
> Emperor desires and commands, Given by Us Captured Dutchmen
> to the Commissioner Tsicungodonne
>
> To: IjnoUije 't Sicungo no Camisamma [sic]
>
> [Having come] from Jacatra [sic] this year on the first voyage to
> look for Tartary, we encountered a violent storm at sea and lost our
> flagship. Therefore, we have come to the coast of Japan to look for
> her and to possibly find her near the same. We did not say we are
> Hollanders, moreover we have fired our guns here and there in the
> Dutch manner, committing in this way (unknowingly) an offense,
> for which we therefore ask to be pardoned. Our ship did not bring
> any Spanish papists, nor did we intend to spy or do any harm. We
> will be punished in the Japanese way if it is ever revealed in Naga-
> saki by the chief factor of the Company that any of the above was
> different. Therefore, we pledge to come back to Japan at any time if
> his Imperial Majesty summons us. For that purpose we have pre-
> sented this document.
>
> On the twenty-eighth Japanese September[43]
> Was signed: [Hendrick Cornelisz Schaep, Wilhem Bijlvelt][44]

In this "contract," as it is called, we see the bakufu's position in a
nutshell. The Dutchmen were guilty of two punishable offenses, to
which they had now admitted on paper: (1) they had not said that they
were Dutch; (2) they had fired their guns off the coast of Japan, even
though they had done so to find their companion ship. Inoue's own
contribution appears in the latter part, for in his capacity as "protector
of the Dutch" he added the clause: "in the Dutch manner," implying that it was forgivable for Dutchmen to act according to "Dutch
manners." Indeed, the clause follows immediately: "for which we
therefore ask to be pardoned." The document ends with the true
fears of the shogun: if it is later found that the Dutch have brought
any "Spanish papists," the men have agreed to die "in the Japanese
manner."

On the way back to the Nagasakiya, the interpreters, as usual, said very little. The Dutchmen thought it was from pride or jealousy of each other. Tōzaemon remarked only: "You have said something wrong, and if it weren't for that, you would been given permission to leave a long time ago." That was not the way to reassure Captain Schaep who knew his own lies all too well. He tried to get the interpreters to explain what was wrong, but the men refused to enlighten him any further. Of course, Tōzaemon was exaggerating, for a release was not in the cards just yet. There were still other purposes the Dutch prisoners could serve.

Chapter 5
Unwitting Witnesses

One hour before dawn on 20 October 1643, the ten Dutchmen left the Nagasakiya to go to Inoue's mansion at Hitotsubashi. They were accompanied by their landlord Gen'emon, his son, Chū'an the apostate, as well as the four interpreters: Hachizaemon and Kichibei (specialists of Portuguese from Nagasaki), and Tōzaemon and Magobei (speakers of Dutch from Hirado). On their arrival, they were first brought to an "elegant room looking out on a strange and beautiful garden," where they had never been before. Later they were taken to their usual spot on the verandah to wait for their interrogators to arrive. Around noon, they were brought into the audience room, where they were seated, all in a row, on cheap mats next to the four European Jesuits of the second Rubino group.

That the Dutch were to be released, eventually, had been clear to the bakufu since their arrival in Edo, but of course the prisoners themselves were not informed of this. For the duration of their detention, they were to serve the bakufu's purposes. One of these, it turned out, was to tell the world about what would happen to Jesuits who were caught in Japan from now on. This was the third time the two groups of foreigners had met in Edo over the past two months.

To recapitulate: the first time had been on 26 August, just after their arrival in the shogun's capital. At that time the Dutchmen had been so afraid that, in their eagerness to establish their enmity toward Roman Catholics in general and to Portugal and Spain in particular, they had not shrunk from spitting at and kicking the Jesuits, who had been—note the gesture!—manacled in their presence.

The second time the two groups had met was on 5 September, at Hotta's country mansion, when the Dutchmen were thrust into the "dark and ugly hole" where the Catholic group was being held. As this joint confinement did not last long, it was clearly a way to demonstrate to the Dutch how differently they were being treated, and to allow them a good look at the fathers just before they were lowered into the torture pits.

Now, the stage had been set for a *Stabat Mater Dolorosa*, conducted by the composer Inoue Masashige himself. His audience consisted of the *toshiyori* Sakai Tadakatsu and the *rōjū* Matsudaira Nobutsuna, as well as the whole Dutch group. They were now being shown how the bakufu's victims looked *after* the torture, and by this time the tone of the Dutch debriefing report has changed. The appearance of the ex-Jesuits must have been so painful ("they look extremely emaciated and desperate because of the terrible torture they had suffered") that even the hardy Dutch sailors, bent on their own self-preservation, could not suppress feelings of pity and indignation at what had been done here.

Again the Dutchmen's first reaction was acute fear, for they had no inkling of Inoue's purpose, which was to have them witness the apostasy of the Jesuits. In the presence of the men from the *Breskens,* the fathers were questioned a great deal about the "power and might of God." Some of them answered very faintly and others a little more firmly. The Dutchmen pretended not to pay attention, "in order not to excite the suspicions of the Japanese gentlemen," so they did not hear everything that was said. But they reported later the following questions and answers:

QUESTION: How can you still believe and trust in your God, now that you see He has forsaken you completely and has no power, but that the Emperor can do with you as he pleases at present (without asking your God anything)?

ANSWER: Our God, indeed, seems (to the world) to have left us and to send our bodies many heavy torments because of our sins, but He never leaves the souls of the penitent, who live in God and cannot be damaged by any humans in the world, and the Emperor may be able to do whatever he wants with our bodies, which God (whose kingdom is not of this world) permits because of our many sins, but when our bodies have died and rest in God our souls will be rewarded with eternal bliss. And there is no salvation outside of God, and no one can be [saved or damned] without His will or permission.[1]

After these answers were given in very soft-spoken voices, Chū'an the apostate was called. He, one of history's first examples of a successful brainwashing, was willing to do Inoue's bidding and spoke these harsh words to the men of the second Rubino group "with a severe look on his face": "You rave so much about the power of your God and your own salvation, why is it that not everybody is saved and how do you know, or who has told you, that you will be saved? Where is your God's power now, of which you boast so much and in which you find support, when you have already had to suffer so much pain (because of your unnecessary presumption and stubbornness), and you are still in the power of the Emperor, who can make you suffer even more (as he pleases)? Why doesn't your God help you then?"

After this question, in the debriefing report the Dutch captain inserted his own lament: "Oh, awful blasphemy spoken by someone who knows better nonetheless." But in spite of their previous apostasy, the Jesuits answered bravely: "In spite of your harsh treatment we believe and trust deeply that nobody can hurt even a hair of someone else without God's will and we know that there is no salvation for the soul (which is immortal) outside of God, and that to forsake God is an inexpiable sin, and that God is calling all sinners who want to convert and live [eternally]." The last phrase about God calling all sinners, of course, was meant especially for Chū'an himself, who stood rebuked in front of the Dutch and did not speak again during this meeting.[2]

The Dutchmen understood from these answers that the Jesuit fathers were not willing to repeat their apostasy in front of them, and concluded that the priests would have to "endure and suffer the threats of the Emperor and the Japanese authorities a while longer (even though they had already been tortured to an extraordinary degree)."[3] But even though Inoue's aim of having the Jesuits recant in front of the Dutch was not attained, he was successful to the degree that he could now be sure that the Calvinist Dutch would carry the image of the tortured priests back with them to the outside world.

The bravery of at least two of the new apostates in front of the Dutch had been extraordinary, for their noncooperation with Inoue indeed meant, as the Dutchmen suspected, that they would have to go back into the torture pit. The *Tokugawa jikki* reports another ominous visit to Hotta's mansion two days later on 2 October.[4] The Dutch debriefing report has an entry for the same day, noting that two of the priests had withdrawn their apostasy.[5] Chū'an, who had already been rewarded for his assistance and granted permission to return to Nagasaki after the group's first apostasy,[6] was ordered to remain in Edo for the time being. If two of the Jesuits withdrew their apostasy on the same day that Iemitsu visited Hotta's mansion, this withdrawal is likely to have occurred in front of the shogun himself. Moreover, it seems reasonable to suppose that these two brave men were the two of the group who died first, that is, Alonso de Arroyo and Francisco Cassola.

The Dutchmen, when it was their turn to be interrogated, continued to grovel before the authorities. After the fathers had been led away, they were ordered to take their seats right in front of Sakai Tadakatsu and Matsudaira Nobutsuna, who ordered the men to "sit upright." From the questions asked we can infer that Iemitsu feared that the foreigners, with their powerful ships, might team up against Japan. Even though I do not think that the shogun's advisors present here were all equally convinced of the reality of such a threat, and in particular of the possibility of an alliance of Portugal and Holland against Japan, the recently concluded truce between the two countries was interpreted as a peace agreement and possibly a first step toward such an alliance. But most important on this occasion was that the Dutch group established they had nothing to do with these Jesuits:

> QUESTION: The Portuguese papists profess that they can help each other by praying and in other ways. Do you believe too that they would be able to help you now?
>
> ANSWER: No, but we do believe that his Imperial Majesty of Japan (whose prisoners we are at present) can grant us our freedom and permission to leave for our friends, and that the captured papists should (now) try to help themselves.[7]

The last remark "made the said gentlemen laugh," and seemed to confirm their impression that the two groups had not been in league together. After this, each of the Dutchmen was again asked individually if they were "papists" or not, to which all of them answered negatively.

On their way back to the Nagasakiya, Schaep asked the interpreters why they had been seated next to the "Portuguese papists," and why the two gentlemen had left in such a hurry afterwards. This time, they were given a straight answer for a change: "Mr. Sanuki Sama [Sakai Tadakatsu] had said: Have the Hollanders come here; I will be able to see from their behavior if they have brought any papists to Japan or not."[8] And the councilors had left in such a hurry because it had been time for them "to appear at the high court in the Castle." The Dutch also asked what Tadakatsu had said when they had first appeared before him on that day. The interpreters answered that he had said: "No, those people are innocent and have not brought any papists to Japan." Of course, this was music to the Dutchmen's ears, and they "praised and thanked the Lord Almighty (in our hearts) that we had so far been treated so well."[9]

~

Some important conclusions can be drawn from this famous meeting.[10] The Dutchmen were present for two reasons. First, they were to be confronted with the Jesuit fathers so that their guilt or innocence might be judged from their overt reactions to the pitiful state to which these men had been reduced in less than two months' time. Apparently, they hid the pity they felt according to their own debriefing report. Second, they were to be eyewitnesses to Inoue's victory over the Jesuits by hearing with their own ears the fathers' denial of their faith. This was, of course, a covert purpose, for officially the Japanese preferred to believe the fiction that none of the Dutchmen spoke any Portuguese or Spanish. As we have noted before, the bravery of two of the Jesuits thwarted Inoue's scheme, and so the message the Dutch carried back to the Western world was ambivalent, giving rise to three hundred and fifty years of polemics on the topic of whether any Jesuits other than Chū'an had really apostatized in Japan.[11]

For the history of Japan during the reign of Iemitsu, however, an even more important conclusion can be drawn from the evidence brought together in this case study, and in particular from the results of this meeting of 20 October 1643. There are indications that this session was arranged well in advance, and we now know that it was done by the order of the *toshiyori* Sakai Tadakatsu to the *ōmetsuke* Inoue Masashige, while Matsudaira Nobutsuna was present as the first of the *rōjū*. This group was the bakufu's pro-Dutch faction. The three men each represented a different side of the shogun.

In the secondary literature on the organization of the early Tokugawa Bakufu, there is much confusion about the exact division of power during the reign of Iemitsu, a confusion usually resolved by the conclusion that Iemitsu had slowly set aside the men who had been put in place by his father and grandfather to assure the continuation of the Tokugawa house, so that he might govern alone.[12] This process is said to have started in earnest after the death of his father, the second shogun Tokugawa Hidetada, in 1632. This explanation, attractive in its simplicity, is both true and untrue. Many signs indicate that, indeed, Iemitsu moved quickly after his father's death to eliminate or neutralize those whom he perceived to be in his way.

On his accession as shogun in 1623, he had already attaindered his ex-mentor Aoyama Tadatoshi, the unyielding veteran of Ieyasu's wars who had been in the habit of scolding the future shogun for his effeminate ways. One story tells how Tadatoshi, when Iemitsu did not seem to be listening to his admonitions, would unsheathe his sword and bare his torso. Approaching on his knees, he is reported to have said: "Will you only mend your ways when my head has been cut off?"[13] Obviously, this kind of sentimental blackmail did not endear him to his charge.

Next Iemitsu forced the suicide of his younger brother, Tadanaga (1606–1633), who, when they were both still boys, had been favored by his mother and hen-pecked father Hidetada to succeed as shogun. Then during the years 1633–1638, in rapid succession, the *rokuninshū* or council of six of Iemitsu's men replaced the *rōjū* or council of elders left from Hidetada's days, a development that has been described several times.[14]

However, as we find in the Dutch debriefing report, the *Tokugawa jikki,* and the Castle diaries on which the latter compilation is principally based,[15] Sakai Tadakatsu remained the foremost power broker in the country until Iemitsu's death in 1651, and continued to be very powerful until his own death in 1662. As we have seen, his cousin, Sakai Tadayo (who was fifteen years older than Tadakatsu), had been, with Doi Toshikatsu and Aoyama Tadatoshi, one of the three mentors put in charge of young Iemitsu's education.

Tadakatsu was born in 1587 in Nishio in Mikawa. After serving Hidetada under his cousin's guidance, he became an adviser to Iemitsu in 1620. Here, obviously, we see the hand of Iemitsu's mentor, Sakai Tadayo, who succeeded in maneuvering (just in time!) his cousin close to the future shogun. From the time of Hidetada onward, such associations with the shogunal heir were to be of extreme importance for the continuation of policies and the endurance of the bakufu itself. All the other power holders (Doi Toshikatsu, Matsudaira Nobutsuna, Hotta Masamori, and the Abe cousins) were men chosen by Ieyasu and Hidetada to guide, accompany, or serve Iemitsu, long before he became shogun. Sakai Tadakatsu was the next to last to be added to this group associated with Iemitsu before he assumed the title of shogun in 1623.

In the first year of Iemitsu's reign Tadakatsu moved his office into the main keep of the Castle and started to participate in the work of the *rōjū*, specializing in matters concerning the ancient nobility of Japan, the great warrior houses, and foreign policy.[16] By 1643, then, Tadakatsu had been involved in foreign policy questions for almost twenty years. There was no one in the country who could compete with his expertise, and it was natural that he was the final arbiter in matters concerning the Dutch.

Tadakatsu is also frequently mentioned in the journal of the Dutch chief factor as the shogun's "supreme councilor and chancellor." The Dutch, while in Hirado, considered him their friend and adviser. Chief Factor Caron called him a "father of the Company," the only one who had advised against the removal of the Dutch to Deshima. Overtwater described him in 1645 as "cheerful and friendly, a completely gray and calm man, much better dressed than Matsudaira Nobutsuna, Abe Tadaaki and Abe Shigetsugu."[17]

Tadakatsu was the only other person in Iemitsu's surroundings who also frequently received personal visits from the shogun. As we have seen in the case of Hotta Masamori, such visits were of great importance in the world of power during the days of Iemitsu. They were a gauge by which a man's real power could be measured. Among the senior retainers competing for such visits, there must have been a real distinction between those who had and those who had not (yet?) been visited by the shogun. The Dutch were well aware of this:

> Contrasting with the countless number of common buildings are the precious palaces of the great lords. Each palace possesses several imposing entrances, among which however one excels above the others: this one is never opened more than once. This is because of respect for the Emperor. For when a distinguished lord founds a palace, he builds a gate, which is covered up with boards. This gate is full of carved sculptures, lacquered and gold-plated. It may not be seen by anyone until the time when in a certain month the Emperor honors him by appearing for a feast in his newly built dwelling. At that moment the planks are removed, and the wrappings put over the gold plate (to prevent it from becoming dull) are taken off. The Emperor alone comes and leaves through this gate. After that time it remains closed, for nobody deserves the honor to pass where the Emperor once passed before, for he never visits the same house more than once.[18]

To be the recipient of more than one visit, then, was extraordinary, and set a man apart from all others in the bureaucratic hierarchy. Only Sakai Tadakatsu and Hotta Masamori occupied such unassailable positions. It is tempting to speculate, therefore, on the importance of the two men for Iemitsu. Hotta's function, as we have seen, was that of Iemitsu's supreme confidant, participant in his phobias, and accomplice in his crimes. Judging from Hotta's *junshi* ("following one's master in death" by suicide) after Iemitsu died, theirs was clearly a relationship that included a death pact.[19]

Tadakatsu's importance to Iemitsu is more difficult to fathom. First of all, he must have represented the supreme example of the trusted Mikawa retainer to the Tokugawa house. By itself that was significant, but not sufficient. The Mizuno, for example, another old Mikawa retainer family, had also supplied a boy lover to the shogun, the third son of Mizuno Katsunari (1564–1651), called Narisada. That relationship had clearly not worked out as intended, for Narisada died in 1650 with the meager income of 3000 *koku*.[20]

What probably saved Tadakatsu's cousin Tadayo from the same fate as Iemitsu's other mentor, Aoyama Tadatoshi, was that he was too busy with the execution of Hidetada's policies to have had much time for the education of Iemitsu. Tadakatsu's association with the future shogun, then, was not burdened with Iemitsu's resentment, whereas the relative lateness of their connection was more than offset by the familial continuity, for Tadakatsu had become Tadayo's official heir. Tadakatsu represented the experience in government that had been accumulated in the Sakai family. The conclusion seems warranted that, whereas the connection with Hotta Masamori may have represented Iemitsu's inner self, Sakai Tadakatsu became the person most closely identified with the appearance Iemitsu wished to convey to the world.

This is made quite clear by Tadakatsu's official biography, in which matters related to the construction of Ieyasu's tomb at Nikkō and the funeral services connected with the shrine continually appear. It is well known how, through the expansion of Ieyasu's mausoleum at Mt. Nikkō, Iemitsu wished to honor his grandfather (who had personally assured his accession to the shogunate) to the whole world.[21] The Korean and Okinawan ambassadors were forced to make pilgrimages there in 1636, 1643, 1644, 1653, and 1655.[22] The Dutch East India Company had presented gifts for the "Emperor's grandfather's grave" before and was to do so again.[23] The Nikkō complex represented the outer image of Iemitsu and, after him, of his Tokugawa successors as well. It was, therefore, Tadakatsu who was in charge of the most important ceremonies there.

On 10 January 1633 Tadakatsu was promoted to close attendant to the shogun *(jijū)*.[24] This rank was reserved for those who had been with Iemitsu since before his succession to the shogunate. It was given by the emperor in Kyoto because it went with the Junior fourth court rank lower grade. Tadakatsu was the first of Iemitsu's close associates to receive it, even before Hotta Masamori (who received it one year later), and ten years earlier than Matsudaira Nobutsuna who became *jijū* only in December 1643, on the accession of Emperor Gokōmyō.[25]

As the first man in the bakufu after the shogun himself, Tadakatsu held, by 1635, multiple fiefs worth more than 113,500 *koku,* with castles in Kawagoe and Obama, and several pieds-à-terre along the Tōkaidō highway, as well as in Wakasa and Echizen. Thus he had been provided with the necessary resources for the overall supervision of the government of Japan, which freed Iemitsu of some of the irksome duties connected with his position. Although the shogun never completely relinquished control, as time went one he began to spend more time pursuing his own hobbies. Other unprecedented distinctions also set Tadakatsu apart from the rest of the shogunal bureaucracy. In 1638, he was excused from regular bureaucratic duties, allowed to keep his hat on in front of the shogun and to sit at his leisure.[26]

If it be objected that Tadakatsu's official biography contains only surface honors without giving information on his real stature within Iemitsu's bureaucracy, this objection may be countered with the simple observation that *all* such biographies concentrate on the honors received from the shogun. Moreover, an analysis of the entries in the *Tokugawa jikki* since the death of Hidetada in 1632 shows that of all the men surrounding Iemitsu, Sakai Tadakatsu is most frequently mentioned among those making policy decisions, more than twice as frequently as, for example, Matsudaira Nobutsuna. And only Hotta Masamori barely surpasses Tadakatsu in the frequency he is reported to be in the shogun's company.

∽

The result of the confrontation of the Jesuits with the Dutch group at Inoue's mansion in Hitotsubashi on 20 October was, as we have seen, another interrogation at Hotta's country house on 22 October in the presence of the shogun. On that occasion the two bravest of the Jesuits had persisted in revoking their apostasy and were forced to go back into the pits. We have no direct evidence when they apostatized for the second time, for the experiment of having the Dutch witness their apostasy was not tried again. However, the debriefing report left by the Dutch prisoners has an entry for 28 October, stating that the apostate Chū'an had received "full permission" to leave for Nagasaki and would do so "in two or three days." [27] Obviously, his duties were considered finished by that time, and we have seen that he had come to the shogun's capital in the company of the second Rubino group to assist at their interrogations. We have also seen that when two of the fathers withdrew their apostasy, Chū'an's permission to go back to Nagasaki had been canceled. It is probable, therefore, that the second apostasy of the fathers occurred between 22 and 28 October, for Chū'an's duties could only be over when all European fathers had conclusively denied their faith.

After their second experience in the pits, the fathers may have been in no condition to answer anyone's questions coherently. They were given two weeks to recover, for Iemitsu only checked on their apostasies again on 11 November, when he visited Sakai Tadakatsu's country mansion in Ushigome.[28] The Tokugawa jikki does not say why the shogun visited on that day, as it usually does in the case of a hunt or tea ceremony, practice or viewing of martial arts, or even when a visit concerns secret policy talks. Happily, the Okachigata mannenki (Ten Thousand Year Record of the Ambulatory Spies) adds that the shogun arrived at one o'clock in the afternoon and stayed until eight o'clock at night to hear the four Southern Barbarian priests, as well as Takeya Chō'emon and four or five other Japanese Christians.[29] We now know what such a visit entailed.

Meanwhile, the prisoners in the Nagasakiya lived from visit to visit, endlessly discussing the different rumors they heard. On 13 November 1643, for example, they heard from the interpreter Hachizaemon and the sons of their landlord that the shogun and his advisers had decided that the apostate fathers would be handed over to the Dutch factor, Jan Van Elserack, on his arrival in Edo, so that they might be deported on a Dutch ship. The Dutchmen thought this was the strangest thing they had heard so far, and they took it to be "empty gossip, half understood."[30] This was also the opinion of the Dutch interpreter from Hirado, Magobei, who came by for a chat on the next day. But five days later Schaep and Bijlvelt again heard the same rumor, this time when they visited Hachizaemon and Kichibei in their room upstairs. The Portuguese interpreters told them they had heard it, a few days before, from the *ōmetsuke* himself, and asked the Dutch what they thought Elserack or the governor general would do with them. They answered: "If they had been caught or captured by us, they would have been chained as our enemies (for Manila is our foe) to do foul stinking and contemptible work (without getting much food), but that we were ignorant of this transport and what his Imperial Majesty and the Imperial Councilors of Japan had in mind with this, and therefore excused ourselves and referred to Mr. Elserack for more details."[31]

The same balloon was floated before Elserack as well, for the rumor also crops up in his journal: "The four apostate papists were threatened by order of the emperor that they would be handed over to the Dutch captain in order that he might do with them as he liked. At this they had started to weep profusely, saying that they would rather die at the hands of their Japanese judges for the Dutch were the biggest enemies they had on earth, by whom they would die more than ten deaths daily. This news pleased the emperor exceedingly and partly alleviated the suspicion he had borne toward our nation."[32]

It is difficult to assess these entries, for it is hard to believe that the Japanese ever contemplated anything of this kind. The rumors may have been designed to see what reaction such a plan would provoke from the Jesuits as well as from the Dutch.

On the afternoon 20 November, the other Dutch interpreter from Hirado, Tōzaemon, came by to see the Dutch group in the Nagasakiya and he also brought news of the Jesuit fathers: "the captured papists have confessed (under torture as well as of their own free will) that more papists will come from Manila every year (in spite of the heavy punishment for it), and that next year two native Japanese (who are also papists, as well as some Spanish ones) will be sent here, and that Manila would never stop sending papists (even if they would be killed by the Japanese for a hundred years) but always continue to do so."[33]

Tōzaemon told them how the "whole Japanese empire was in an uproar" over this, and that the shogun was very alarmed because of the many Japanese Christians who were being discovered every day, and of course about the fact that Hollanders had been caught in the north and Roman Catholic priests in the west at almost the same time.

For all of these reasons, Tōzaemon said, the shogun "did not trust anyone and was usually present himself at all meetings when prisoners were being interrogated or examined."[34]

On 24 November, on his way to Edo where he had been summoned by the bakufu, Chief Factor Jan Van Elserack noted down more news of the fathers in his journal. He had heard that the Portuguese "padres" had finally denied their Savior, but that they were still in prison where they "enjoy good treatment, and have been promised by His Majesty five bags of rice a month and one hundred *taels** in silver for their sustenance for as long as they live, for which they will have to serve in Nagasaki (like the apostate father Chū'an)."[35] The factor added that only time would tell what the authorities were planning to do with these men. Realizing how unusual the Japanese ability was to bring Jesuit fathers (soldiers of God!) to recant their faith, he added: "This will sound strange to those in Macao, Manila and elsewhere, for these are things that have never happened before, that each of them has denied his Lord because of his fright of temporary torments, and now they have to betray other Christians, which they have already started to do by naming two merchants (one living in Miyako and the other in Fushimi) as Christians. By order of the Emperor these men have been tied up and brought to Edo. How this will end, we cannot know yet."[36]

The apostasy of the fathers was just a beginning, as far as Inoue was concerned. For after their recantation and their employment by the bakufu, the fathers were supposed to take on a Japanese identity, just as Chū'an had done, and assist in the war on Christianity. The ultimate aim of the elaborate torture to effect apostasies was to create living proofs of God's impotence in the realm of the shogun, but the ferreting out of Christians remained the main task. For their apostasy, the former priests had been rewarded with money in silver and a monthly stipend. From then on, in Inoue's eyes, there could never be enough proof of the sincerity of their recantation.

On 29 November, ten Japanese women were brought to the jail where the Jesuit group was kept to serve as spouses for the fathers and their followers. The first reaction of the four apostates to this ulti-

---

*In this context, a *tael* is a unit of currency, equivalent to 285 Dutch cents.

mate humiliation and negation of their former selves was to refuse to share their cells with the women. Their Asian converts, however, who had never been ordained as priests, did not have the same qualms. Inoue and his henchmen were not pleased with the stubbornness of the foreigners. The apostates, who had been living in relative comfort during the month of November, were made to feel miserable again.[37]

In the end, however, three of the fathers yielded to the temptations of the ōmetsuke. Inoue himself has left a record of this, the *Kirishitoki*, a document detailing how to deal with Christians, which the ōmetsuke compiled for his successor on his retirement. According to this document, Alonzo de Arroyo lived only twenty more days after he had been forced to share his cell with a woman.[38] In these three weeks he starved himself to death, which must therefore have occurred around 17 or 18 December. Indeed, there is indirect evidence from the Dutch factor's journal confirming this. On 18 December, Elserack noted that at two o'clock in the afternoon he had received a visit from Inoue's "highest collaborator," probably Okabe Iori. The man had a strange request: "He told us how the said papists had been ordered by His Majesty to take and use women. However, even though they said they had apostatized and become Japanese, they could not be forced to touch women. His Majesty and the High Authorities (who daily grow ever more embittered against these bad people) are pondering all the time by what means the apostates could be tortured further while still keeping them alive, so that the principal reason for his visit to the Dutch factor today was to see if there were any Dutch ways of torture, by which one can cause much sorrow but keep the criminals alive."[39]

The factor answered that "it was the Dutch custom to punish each criminal according to the degree of his guilt, after they, having been tortured, had confessed the crimes they had committed." After this pious statement, he added that the Dutch in the Indies were used to "chain their enemies and evil-doers, two by two with heavy irons, forcing them to slave from morning till night at filthy jobs, giving them nothing but bad rice to sustain themselves, making them sleep in jail with their legs chained together, and beating them with the rod as much as we know a man can bear and stay alive."[40]

Nothing innovative here. Inoue's henchman told him that he had heard as much from the prisoners from Nambu, but that he had hoped that Elserack would know of another torture. Was Inoue getting desperate, to ask advice about torture from the Dutch? We have already seen that it is likely that Alonzo de Arroyo had starved himself to death around this time. Although Inoue's man did not own up to it, his visit may have been prompted by Arroyo's death that morning or the day before.

We find more news of the fathers in the chief factor's journal of 14 February 1644, when the two Portuguese interpreters, Kichibei and Hachizaemon, finally returned from Edo to Nagasaki. They told Elserack that the Portuguese fathers were still "treated evilly and tormented in all imaginable ways, being held at the home of the Commissioner Chikugodono [i.e., Inoue] in a dark room, and [being brought out] from time to time at the pleasure of the Japanese gentlemen to pass the time torturing them."[41]

The Nagasaki *bugyō*, Baba Saburōzaemon, returned to his post on 22 May 1644, and again the Dutch factor received news about the Jesuits: "We also heard how the apostate priests so far have not been willing to touch women. Therefore, they are still tortured daily with water as well as in other ways (to the amusement of the Japanese noblemen)."[42] Which of the "Japanese noblemen" were amused here should require no further explanation.

Arroyo had been the first of the second Rubino group to die, but if we may believe Inoue's own testimony, he finally scored another triumph with Cassola: "Francisco [Cassola] was locked up alone with a woman, and became friendly with her. When they both admitted this, we made it known to all the inmates of the prison. Everyone was notified that the marriage of a father was a rare occurrence. We had them exchange marriage cups, and then moved them to the manor of Chikugo no kami, where they were held until they died."[43]

In the last entry concerning the fathers in the journal of 1644, the chief factor noted that he had heard from the interpreters that two of the fathers had died and the other two were ailing but were still tortured from time to time, being kept in a heavily guarded and dirty prison. On 14 January 1645, however, we read in the journal the depressing news that Chiara and Marquez had both married as well, and that the latter, seventy-three years old, had made his wife pregnant.[44]

In 1646, Inoue's country mansion at Koishikawa was fixed up as quarantine quarters for apostates, foreign as well as Japanese.[45] Here

Pedro Marquez lived until 1657 and Chiara (or: Okamoto San'emon) almost thirty years longer.[46] When the latter died on 24 August 1685 he had pathetically managed to save twenty-eight *ryō* and three *bu** in gold and silver pieces.[47] One would like to know what he was saving for.

∾

The landing of two groups of Christians, one Roman Catholic and one Calvinist, at the two extreme ends of Japan within a little more than a month from one another was pure coincidence. The arrival of the two groups in Edo, within one day of each other, cannot have been foreseen either. To deal with these two unexpected events the bakufu had to improvise its response. And although the power brokers tried to observe their usual discretion, two independent sets of primary sources were being created when it was decided to let the Dutch group go free.

Both sets of sources, Japanese and Dutch, have their own surface bias. The common denominator of the Japanese sources is their desire to represent the shogun as an infallible, godlike being. The Dutch sources, on the other hand, are concerned with such mundane matters as the approval of the behavior of the company's employees by their directors in Amsterdam. The particular attractiveness of both the debriefing report left by the prisoners from the *Breskens* and the factory journal kept at Deshima, however, is that their surface bias does not interfere with our study of Japanese history. Junior Merchant Bijlvelt (the keeper of the record of the prisoners) and Captain Schaep (who was responsible for its contents) had no reason to dissimulate except where their own behavior was concerned. But, as prisoners in Japan, most of the time they had no choice of their own, and therefore they left a record of how they were moved around rather than of how they moved.

The fate of the second Rubino group can only be traced through a careful comparison of the Japanese sources with those left by the employees of the Dutch East India Company. However, while tracing the fate of the second Rubino group, we necessarily recreate in detail the response of the bakufu to this new challenge. Thus a study of the fates of the Dutch and Jesuit groups offer us a rare glimpse into the inner workings of the Japanese power structure in the 1640s. For one thing, the story of the Jesuits allows us a close look at the compulsive

---

*A *ryō* is a gold coin worth four times the *bu*, a coin minted in gold or silver.

behavior of the shogun himself, whose very personal obsession with his war on Christianity is revealed all the more clearly through the testimony of the Dutch. Such behavior cannot be called rational anymore, and to state that the shogun was engaged in assuring "Japanese security, Japanese sovereignty, and Tokugawa legitimacy" is to completely misunderstand the personal nature of the power structure of the early Tokugawa Bakufu.[48]

This power structure had two aspects. To begin, those within it were exclusively men who had been put into place by the two previous shoguns, Ieyasu and Hidetada. Second, only those among them who had proven their unconditional loyalty to Iemitsu had survived in positions of power by the 1640s.[49] Consequently, this power structure was determined by Iemitsu's Tokugawa heritage as well as by his own preferences. Very literally, then, all the men in high positions during this time were Tokugawa Iemitsu's men, and each of them represented a particular aspect of the shogun's mental makeup.

This realization has important implications for a proper understanding of who these men around Iemitsu were. There were two in particular whose function we have analyzed above. We found that Iemitsu most freely visited and used the private mansions of Hotta Masamori and Sakai Tadakatsu. Both these men fulfilled particular needs of the shogun, Masamori being the shogun's intimate confidant, connected with Iemitsu's inner self; and Tadakatsu his official representative, standing for everything associated with the Tokugawa family name. It is not surprising, therefore, that after the shogun's death in 1651 the good fortune of the Sakai family continued unabated, whereas the Hotta, after Masamori's *junshi,* immediately went into (temporary) decline.

Disguised as samurai, the second Rubino group had tried to enter Japan unnoticed. It is unclear, really, what they planned to do other than to get caught. But if that was all they wanted, why did they try to disguise themselves? I suspect that they did not know themselves that they wanted to get caught until Jin'emon shot his warning arrow at them. There were some definite advantages to getting caught. For one thing it was the surest way to come into contact with those in Japan the men wanted to convert: the shogun and Chū'an the apostate. For another, obviously, the men had come looking for the glory of martyrdom.

The samurai disguise, therefore, must be considered a prop that had helped them during their preparations by sustaining the illusion that their mission would initially succeed. Subconsciously, the disguise may also have prevented the weakest members of the group from doubting the meaning of the journey to Japan. It was proof of strategy, employed by samurai of Christ, confident in the knowledge that they were doing God's will, and that God would help them succeed. But in Japan, the expression "God's will" had no longer any meaning.

The Jesuits seem to have had no idea who they were up against. Their disguise as samurai becomes painfully ridiculous when it is compared to the true samurai they had to face. There could likely be no more complete misunderstanding as that which existed among the men of the second Rubino group about conditions within Japan, which had been shaped by several centuries of civil war. The men of Inoue's office felt no compunction at all in causing suffering. Suffering was their tool. They were so familiar with death they had made it their ally. Never was death allowed to comfort those who were suffering. When on the very edge of dying, the victims were nursed back to life so that the torture process might be started anew.

For the men of the second Rubino group, the greatest disappointment must have been the realization that they were not even going to be allowed to die for their beliefs. This may have been the moment Inoue and his henchmen were waiting for. If they could make their victims realize that it was the truth of their childhood, of their education, of their whole life as they had lived it before coming to Japan, that was making them suffer and would continue to do so, they would be ready to abandon it. Between continuous suffering and not suffering, there really is no choice at all for any human being. For the Jesuits there were only two choices left: suicide or apostasy.

For the Jesuit order, the existence of the apostates in Japan represented an ugly defeat as well as a stain of possibly devastating import for its worldwide counter-Reformation offensive. It is understandable that the order has done all it could to deny, misinterpret, turn around, sow doubt, and scoff at all the evidence available.[50] If China represented the limit of Jesuit power, the apostates in Japan clearly proved that the island empire had become completely beyond the reach of the order, and therefore the truth it propagated could never make a real claim to be universal.

Chapter 6
A Magnanimous Gesture

During the month of November 1643, the shogun and his advisers put the *Breskens* affair aside until Elserack, who had left Nagasaki on 8 November, would arrive in Edo. For the prisoners from Nambu this time of inaction and uncertainty about their fates must have been especially hard to bear, although the men from Inoue's office seem to have gone out of their way to reassure and comfort them. On 29 November, for example, the interpreters Kichibei and Hachizaemon visited the Dutchmen. They urged them to write a secret note to Elserack, which they promised to give him when he arrived. After the two Japanese men had left, the men discussed their proposal. At last, they decided to trust the interpreters and to make use of this opportunity to write a letter with everything they had said during their interrogations.

The next day, they were summoned to Hotta's country mansion again. On their arrival, they had to wait a while, and then Schaep and Bijlvelt, accompanied by Tōzaemon and Magobei, were brought to "a large, open court yard with a pleasant garden in front of a splendid chamber and a wooden verandah of excellent workmanship (where the councilors were seated in extreme magnificence.)"[1] Among the councilors was the shogun himself.[2] Sakai Tadakatsu and Matsudaira Nobutsuna were not present, for they had left for Kyoto, as the shogun's envoys, to attend the inauguration of the new emperor on 2 December. Apart from Inoue's presence, then, this time the Dutchmen were facing a predominantly antiforeign faction of the bakufu: Iemitsu, Masamori, and the Abe cousins, Shigetsugu and Tadaaki. That both Masamori and Shigetsugu would commit suicide on Iemitsu's death in 1651 testifies to their close involvement with the shogun's obsessions.[3]

The interrogation started with threats of violence: "You, captain and merchant," said the ōmetsuke, "we order you unequivocally to speak nothing but the truth, for if we hear something else from Captain Elserack (who may arrive in Edo any day now), a terrible and heavy punishment awaits you."[4] The men answered that they would reply truthfully to the extent of their knowledge, just as they had done "continually" so far.

This time the questions concentrated on the perceived threats to Japan's security: ships had been appearing and disappearing off the coast of Japan all year long. The latest reports had reached Edo from Matsumae in the extreme north and from Kyushu in the south. The Castricom had been sighted and visited by a pelt trader on the south coast of Hokkaido.[5] The man was brought to Edo to be interrogated, together with the articles he had acquired from the crew of the ship.[6] Next, Akizuki Taneharu, a daimyo with a fief of 30,000 koku in Hyūga on Kyushu's east coast, reported on 28 November that his lookouts had sighted two ships.[7] Two and a half weeks earlier, by an amazing coincidence, the Castricom and Breskens had found each other again off the coast of Shikoku.[8]

Today, Schaep first had to answer questions about the Castricom. Why had the ship been heading east from Hokkaido? When was the right time to sail from Japan's northern extremity to Java? And where did the two large ships, seen near Satsuma a few days earlier, come from? Of course, Schaep could not have known about the miraculous reunion of the two ships, but he answered that the ships sighted might have belonged to the fleet bound for Nagasaki this year.

More evidence of a possible Dutch-Portuguese alliance had been supplied by the apostate fathers: "Did you know," Inoue asked, "that Dutch soldiers and sailors have been sent by the Prince of Orange from Holland to assist the king of Portugal in his struggle with Spain? And that, some time ago, these soldiers had mutinied against that king over back pay, and had started a new war inside that country?"[9] The men from the second Rubino group had departed from Manila sometime in April or May, months after the men from the Breskens had left Batavia, so they may have had more recent news from Europe. Schaep had to admit that he did not know about this. But the implication was clear: the Dutch were cooperating with the Portuguese, archenemies of Japan, on many different levels.

From the dangerous topic of an alliance with Portugal, Inoue moved smoothly to the even more dangerous topic of Christianity: "Do you Hollanders ever sell any merchandise for the Portuguese? What is the meaning of the signs and crosses which are sometimes found on the packing of European commodities? Do you also have crosses and crucifixes on your ships?" Schaep blandly denied everything. "We never sell any merchandise for the Portuguese," he said, "and the crosses that are found on our European wares are the coats of arms of the cities of Holland where they are manufactured."[10]

But more theology was on Inoue's agenda. "Is your God the same as the Deus of the Portuguese and Spanish? How do you call him? Who has seen him? How do you know he has existed? Where did he live? And on what authority do you believe this?"[11] These were all questions a staunch Calvinist like Captain Schaep, who was torn between saving his skin and his soul, would have liked to avoid. Schaep had to admit that the God of the Portuguese and the Spanish was the same God the Dutch worshipped. "Are your holidays the same as those of the Portuguese and Spanish? How do you call them? Do you have as many? And do you observe days of fasting, when you refrain from eating certain dishes, like they do every year?"[12]

The direction of the questions seemed to indicate that, in Japanese eyes, there was little difference between the religion of the Portuguese and that of the Dutch: "Don't you have papists, priests, or teachers in Holland as well, who preach to and teach the common people as they do in Spain and Portugal? How powerful are they? Who pays them? Do they have any say in the government?" It turned out to be hard to explain what was so different about Protestantism, especially in view of the large number of Roman Catholics living in Holland. "If your God is the same as the God of the Portuguese and the Castilians," Inoue continued implacably, "and you observe the same Sunday, what then is the difference between your and their religion?"[13]

The best policy seemed to be to stress the number of gods deemed worthy of worship: "The Portuguese and Castilians have, apart from their God in Heaven, also a god on earth. That is the pope of Rome, of whom they say he can forgive all sins completely. They worship and believe in many saints and images, but we don't. We have only one God in Heaven, in whom we put all our trust and to whom we look for salvation. There are several other points in which their and our religions differ, but we cannot explain them to your Excellencies, as we are not scholars."[14]

That the Dutch did not worship the pope was a point in their favor, to be sure. In the Japanese sources, fear of the *papa*'s power crops up regularly.[15] More questions dealt with the Dutch presence on the island of Java, its inhabitants and native rulers. During this interrogation, then, the Dutchmen were questioned not on their own particular case but rather only as potential allies of the Portuguese, as Christians similar to the Iberians, and as colonists indistinguishable from the Spanish. The slant of this interrogation suggests that the shogun still had doubts about continuing his relationship with Holland and had decided to take another look at it, while the other two members of the pro-Dutch faction (Tadakatsu and Nobutsuna) were safely out of the way in Kyoto.

When Schaep and Bijlvelt came back to their men, they found more than thirty Japanese prisoners sitting next to them, some of them shackled with handcuffs and others with their arms trussed up underneath their clothes. Perhaps they were talking among themselves, the Dutchmen guessed, about whether they were treated justly or unjustly. Later they saw them brought, two at a time, to the place where they themselves had just been questioned. While waiting for permission to return to their lodgings, Schaep asked Magobei what crimes all these people had committed. The interpreter answered that he did not know off-hand, but that he had heard them say that they or their parents had been Christians, and that they had already spent a long time in prison. This was clearly visible from the pitiful condition they were in. The Dutchmen had merely been the first that day in a long line of suspects in Iemitsu's private war on Christianity, whose cases the shogun was reviewing.

The next morning, 1 December 1643, Schaep had a servant secretly call Kichibei to their room. When the interpreter came, the captain handed him two letters, one inside the other, to give to Elserack on his arrival. The interpreter promised he would do so.[16] That this secret communication between the prisoners and Elserack via the Portuguese interpreters is not mentioned anywhere in Elserack's journal does not necessarily mean much. Elserack surely read the debriefing report before it was submitted to the authorities in Batavia, so we have to assume he knew about the letter. We may also infer that the letter was, indeed, delivered to him, otherwise we would have found some indication to the contrary. Of course, we can only guess at the contents, for, not surprisingly, this letter has not been preserved. It probably contained a more honest and complete record of the questions asked and the answers given than we have in the official debriefing report, for at this point all the prisoners cared about was that the chief factor from Nagasaki would give the same answers as they themselves had.

Furthermore, it is unlikely that the Portuguese interpreters would initiate such a step exclusively on their own authority, for if it ever became known they were sure to pay for it. Therefore, they must have been *instructed* to give the Dutch this secret channel of communication. Only Inoue Masashige had to power to do so and be assured of the interpreters' cooperation, and even he may have had orders from Sakai Tadakatsu, before the latter had departed for Kyoto, in order to make sure that Elserack's story would corroborate what the prisoners had said.

The shogun's orders had been that no communication be allowed between the prisoners and the chief factor, and that is why the men from the *Breskens* had been moved away from the Nagasakiya, on 27 November, to different quarters.[17] Sakai Tadakatsu, however, seems to have decided that it was in Japan's best interest for the Dutch traders to continue to come. Inoue was of the same opinion, and the interpreters undoubtedly agreed, for the presence of the foreigners in Japan was the basis of their livelihood. If Iemitsu were to find Elserack's story to be different from that of the prisoners, and the latter were executed by his order, a continued Dutch presence in Japan would clearly become impossible, and a Dutch-Portuguese alliance against Japan might actually materialize. On this occasion, then, the shogun's subordinates protected Japan against the excesses of his obsessions. We must conclude that even Iemitsu's power had its limits.

In the afternoon of 2 December, Schaep and Bijlvelt were summoned again to Hitotsubashi. After they waited a little less than an hour, the chief secretary of the *ōmetsuke* came to sit with them. He had brought paper and writing utensils and warned them that this time all their answers to the *ōmetsuke*'s questions would be written down and compared to what Elserack said. The men answered that they would reply to all questions truthfully.

This was it. Their formal examination was all done exclusively on paper, for the men did not even see Inoue and the Nagasaki *bugyō* this time. The secretary went over all the old questions once more, about where they had come from and where they were going, and the Dutchmen answered these as they had before, withholding their discovery of the Kuril Islands, northeast of Hokkaido. After that, the questions concentrated on the differences between the two ships. What did the officers of the *Castricom* look like? How old were they? What were their names? Had any of them been to Japan previously? Did Elserack know them? What cargo did the ships carry? When and where had they last seen Elserack? Did he know the contents of their cargo?[18]

All of these questions could be answered with complete honesty. After their answers had been written down, the secretary took the documents inside. He stayed away for a while. When at last he came back, he asked them if Elserack would know the date of their departure from Batavia and the fact that they had been sent to Tartary. He also asked if the men would be prepared to confirm with their signatures that Elserack would surely know these two details.

Here again we may discern the hand of the helmsman, Inoue Masashige. Convinced that these two details must have been among the information provided to Elserack in the secret letter from the prisoners, he insisted that they sign their names to the fact that Elserack would know them. In fact, the information that the ship had been heading for Tartary had, as we have seen, been first conveyed to the Japanese authorities by Elserack himself. So, of course, he knew that fact. But there was a problem here, for on 10 September, in his first communication on the affair with the Nagasaki *bugyō*, Yamazaki Gompachirō, Elserack had stated that the ships had left in March of that year.[19] The departure date provided by the prisoners, however, had been 3 February 1643.

The prisoners may have been aware that something was afoot, but if so they did not mention it in the debriefing report. They answered the question of Inoue's secretary: "Yes, we are quite sure that His Hon. was informed about our voyage, and trusted that he also knew the date of our departure from Batavia."[20] From this confident response it seems likely that they had taken care to include these details in their secret letter to the chief factor.

That night, in his room in the Nagasakiya where he had checked in the previous day, Elserack noted in his journal that he had been informed about the strict interrogation that had taken place that afternoon. His interpreter Shōsuke gave the chief factor a complete synopsis of the questions that had been asked, including the one concerning the departure date from Batavia.[21] As we can see, Inoue was leaving nothing to chance, and the apparent separation of the prisoners from the representative of the Dutch in Japan was, therefore, nothing but a formality designed to please and deceive the shogun.

~

At dawn the next morning, the chief factor left for Hitotsubashi in his palanquin. Elserack later noted proudly that, after only a short wait, Inoue had welcomed him in one of his main reception rooms. The *ōmetsuke* had smiled and congratulated him on his speedy journey and the fact that he had arrived in Edo in good health. He then went on to tell the factor that "the reason why he had been summoned to the Court so early was that, now four months ago, two Dutch ships had been near the Japanese coast north of Edo, sailing back and forth without anchoring or coming ashore, which has caused the Emperor and the Lords of Japan to suspect that those ships were up to no good, but might try to bring papists ashore somewhere and cause trouble. For that reason, a strict guard had been kept along the whole coast to keep an eye on these ships, and finally one of these anchored near a city called Nambu in the country of Masamij."[22]

The disinformation policy continued. The extent of the Japanese coastal guard was greatly exaggerated. The geographical indications were so vague as to certainly cause problems if they were ever used in attempts to bring priests ashore in Japan. Inoue continued: "The captain and merchant, having gone ashore with eight of their men, could not be understood, for lack of interpreters, when they had been brought before the Governor of that place. For that reason, all of them had been sent to Edo in order that an investigation could be conducted into what kind of people they were and what they had in mind. Meanwhile, the ship had left and was not seen again. The Dutchmen who remained behind have been interrogated and examined several times (by the High Authorities and by us), and we have now summoned you here [to check] whether they have told the truth and did not lie to us."[23]

The story sounds innocent enough. The Japanese had been at their most reasonable, it seemed. Note how the prisoners are called "the Dutchmen who remained behind," shifting the blame and suggesting that they were still in Japan because their own shipmates had abandoned them.

Shortly afterwards, the Nagasaki *bugyō* Baba Saburōzaemon arrived. But Elserack's exchange of mutual compliments with this official was rudely interrupted by the arrival of Makino Sado no kami Chikashige, who had been sent by Iemitsu to represent the shogun at Elserack's interrogation. Son of Makino Takumi no kami Nobushige, he was thirty-six years old at this time, and had entered the ranks of Iemitsu's pages at an early age. On 25 February 1633, at the age of twenty-six, he had been appointed *gozenban,* the official who served the shogun his meals, a position of great trust. In view of what we have seen about Iemitsu's habits, we may safely assume that, by then, Chikashige had given the shogun ample proof of his obedience to all his wishes. On 18 April 1642, his power had been increased with a captainship in the body guard *(goshoinban).*[24]

He was introduced to Elserack as "a great friend of the Company,"[25] who was held in high esteem by the shogun, "far more so than his father had ever been." For these reasons, he was accorded the room's principal seat and treated with the utmost respect by the *ōmetsuke* and the Nagasaki *bugyō.* The three men conferred with each other for a short time, and Inoue had his secretary bring in the minutes of Schaep and Bijlvelt's last interrogation and the declaration signed by them two days earlier. The *ōmetsuke* started with the latter.

He asked the chief factor if he knew about the two ships that had appeared off the Japanese coast four months earlier. He wanted to know the purpose of their presence there. Elserack answered he did know about the ships, and explained that they had been on their way to Tartary. Inoue continued: "Did the captain know when these ships had left Batavia?" Elserack answered: "On the third of February, which was the fourteenth day of the twelfth month [of the previous Japanese calendar year]." This was extremely precise, a little too precise, for Elserack's conversion of the date to the Japanese calendar is off by one day.[26] Nobody seemed to notice. The Japanese date had probably been supplied to Elserack by the interpreters, and therefore ultimately may have come from Inoue. Perhaps the *ōmetsuke* himself had miscalculated.

Elserack's responses to other questions about the crews of the ships, their officers, and cargo also agreed with the answers given by Schaep and Bijlvelt. Then Inoue asked if the chief factor knew why the *Castricom* had approached the shore at night and put out to sea again during the day, and why she had shot her guns and muskets, as though she were up to no good. It should be well known, he lectured ponderously, that the shogun had permitted the Dutch to "freely conduct their trade in his realm."[27]

Elserack answered this disingenuous accusation by stating that he could not be sure why this had happened, but that he presumed that the ship was forced to do so for lack of fresh water. Her officers might have been hesitant to come ashore, he added. It was true that the shogun had permitted the Dutch to come to Japan, but the men on these ships may have understood that to mean that they were allowed to come to Nagasaki and nowhere else. That the ships had sometimes fired their guns, Elserack believed, had been to signal someone to come aboard and see whether they would be allowed to enter a harbor to procure the things they needed, as was the practice in Europe and other places.

All of these answers pleased the gentlemen well, and they announced that they had been in accordance with the confessions of the Dutchmen from the *Breskens*. The entire affair had been a consequence of the "Japanese system of justice," they said, and the Dutch should not "take offense in their hearts." Again we have a sign here that at least some men on the Japanese side were well aware that they had been playing with fire, if they valued the continued coming of Dutch ships. The treatment of the *Breskens* matter shows clearly that those making most decisions in foreign policy did indeed value the presence of the Dutch in Japan. Both Sakai Tadakatsu and Inoue Masashige were highly educated and fully aware of the usefulness of a European contact, quite apart from what the Dutch could contribute in the inter-Asian trade.

It is clear, moreover, that the Chinese could easily have provided Japan with the silk it wanted, and that the Dutch were not really indispensable intermediaries.[28] But after the expulsion of the Portuguese and the continued (or presumed) presence of southern European Roman Catholic missionaries in the country, the Dutch were the only channel of communication with Europe that Japan had left.

On 5 December 1643, the weather in Edo was "fine and clear."[29] Around two in the afternoon, a messenger arrived at the Nagasakiya and announced that Inoue and the Nagasaki *bugyō* had summoned the Dutch factor and his party to come to Hitotsubashi immediately. A similar message had been delivered to the Dutch group from the *Breskens* in their new apartment. The latter arrived in Inoue's resi-

dence *(yashiki)* before Elserack did, and were told to wait: the sailors in their Japanese clothes in the *genkan* (entrance hall), and Schaep and Bijlvelt in their Dutch costumes a little further inside.

When Elserack arrived, he was shown to a room where he and his men were to wait for the *ōmetsuke* and the Nagasaki *bugyō*. Soon, the two Japanese officials came with a large number of men in their wake, easily surpassing the meager retinue of four Dutchmen that the Dutch *kapitan* had brought. Schaep and Bijlvelt were called to the same room, and then the Japanese officials asked: "Elserack, here are the ten Hollanders whom you have said you know. Are they the same people that they pretend to be?" The chief factor answered affirmatively, "Yes," and pointed with his finger: "That is Captain Hendrick Cornelisz Schaep and that is the Junior Merchant Wilhem Bijlvelt."[30]

The officials continued: "Are you willing to affirm and guarantee with your own person that these are the people and officers of one of the ships that were ordered to sail for Tartary, and not in order to harm the Japanese empire by bringing papists or in any other way?" Elserack nodded again. "Because your words have checked out completely with what the prisoners have said, His Majesty has ordered to hand them over to you, on the condition that you sign a paper that all of you are Dutchmen employed by the East India Company." Elserack declared he was ready to do so, and that moreover, he would be prepared, if necessary, to pledge "all the ships that come every year to Nagasaki as additional securities."[31]

This answer shows that Elserack was relieved as well, going overboard as he did here with promises that had not even been requested. Of course, his answer pleased Inoue, who felt himself suddenly on more solid ground. He notified Elserack that he would have to appear in the Castle before the shogun and his councilors the next morning to confirm verbally as well as in writing what he had said just then. The Dutchmen were delivered to him now, and he was free to talk to them as much as he wanted.

Elserack thanked the Japanese officials profusely, and assured them he would be ready the next morning to go to the Castle. The Dutchmen then left the reception room and went back through the hall to the entrance. There all the captured Dutchmen again bowed their heads to the ground in front of the *ōmetsuke* and the Nagasaki *bugyō*. Elserack told them: "Men, you have been released."[32] On hearing this, the sailors were all so overcome with emotion that they could not hold back their tears. They thanked Elserack and the Japanese officials, and then were amiably given their leave.

~

The next morning, 6 December, the chief factor crossed the wooden bridge over the Castle's outer moat around ten-thirty. He passed through the Tokiwa gate with his two interpreters, Kohyōe and Shō-suke. Seeing great numbers of guards armed with halberds, muskets, bows, and arrows, they continued toward the Ōtemon gate. Before crossing the bridge leading up to this gate, Elserack had to get out of his palanquin and walk the rest of the way. Passing through the gate, the men turned left and walked up the slope toward the next gate, the Nakanomon or inner gate, and then right again to approach the main keep. Shortly before eleven, they entered the *genkan* and were brought to an "exquisite" antechamber, where they were told to wait until called.

This was the *toranoma* (tiger room), the office room of the shogun's body guard *(shoinban)*, which on such occasions served as antechamber where all chief factors had to wait for their audiences with the shogun. Here Elserack waited for two hours, during which time "many lords and other noblemen" came to see him. Finally, one official took him by the hand and led him through several other "exquisite" halls until they came to the verandah in front of the "council of the highest authorities." Elserack would write later: "The Commissioner Chikugo no kami and the Governor Saburōzaemon and a swarm of other gentlemen sat down in the lacquered wooden corridor. The said council consisted of more than forty people, who were all seated according to their ranks in an excellent hall that had been preciously decorated with gold and many other colors."[33]

Apart from the *rōjū*, some of the *tozama daimyō* were present to witness the proceedings from their usual spots in the *ōhiroma* (great and wide hall). The corridor was filled with other officials, mainly *metsuke* such as Inoue and probably also the superintendents of shrines and temples *(jisha bugyō)*, while some of Iemitsu's close associates, such as Makino Sado no kami Chikashige and others we have met so far, would also have been present among them. The shogun himself was present incognito: "His Majesty was, at a distance of fifteen feet away, continually looking at us through the sliding doors (which had been opened one foot wide), and heard everything said on both sides. The main lords were Bungo no kami [Abe Tada-aki], Tsushima no kami [Abe Shigetsugu], and Hotta kaga no kami [Masamori], who ordered the said commissioner and governor to interrogate us."[34]

From this we see that the sliding doors of the lower step room *(gedan no ma)* had been half closed, so that the shogun could see and hear everything that happened in the lacquered corridor in front of him as well as spy on the Dutchmen who were sitting on the outside verandah. Again, as we have seen in Hotta's country mansion, the seating arrangements made visible the social position of each man present. The Dutch *kapitan* occupied the lowest place in this Japanese hierarchy and thus sat furthest outside. Although officially not present, the shogun sat furthest inside, and everyone else had his proper place in between.

Inoue had a roll of paper in his hand and addressed the factor in the following manner, reading the words of the shogun himself, as drafted for him by the *rōjū:*

> The Dutch received permission from the previous Emperor Gongen Sama [Ieyasu] to freely enter all harbors of Japan (for he had found them to be a sincere nation). [This being the case,] why then did two ships sail to and fro [off the Japanese coast] without daring to enter a harbor to provide themselves with rice, water, or other necessities (which they say they needed), but hesitating to do so like untrustworthy characters? The ten Dutchmen, who have been brought from the said ships from Nambu to Edo, would have been tied up and tortured with water or in other ways according to the law of Japan (as happens in such cases with other foreigners) but as we have found you to be sincere men prepared to serve His Majesty at all times, we have treated them well and we will hand them over to you now on your cognizance.[35]

The truth had, of necessity, been turned around. With the peculiar logic of those in power, the shogun said, in fact, that because the Dutch had a right to enter any harbor, they had been arrested. In other words: they had a right to be arrested. Period.

Dutch historians (not notable for their knowledge of Japan) have eagerly jumped on the phrase found here about the Dutch being such a "sincere nation." In all Dutch accounts of the *Breskens* affair, we find the statement repeated ad nauseam, that the Dutch were released because of their "honesty" or "sincerity."[36] However, the Inoue's reference to the so-called Dutch "sincerity" was nothing more than wily flattery, employed to make everyone lose sight of the real issues here. The *ōmetsuke* was an amazing psychologist.

The *Tokugawa jikki* reports this occasion as follows: "[The shogun] inquired about the situation of the Dutchmen who had been stranded last [*sic*] year in Nambu. They said that while on their way to other countries for the purpose of trade they had encountered a violent storm and had drifted ashore. They had not crossed the seas to spread the Evil Religion."[37]

The *Kan'ei nikki* is a little more precise, quoting the diary kept by the Tokugawa house of Ki, which was routinely informed of the shogun's activities: "Today one of the Dutchmen who had come to Nagasaki [i.e., Elserack] was invited to appear before the shogun in the *ōhiroma* to be questioned about the affair of the Dutchmen who had come to Nambu. He affirmed that no one had come to work for any religion, but that they had been on their way somewhere when they were thrown off course by a storm and had come to Japan. He said that they were from the same country as he was and that he knew them well, it is rumored. It is not known what decision was taken in the presence of the shogun."[38]

After this, Elserack was told to leave and wait in the antechamber again, where both the *ōmetsuke* and the Nagasaki *bugyō* joined him shortly and said that he was expected to return to the Castle in two or three days. He was to keep himself ready to do so, and in the meantime refrain from contacting the ten Dutchmen from the *Breskens,* "to prevent the High Authorities from getting a bad impression."[39]

The weather held until Tuesday, 8 December 1643. At ten in the morning, Elserack left the Nagasakiya with his two interpreters again. He took the same route to the Castle as three days earlier, and was told to wait in the *toranoma* once more. This time he waited three hours.

That same morning, the men from the *Breskens* had been visited by Hachizaemon, who announced that they would receive their "complete freedom" on that day. He had scarcely left their lodgings when the men were ordered by Gen'emon's son to dress and get ready to go out. At first the men did not know where they were going but then they noticed they were being walked in the direction of the Castle.

When they arrived at the *genkan,* the men were seated outside on mats spread along both sides of the entrance and ordered to wait there. Fujii Zen'emon, the *kachimetsuke* (ambulatory spy) who had come to get them in Morioka on behalf of the shogun, and the two Dutch interpreters, Tōzaemon and Magobei, kept them company. Zen'emon pointed at the wooden gate *(heichōgomon)* in the wall to the left of the *genkan,* and said that the men would go through it to be led before the shogun. This was a way through the garden to the ōhiroma, which avoided the awkwardness of having such lowly creatures as the Dutch sailors actually enter the main keep.

For an hour or so, the men observed "the great pomp and exceptionally polite manners of the great many lords, secretaries, and courtiers who were passing to and fro."[40] Then Zen'emon led them through the wooden gate over a "pavement of cobblestones," until they came "in front of a beautiful, gilded gallery," where they were ordered to kneel down with their faces to the ground. Soon afterwards, they saw Elserack on the same verandah, and behind him the "highest councilors of Japan."[41]

The scene was mostly a repeat of two days earlier, only this time the shogun does not seem to have been present, not even incognito, and neither were the tozama daimyō. The matsunoma or (pinetree room), a part of the ōhiroma, was filled with the tairō Ii Naotaka, Doi Toshikatsu, Hotta Masamori, the Abe cousins, and various department heads and captains of the guards.[42] Again Chikugo no kami asked Elserack the same questions as he had before, to which Elserack politely gave the appropriate answers.

Then Inoue addressed the chief factor as follows: "Kapitan Elserack, there sit the ten Dutchmen who have been brought here from Nambu and all deserve to die, according to His Majesty's laws. However, having heard their confession as well as yours, which we have found to agree with each other, His Majesty has decided to let them live and to hand them over to you, on condition that you will sign a paper that guarantees with your own person and all the property of the Company in Japan that these men did not bring any papists or other Christians ashore anywhere, and that you have answered our questions in accordance with the truth."[43]

Obviously, the ōmetsuke (who had only demanded a written declaration that all men were Dutch and employees of the Company three days earlier) had been happy to incorporate Elserack's own over-enthusiastic suggestion of putting up the company's property as a guarantee for his own truthfulness. The stupidity of this suggestion did not lie in the fact that the company's property could ever be endangered in this way, for the men indeed had had nothing to do with bringing priests ashore. Rather it lay in the admission, implicit in the act of pledging the company's property, that the Japanese had good reasons for their suspicion.

This was a boon Inoue had not expected, and it cannot have increased his admiration for Dutch diplomacy. The fact that Elserack had shown himself so overly accommodating would, as we shall see, lead to more trouble over the *Breskens* affair later on, for the Japanese side did not fail to try and exploit the advantage gained.

Elserack promised the *ōmetsuke* to do so "in all humility and with a face showing excessive joy," for that was how this "expert" on Japan thought it was best to treat the Japanese authorities. He thanked "their Highnesses with many words for the mercy they had shown to these men." Then Inoue directed himself to the prisoners and said: "Today, you are freed by the Emperor, released, and handed over to your lord and *kapitan*. Therefore thank his Imperial Majesty!" The men, who felt as if they had "arisen from the dead," did not hesitate to do so.[44]

Elserack was the first to retire to the *toranoma*, where shortly afterwards he was congratulated by the *ōmetsuke* and the Nagasaki *bugyō* for "the release of the Dutchmen and the satisfaction he had given to His Majesty, who had come to have a better feeling than ever before about the Dutch nation." They said they rejoiced with the *kapitan* over this happy ending. Elserack could not resist and went overboard again: "thanking the gentlemen with all imaginable humility for the honor and efforts they had taken over this affair." His heart and tongue, he said, could not express how much this honor would be valued by the Dutch.

Then Saburōzaemon cut in with a revealing remark: "Elserack, when you go to Batavia and back to your country, your management of this affair will not be to your credit." But Elserack did not understand. He answered: "Yes it will, and [Japan] will be held in high esteem by our people, something that transcends all riches of gold and silver."[45] Coming from a merchant, that meant a lot.

The Castle record of the *Kan'ei nikki* has no entry for this day, but for unfathomable reasons reports the same events on 10 December, quoting the diaries of the Mito and Ki families. The *Tokugawa jikki* follows suit. That there can be no mistake about the date, however, is proven by the *Hitomi shiki* or Private Record of the Hitomi Family, which agrees with the Dutch sources about the date of the formal release. It has the following entry for 8 December: "Today, the ten Dutchmen who had been caught in Nambu because they had engaged in unseemly behavior were pardoned, even though this was certainly a criminal affair. However, when the *kapitan* Ensaraki [Elserack] was questioned he had stated firmly that they had sailed from Jacatara, without a doubt, and had brought no Christians etc. [to

Japan]. The shogun has heard and understood this and because the affairs of the Dutch have been treated with pity by generations of shoguns, and moreover, because they were foreigners he pardoned their improper behavior and ordered them sent back to Holland."[46]

This, then, was the official line put out. The Japanese had treated the Dutch "with pity," as behooved good Buddhists like Iemitsu.

Each time the men from the *Breskens* had been interrogated on a certain topic, they were first asked the main questions informally. Later, these were repeated on a formal occasion before the councilors and in the presence of the shogun himself. In other words, the interrogations were rehearsed beforehand. When the group first arrived in Edo, the main question had been whether they had been in league with the second Rubino group, which had just arrived off Kyushu. They were first confronted with the Jesuits on 26 August at Inoue's mansion in Hitotsubashi, and later on 5 September, before the shogun and his councilors at Hotta's country mansion in Asakusa. On both occasions, the Dutchmen established their enmity toward the Roman Catholics to the satisfaction of their Japanese judges, and it was clear that the two groups had not been in cahoots.

Then, on 27 September, the news reached Edo from Nagasaki that the ship had been on its way to Tartary. Three days later, the Dutch interpreters Magobei and Tōzaemon arrived from Hirado, and a more detailed investigation of the true reasons for the ship's presence off the coast of northern Japan became possible. On 1 October, therefore, Schaep and Bijlvelt were called to Inoue's mansion to rehearse the questions about their arrival, their goals, and their behavior off the Japanese coast. It is unclear from the debriefing report how detailed Inoue's questions were on the subject of their first arrival in Yamada on 10 June.

As established from an analysis of the local documents in chapter 2, there was more to the *Breskens'* return to Yamada than a simple desire for fresh vegetables and supplies. But in the pages of the debriefing report, covering the questions and answers of the interrogation, we find, strangely enough, not one question related to the events leading up to and including the arrest of the Dutch group on 29 July, although all other matters were investigated and reported thoroughly. It is, of course, very unlikely that Inoue would not have heard the

Dutch on these topics, even though he must have had Japanese reports, notably that of Urushido Kanzaemon, as well.

On 9 October, Schaep and Bijlvelt were first questioned in detail by the shogun and his councilors. On the next day, Inoue followed up with more questions, again undoubtedly prompted by the shogun. On 20 October, the Dutch group was once more brought into contact with the apostate Jesuits in front of Sakai Tadakatsu and Matsudaira Nobutsuna. Although they were not aware of it, this time they were among friends, who were preparing their release and thinking primarily of the message the Dutch were going to take back to the outside world.

All the interrogations revolved around the same theme: were the Dutch in league with the Portuguese and Spanish or not? This must have been Iemitsu's particular obsession. Were the Dutch in the pay of the Iberians to bring priests ashore, or to spy for good places to do so, or as the vanguard for a joint attack on Japan? Iemitsu may have considered the recent truce between Portugal and Holland as the first step toward such an alliance directed against Japan. The reports of ships firing their guns off the Japanese coast, together with the capture of a group of determined Jesuit priests off Kyushu for the second year in a row, may have been perceived by the shogun as indicative of a grand European design—headed by the Pope and the King of Spain and supported by Portugal and Holland—to dethrone him in revenge for the persecutions of Christians in Japan and the execution of the delegation from Macao in 1641.

The discussion within the bakufu pivoted on the following questions: Was Holland preparing to ally itself with Portugal? In that case, the shogun had reason to fear their combined sea power. Was Holland willing to become Japan's vassal? Then the prisoners needed to be treated with care. The less factual support there was for the idea of an evil alliance between Holland and Portugal, however, the more awkward it became for the Japanese side to admit that they had arrested their own "friends." It was, therefore, necessary to establish the existence of some other illegal act that could serve as the reason for the arrest. Hence the insistence, during the interrogations, that the shooting of guns off the Japanese coast had been contrary to the shogun's laws.

Although there are no Japanese sources left that report this discussion, we find all the arguments of the anti-Dutch side reflected in

the questions asked of the prisoners from Nambu during their interrogations. However, the eventual release of the prisoners and the
continuing relationship with the Dutch East India Company are
clear evidence that the pro-Dutch side within the bakufu finally carried the day.

In theory, the shogun's power was supreme in Japan, but the
resolution of the *Breskens* affair shows that even Iemitsu's megalomania had its limits. In spite of all the insinuations of a Portuguese-
Dutch partnership, in spite of the resemblances found between Cath-
olicism and Protestantism, and between the Spanish city of Manila in
the Philippines and the Dutch city of Batavia on Java, in the end
common sense prevailed over paranoia. For this containment of the
shogun's suspicions, it is clear we can primarily credit three men: Sakai
Tadakatsu, Matsudaira Nobutsuna, and Inoue Masashige. And with
this realization we have also defined who among Iemitsu's top advisers
were principally responsible for Japan's foreign policy during the reign
of the third shogun.

Chapter 7
Elserack's Promise

Elserack's visit was not yet over. With the release of the prisoners from Nambu out of the way, the next point on the chief factor's agenda was the presentation of the yearly tribute from the Dutch East India Company to the shogun. By a lucky coincidence, this year the company's preparations had been especially lavish. The most important gift was a massive brass lantern, standing ten feet tall and weighing a total of 4,523 pounds, which had been ordered cast for the shogun at Amsterdam and had arrived in Batavia in 1642.[1] The lantern still exists and stands near the Yomeimon gate at Nikkō, opposite the bell offered by the Korean ambassador Yun Sunji, who had come to Japan in the summer of 1643.[2]

For the occasion, the lantern was assembled in the Castle garden outside the *ōhiroma*, on 10 December.[3] The following day was the first day of the eleventh month, according to the Japanese calendar, and therefore the day of the biweekly, compulsory court attendance for all the *tozama daimyō* in the city. The stage was thus being set for another round of Tokugawa bragging in front of their competitors for power in Japan, showing that the shogun's power reached "far across the seas."[4] With the lantern in its full splendor in the background, the rest of the Dutch tribute was displayed on low tables, especially made for the occasion, placed in the corridor before the lower step room (*gedan no ma*) in full view of everyone present.

Again, after waiting in the *toranoma* on the morning of 11 December, Elserack was led by Inoue through the Castle and was told to pay his respects from the corridor. The Dutch factor knelt down before the shogun, who was sitting some sixty to eighty feet away from him in the upper step room *(jōdan no ma)*. This being a formal audience, the sliding doors were open, but, because of the distance, Elserack did not get a good look at the ruler of Japan. He later wrote in his journal: "He was dressed in a black gown, and wore a black cap on his head. I could see he was short and skinny."[5]

There is a much better description of the shogun in Chief Factor Versteegen's account of 1647: "His Majesty was seated in the inner room [*jōdan no ma*] close to the separation with the outer room [*gedan no ma*]. His head was bare and he was sitting on the mats on his knees with the soles of his feet under his behind, without a throne or any elevation at all, dressed in black with a blue net-like shawl [over his kimono]. He did not look very different from the other [lords]. He was fair skinned and handsome in the face, not really fat, but rather rosy looking according to their standards. He was tall rather than short, his face elongated rather than round. He looked a few years younger than he was."[6]

The presence of the Dutch chief factor was announced by Inoue in a loud voice: "Oranda Kapitan!" To this single exclamation Elserack added later in his journal ". . . pays his respects and expresses his gratitude to His Majesty." He obviously was not pleased to have been introduced with a grand total of two words. Then Elserack was ordered to open his coat so that the shogun might view his clothing. After sitting still for a moment in this posture, he felt Inoue take hold of his coat lapel, and both men retired toward the *toranoma,* bowing all the way.

Again the chief factor was congratulated by the *ōmetsuke* and the Nagasaki *bugyō* on his "worship of His Majesty's countenance," the release of the Dutchmen from Nambu, and countless other honors and proofs of respect, "more than had ever been shown to any foreigner (yes, even the ambassadors from Korea)."[7] A personal audience of the Dutch factor with the shogun had not happened since 1636. In the years immediately preceding the *Breskens* affair, the chore of receiving the Dutch delegation had usually been taken care of by the councilors Matsudaira Nobutsuna, Abe Tadaaki, and Abe Shigetsugu. Considering the high value the Japanese themselves set on a personal interview with the shogun ("worship his countenance"), the bakufu was giving a clear signal of favor to the Dutch.

The Japanese Castle records are, again, silent for this day. And, again, the *Tokugawa jikki* follows suit. The *metsuke* in charge of these records may have been of the opinion that official receptions for the Dutch were all very well, but to have three of these in the *ōhiroma* within a period of five days (and, as we shall see, another one six days later) would be too much honor to record separately, even if the shogun himself had been present on two of the four occasions. I suspect that this is the reason why these four meetings were reduced to two in the official record.

On 6 December, the "inspection" of the Dutch tribute was recorded (but of the much-appreciated lantern there is not a word), and on the tenth the official release of the prisoners was announced. One cannot escape the impression that the shogun's honor overrode all considerations for truthfulness. The latter concept may, indeed, have been of but limited concern to the record keepers.[8] However, this still does not explain why the date of 10 December appears in the record, when there had been, in fact, no meeting at all with the Dutch in the *ōhiroma* on that day. Possibly on 10 December the shogun had actually engaged in activities that were better covered up by the announcement of the magnanimous release of the Dutch prisoners. We shall never know.[9]

The next day and the day after, Elserack was busy delivering gifts to the councilors and other power brokers in the Tokugawa bureaucracy. He was carried around in his palanquin through the daimyo quarter inside the Castle's outer moat. His report is dull. Some councilors refused the presents, others accepted them at first but sent them back the next day. To Elserack, after he had been the recipient of so many important honors, it looked very much like they were turning a cold shoulder on the Dutch. It may have been Japanese policy to keep the Dutch guessing about their standing in the country. So "honors" and slaps in the face were alternated as the occasion required. The *Breskens* affair was far from being over.

On 17 December 1643, Elserack visited the Castle for the fourth time in eleven days. He went to receive from the shogun some new orders, some counter-gifts, and his leave to return to Nagasaki. Together with the interpreters Kohyōe and Shōsuke, Elserack waited for an hour in the *toranoma* before he was called to his usual place on the verandah in front of the *ōhiroma*. Waiting for him were Hotta Masamori, Abe Tadaaki, Abe Shigetsugu, and Doi Toshikatsu, who ordered Inoue to address the Dutch factor.

Elserack was first informed of the new regulations. First, the Dutch were promised that they would be treated well wherever they came ashore in Japan. However, they were obliged, from now on, to immediately tell local authorities their nationality, as well as the number and names of their crew. If they were in need of rice or water they would be allowed to buy what they needed. In case they had had an accident or had suffered damage during a storm they would be helped with materials and labor to repair their ships.

Second, the next time that any Dutchmen were caught, as they had been, sailing along the coasts of Japan and shooting their cannon without identifying themselves, they would be executed without pardon. Moreover, the chief factor residing in Nagasaki would be held responsible.

Third, if the Dutch in Batavia, Taiwan, Holland, or anywhere else were to hear of plans to send "papists" to Japan or of Spanish or Portuguese plans to attack the country, they should inform the Japanese authorities, "which would serve the shogun and be of advantage to the Dutch." Inoue stated that these new rules amounted to a "new pass of his Majesty's,"[10] and that he would hand them over to Elserack so that they could be translated into proper Dutch. After this the chief factor was given his leave to retire to the *toranoma*.

Shortly afterwards, the *ōmetsuke* and the Nagasaki *bugyō* came to escort him to another room where the shogun's counter presents were on display. Elserack was given "two hundred bars of silver and twenty silk gowns" and was told that the shogun had appreciated the gift of the brass lantern for his grandfather's grave as well as the other gifts that had been presented this year. Next, Elserack received another twenty silk gowns in return for the presents that had been presented to Iemitsu's successor, Ietsuna, and he was given permission to return to Nagasaki.[11]

The departure date of the Dutch train was set for Christmas Eve. This probably was not a coincidence, for it gave the Dutch an opportunity to prove they did not mind traveling on Christ's birthday. The day before they left, when Elserack had stopped by Inoue's at Hitotsubashi to say good-bye, he was told that, in addition to the three previously issued regulations, there was now a fourth. It was an elaboration of the article stipulating that the Dutch would be helped with repairs to their ships. However, said the fourth rule, the ship would not be allowed to leave in such a case until the Dutch factor had come from Nagasaki to Edo and had convinced the authorities that the ship was indeed Dutch. The shogun would bear all costs of such delays.[12] But by another calculated "coincidence," this promise (that the shogun would bear the costs of the stay of shipwrecked sailors) was added only *after* the Dutch factor had already paid the bills at the Nagasakiya.[13]

The experience with the *Breskens,* then, resulted in Japan's specifying future treatment of shipwrecked Dutch sailors. It is not surprising that this regulation was hailed as a great success by the Dutch, for in their eyes it proved that the Japanese were serious about having a long-term relationship with them—something many had come to doubt after the expulsions of the other Europeans from Japan. The *Breskens* affair had forced the shogun to rethink his relationship with the Dutch and this was the result. But it was a two-edged sword that had been employed here. As we shall see below, from now on the Japanese held on to this new interpretation—that the men from the *Breskens* had been "shipwrecked" and subsequently "saved" by the Japanese. All during the 1640s this twisting of the truth was to cause the Dutch in Nagasaki and Batavia many headaches.

On the Dutch side, Elserack summarized the *Breskens* affair in a letter addressed to Governor General Van Diemen, dated 15 October 1644.[14] This letter is important in revealing Batavia's perception of what had happened. Elserack drew the following conclusions from the affair. In the first place, he was convinced that Van Diemen's letter to the *rōjū,* dated 28 June 1642, had been known to the shogun and his councilors. In this letter Van Diemen had surveyed the recent state of the Dutch East India Company in Japan, after the forced move from Hirado to Deshima.

Van Diemen's argument culminated in the following passage: "Whether we leave Japan or continue to come, we remain prepared to send next year a person of quality and some rarities to Nagasaki in order to reverently take our leave from His Majesty and Their Highnesses, or, in case we are ordered to keep on coming to trade in Japan, with the restoration of our previous freedoms, in order to show our gratitude in the proper manner. However, as we are unsure whether such an embassy would please the authorities, and whether our representatives will be received with the appropriate respect, we request your Highnesses to react to this proposal, for we are firmly decided to follow your advice and wise council in this matter to the letter."[15]

Because the Nagasaki *bugyō* had refused to send this letter on to the *rōjū*, it had, officially, been held up in Nagasaki. Nachod has speculated, following Von Siebold (who in turn may have been mouthing the interpreters' line), that this was done because the *bugyō* were afraid of being found to have been too strict with the Dutch in Nagasaki.[16] After the evidence presented here it should be clear to any student of the bakufu that the Nagasaki *bugyō* worked closely together with Inoue Chikugo no kami, who was directly responsible to Sakai Tadakatsu and Iemitsu himself.

All measures taken to curb the freedom of the Dutch, then, must be considered as having been directly inspired by the shogun. This fact in itself doomed all protests of the Dutch from the very beginning. By refusing to send through official channels their insolent letter to the *rōjū* (with its ultimatum of "restore our previous freedoms or we will stop coming to Japan!"), the *bugyō* were, rather than obstructing communication, in fact protecting the Dutch from their own ignorance.

However, even if this letter was not officially delivered to its addressees (and thus, conveniently for the Japanese side, required no answer), Elserack was certain, as he wrote in his letter to Van Diemen of October 1644, that its contents were "still studied every day." The shogun and his councilors, Elserack continued, had previously been convinced that the Dutch could not survive in East Asia without the Japanese trade, but because of Van Diemen's sharp letter they now perceived the situation to be quite different.

Secondly Elserack concluded that the captivity of the men from the *Breskens* had given the Japanese authorities their first sustained and close look at the Dutch nation ("which would not have been possible otherwise, or [if possible] would have taken years of arduous effort"). The shogun himself had been eager to hear in person the interrogations of the Dutchmen, who had been able to satisfy his "suspicious nature." The men themselves had behaved in an exemplary manner. For this reason, they had been treated well, and the Japanese authorities had praised their patience and good behavior to Elserack, requesting him to write this to the governor general so that they might not get into further trouble after their release by the Japanese.

Elserack's third and final conclusion was self-congratulatory. The Dutch had recently obeyed all Japanese orders concerning trade and had obtained much goodwill from traders and authorities alike, for which "they" had been rewarded with a personal audience with the shogun: "It is no small matter to appear in front of the person of His

Majesty. No one is allowed to do so unless he is highly valued by His Majesty. A king, councilor, vassal or other great dignitary who is in trouble or disgrace is never allowed to gaze on his countenance before the difficulty is solved and the man has been restored to favor."[17]

As we have seen, Van Diemen's letter of 1642 had "not been delivered." Therefore, if there was an improvement in the trade of that year (which according to Nachod and others there was),[18] this ostensibly had nothing to do with Van Diemen's letter of protest, even though this improvement undercut its main complaint, namely, that the return on the investments did not warrant the great effort that coming to Japan entailed. But indirectly, by improved profits, the bakufu had given the Dutch a sign, and the sign said: Please keep coming. The bakufu's handling of the *Breskens* affair was dominated by this desire.

Obviously, the Dutch and the Japanese perceptions of the *Breskens* matter differed greatly. The Japanese, it appears from several entries in the *Daghregister,* were rather pleased with their handling of events and did not cease to congratulate themselves on the "magnanimity" of their shogun who had consented to release the Dutch prisoners even though "they were guilty of an offense punishable by death according to Japanese law."[19]

Exactly what this offense was, and which law applied to it, was never made clear. Sometimes it was said that the Dutch had misbehaved, and had shot their guns. At other times, it was given out that the Dutch had entered forbidden territory. None of these reasons was accepted by the Dutch management in Batavia, for neither the *Castricom* nor the *Breskens* had threatened anyone with their guns, and, according to Ieyasu's pass of 1609, there was no place in Japan specifically forbidden to them.[20]

To the Dutch the events mainly showed that one had to be extremely careful with the Japanese, because "law" as it was understood in Europe was nonexistent or not applicable to foreigners in Japan. The men from the *Breskens* had obtained consent from the local authorities in Yamada to go ashore, yet as soon as they had left the relative safety of the protective shield provided by the guns of their ship, they had been treacherously arrested.

The Dutch position in later years was perhaps best expressed by an aside in the *Daghregister* kept by Reinier Van't Zum, chief factor in

Japan in 1645–46. On 8 March 1646, during his visit to the shogun's capital, Van't Zum had been called by Chikugo no kami for a last interview before he left for Nagasaki. He was told, among other things, that such an important matter as the release of the Dutch prisoners was not being valued enough by the Dutch. Van't Zum politely answered the *ōmetsuke* that the Dutch always tried to obey the shogun's orders in all matters and that they had never transgressed against them.

Contrary to what Chikugo no kami was being told, Van't Zum said, the Dutch did indeed value the release of their fellow countrymen highly and would never forget His Majesty's benevolence. Between parentheses in his account then follows this revealing remark: "(I thought it best to answer in this manner even though it went against the feelings in my heart, for I would rather have protested against the violence and the wrongdoing of the Japanese, which would have been clear if the matter could have been brought before impartial judges)."[21]

In other words, the Dutch professions of gratitude for the release of the prisoners from Nambu masked their indignation about the treatment of the men at the hands of the officials of the Nambu domain, who had used trickery and force in order to detain as many sailors as possible from a ship of a friendly nation.

However, in the wake of the release of the ten prisoners into the hands of Chief Factor Elserack, the main feeling among the Dutch was one of relief and willingness to forget the whole distasteful affair as soon as possible in order to get on with business. The Dutch were therefore happy to remain polite to the Japanese authorities to the point of obsequiousness. But alas, forgetting the matter was exactly what the bakufu was not willing to do.

Nothing much seemed amiss when Overtwater, the chief factor who succeeded Elserack, visited Edo during the winter after the release of the men from the *Breskens*. His conversations with the *ōmetsuke* did, of course, touch on what had happened with the *Breskens,* for Inoue asked whether Schaep and his men had safely arrived in Batavia. Overtwater confirmed that they had. Inoue then asked if the Dutch were planning to send more ships to Tartary, and Overtwater answered that he doubted there were such plans at that moment.

The tone of the conversation was so relaxed that Overtwater, foolishly, thought he might be able to win favorable notice in Batavia if he managed to obtain permission to establish a new factory in northern Japan. The interpreter, knowing the outrageous impression such a proposal would make, at first refused to translate it. Only when Chikugo no kami, noticing some difference of opinion between the chief factor and the interpreter, ordered the latter to interpret, did he get the full story. Inoue must have laughed in his beard at the preposterous notion, for Iemitsu would never have consented to the establishment of another Dutch factory, let alone one on the territory of a minor *tozama daimyō*. The whole idea proves how little Overtwater understood of the Zeitgeist reigning in Japan at the time.[22] Outwardly, the *ōmetsuke* remained noncommittal and simply changed the subject.[23]

One year later Van't Zum arrived in Edo. His superiors in Batavia, that is, the Councilors of the Indies (for Van Diemen had just died and the appointment of the next governor general had not yet arrived in Batavia), charged Van't Zum to officially thank the Japanese for the release of the men from the *Breskens*. In his journal entry of 9 February 1646, Van't Zum noted his surprise when the interpreter refused to go and inform Chikugo no kami that Van't Zum had come "to present gifts to the shogun and his councilors and to thank them for the release of the Dutchmen from Nambu."[24]

The reason the interpreter gave for his refusal was that this was against protocol, because the chief factor should wait until he was called by Inoue before he made his presence and intentions known. This, however, was merely an excuse on the part of the interpreter who did not want to be the bearer of unwelcome news, but Van't Zum was unaware of this. Three days later, on 12 February, Van't Zum was interviewed by the *ōmetsuke*:

QUESTION: Had the matter of the release of the Dutch caught in Nambu two years ago been completely and accurately reported to the governor general?

ANSWER: It had been, completely and accurately.

QUESTION: Was this release being highly appreciated, for those men had with shooting and other inappropriate behavior sinned against the Japanese laws and had therefore deserved to die?

ANSWER: This was being highly praised and appreciated by the governor general and by the whole Dutch nation. Yes, it was as if those ten Dutchmen had already been dead but had been called back to life, and we will always remember this and remain grateful for such bounty, for we clearly perceive the shogun's great affection towards the Dutch nation.

QUESTION: Had Elserack himself discussed the affair with the governor general, and left for Holland to make the details known
over there as well, and would he be coming back to Japan?

ANSWER: Elserack had met with the governor general himself and
discussed the affair, that we knew for sure, but the reason for
his departure to Holland and whether he would come back I
did not know for I had been in Siam at the time.[25]

Before Van't Zum had his audience in the Castle on the next day,
13 February 1646, he was interrogated by Kuze Yamato no kami
Hiroyuki, someone not usually involved in the affairs of the Dutch,[26]
but a personal secretary of Iemitsu since 1640.[27] Therefore the information was sure to reach the shogun directly. The importance of this
entry in the *Daghregister* cannot be overstated. In particular, Van't
Zum was asked one question of great significance: "Had the Hon.
Elserack left for Holland in order to explain the situation of the
prisoners from Nambu there? And will he come back, for he has
promised he would return to thank the shogun and his councilors in
connection with that affair."[28]

Van't Zum had to admit that he was not informed about this.
And neither are we, for this, more than two years after the release of
the prisoners, is the first mention of such a promise by Elserack in all
the company's voluminous paperwork connected with the *Breskens*
affair. Among Elserack's own papers, one will look in vain for such a
promise. Neither is there any clue in this direction in Overtwater's
journal or the letters sent from Nagasaki during the years 1644 and
1645.

It is possible that Elserack had promised to inform the governor
general in person, and he may even have mentioned he would ask
him for a special envoy, as Van Diemen had been planning to do anyway, according to the letter I quoted above. But that he had promised
to return himself as an ambassador from Holland is totally out of
the question. For that Elserack knew his own place inside the company too well: he would never have been chosen for such a mission.
Furthermore, it is clear from his long experience with company in-
fighting that Elserack would not have stuck his neck out that far.
Although overly obsequious in his dealings with the Japanese, he was
a careful man.

But if it is highly unlikely that Elserack made such a promise and
then kept complete silence about it, who gave this impression? Was it
an interpreter who misunderstood the true significance of what he

was saying? That, too is very improbable, for if a promise like this had been given, Inoue would have made sure it was repeated over and over again, to avoid "unpleasant misunderstandings," and we would find some reflection of it in the discussions reported. Such repetition had been Inoue's method, as we have amply seen, in dealing with the prisoners from Nambu, and such was his method with every chief factor he interviewed thereafter.

It is also certain that no one in Batavia, let alone in Holland, had even begun to think that the release of the men from the *Breskens* warranted a special embassy. To the Dutch with their license of free trade throughout Japan, the Japanese had absolutely no judicial ground to stand on with their capture of the men from the *Breskens*. But because they were aware of the fact that in Japan "law" was nothing but a label for the shogun's caprice, they did not insist on their own conception of international law and diplomatic usage. Their words of gratitude, however, did not imply they felt they owed the shogun anything in this affair, and certainly they did not owe him an embassy, polite phrases notwithstanding.

But if Elserack did not promise an ambassador, where did this idea suddenly sprout from? Here I must again stress that the first time this promise appears in the *Daghregister* it does not come from the lips of the *ōmetsuke,* as one would expect, for he was the bakufu's official mouthpiece to the Dutch in Edo. Rather, it comes from one of Iemitsu's own close attendants. The setting inside the Castle, just before the solemn occasion of an audience with the shogun himself, is also not without its own profound significance. This was not a time when the chief factor would be likely to contradict a highly placed shogunal official, and so jeopardize the successful conclusion of his visit to the shogun's capital.

In other words, this was the perfect setting for an "adjustment of the truth." It seems to me, therefore, that Van Diemen's original proposal of 1642 had finally germinated in the mind of our so-called "lover of the Dutch," the most benevolent and magnanimous shogun himself. Elserack's "promise" was in all likelihood nothing other than Iemitsu's own invention, his personal contribution to the conduct of Japanese-Dutch relations. Thus, our next task is to discover just how Iemitsu's faithful servant, Inoue Masashige, managed to strong-arm the Dutch into sending an "embassy from Holland."

To return to Van't Zum's visit to the court: a few minutes before his audience with Iemitsu, he was again asked, this time by Baba

Saburōzaemon, whether he was presenting his gifts and paying his respects to the shogun because of the release of the Dutch prisoners from Nambu or in the usual manner. Van't Zum answered that he was presenting the gifts and paying his respects in the usual manner, "and that he come to transmit the Dutch gratitude over the release of the prisoners at the same time."[29] Baba countered tartly that Van't Zum should only present the gifts and pay his respects "in the usual manner."

By this time, it should have been clear to both parties that they had different views on the same topic. To the Japanese, following the shogun's lead, the release of the men from the *Breskens* warranted an ambassador from Holland, whereas the Dutch were convinced that saying "thank you" by the chief factor should suffice.

The next year, in 1647, Willem Versteegen, son-in-law of Melchior van Santvoort, made the trip to Edo. (Van Santvoort was one of the longest survivors of the *Liefde*, the first Dutch ship to have reached Japan in 1600, and Versteegen was married to Van Santvoort's daughter by his Japanese wife.)[30] Because of his long experience in Japan, Versteegen's journal is unusually detailed and varied. However, when it came to dealing with the shogunal officials, Versteegen proved no match for their charm. After he had been received in audience by Iemitsu, Versteegen was questioned at the residence of Makino Takumi no kami Nobushige by his son Makino Chikashige, whom we have already met in the same capacity as interrogator of the Dutch factor and as a close confidant of the shogun.[31]

Again, the questions touched on the prisoners from Nambu, whether the release was being valued by the Dutch, and whether Japan could expect an ambassador "as promised by Elserack that he would be sent back as such."[32] Thus, the second time the matter of Elserack's promise crops up in the *Daghregister*, it is again not from the lips of the *ōmetsuke*. It seems as if everyone in the Castle knew of this promise except the Dutch and their "protector."

Versteegen answered politely that the release was highly valued by the Dutch, but that he did not know if Elserack was on his way back to Japan. He noted, in an aside, that he tried to answer these questions as simply as possible, because details would only involve more questions: "for they have their spies everywhere and know how to investigate a matter from unexpected directions so that one is unprepared for them, for which one has to guard oneself here."[33]

The day before his departure, 22 January 1647, Versteegen noted that Inoue had made clear to one of the interpreters that he should tell the Dutch factor that the Japanese authorities were "surprised" that the Dutch were not "honoring Elserack's promise."[34] Even to Versteegen, then, the ōmetsuke did not dare to use this lie face to face, but only through one of the interpreters. Furthermore, Inoue instructed the interpreter, Versteegen should be aware how highly the Dutch were estimated in Japan. None of the other foreigners were treated here like the Dutch were. The Koreans were the shogun's vassals but they were not allowed a personal audience with him, Inoue said. And even outside the court, the Dutch were treated with great pomp.

Versteegen commented in his journal:

> According to the interpreter, they do not want to *order* us to send an embassy, but they make it sufficiently understood that someone of us has to appear to honor the promises made in connection with the release of the prisoners from Nambu, with some special gifts, which will then be divided into two parts: one part as the usual gifts for that year and the other exclusively to show our gratitude for the release. This is the only thing in which we have been remiss, which makes the emperor and his councilors think our words and deeds do not coincide. This should be given due consideration. And he [the ōmetsuke] recommended I should do my best to make this happen. He [the interpreter] answered that last year the Hon. Van't Zum had come to do just that, but Inoue only laughed a little at that and said: "The gentlemen know better!"[35]

From this entry we may draw two conclusions. First, Versteegen was not aware that Elserack's so-called promise was a figment of the shogun's own imagination. Second, it is clear that Inoue was uncomfortable with the lie he had been saddled with. Wily as he was, Inoue did not ordinarily use outright lies in his dealings with people.

In this connection it is interesting to consult a passage from Inoue's *Kirishitoki*. Among the admonitions he left for his successors on how to deal with prisoners, Inoue wrote the following: "In every particular during the inquest the *bugyō* is to take care that the religionists in prison or in the pit know he speaks no falsehood and does not alter what he has once said. Otherwise they will mistrust the *bugyō* and will be reluctant to speak out, in informing on their relations as in their own apostasy. This must be made clear down to the lowest grade of those charged with the scrutiny."[36]

It was obviously Inoue's opinion that outright lies were counter-productive, although "confusion" and "misunderstandings" were helpful in Japanese-Dutch diplomacy. So we can understand his hesitation to repeat "Elserack's promise" in front of the Dutch. But the poor ōmetsuke had no choice but to play out the game initiated by the shogun himself, until the bitter end.

It was only the next year, 1648, during the journey to the shogun's court by Frederick Coijett, that the differences in perception of the true importance of the Breskens affair caused the first open difficulties for the Dutch in Japan. Excuses were found to embarrass the new chief factor. To begin with, the Dutch were led to believe that the fact that they had given help to the Portuguese ambassador, Gonçalo de Siquicira de Souza (who had come to Japan in the previous year), was reason enough for the shogun to refuse to hold the usual audience with the Dutch factor. As allies of Japan, they should not help those whom Japan considered its enemies.[37]

On 24 December, Coijett was asked by Inoue whether it was true that the Portuguese ambassador had received help in Batavia. Coijett had to make a hard choice: was he to admit the truth of the affair and possibly jeopardize the company's standing in Japan and his own audience with the shogun? Or was it possible to deny everything and bluff his way out of this predicament? Inexperienced as he was in Japan and unfamiliar with his adversary Inoue, Coijett opted for the latter course.

He pretended that the ambassador had never been to Batavia, and therefore had never been given help by the Dutch. The Japanese must have been misinformed, he continued, for the only Portuguese who had received assistance from the Dutch in recent years was a certain Antonio Fialho, who had been on his way to Macao.[38] That Fialho had been the captain of the St. Andreas, which was carrying the ambassador from Portugal to Japan, remained unsaid here.[39]

Most of the negotiations between Coijett and Inoue this year were taken up by discussion of this "new evidence" that the Dutch were in league with the Portuguese. It took a lot of effort on the part of Coijett to make Chikugo no kami accept the possibility that the bakufu was misinformed. For his part, Chikugo no kami was also playing a game; he probably had orders from the rōjū, or even from Iemitsu himself, to stall the Dutch because the "promised" ambassador had still not materialized.

Serving as his master's spokesman, Inoue also changed, chameleon-like, from Versteegen's close "friend of the Dutch" of the previous year to a cold and distant administrator. This year he did not want to see the Dutch factor, but interrogated him via an interpreter who walked from one room to the next in the *ōmetsuke*'s residence.[40] Inoue's charm could be turned on and off at will.

On 16 January 1648, after having waited in Edo for over a month to have his audience with the shogun, Coijett was again hastily summoned to Hitotsubashi, where he found both Inoue Masashige and Baba Saburōzaemon. At long last, Inoue told the shogun's truth to the chief factor's face:

> The old emperor Suruga [Ieyasu] had consented to grant the Dutch free trade in his empire. His descendants have continued to do so as well, and the present shogun has, on top of that, in his great magnanimity and because they were Dutchmen, released and clothed against the cold some Dutch prisoners who had come to Nambu against his orders and whom he could have sentenced to die according to the laws of this country.
>
> This having been now three [*sic*] years ago, His Majesty still has not received any gratitude as promised by Elserack. And now, according to the Portuguese ambassador, the Dutch seem to have helped him to come to Japan by lending him a pilot and some sailors. Even if it was now more or less believed that this assistance had not been given to the ambassador but to Antonio Fialho . . ., all of this has caused suspicion against the Dutch on the part of the Emperor. Today, being an important Day of Judgment, he has decided not to accept any presents from you, to send you back to Nagasaki, and to leave this affair at that until next year. I have done what I could on behalf of the Dutch, and even personally told the shogun many good things about them.[41]

The last sentence here provides proof of what has been postulated above, that is, that Inoue had personal access to the shogun when needed. On this occasion, his interference had been resented by Iemitsu. We read later in the *Daghregister* that the shogun had snarled at the *ōmetsuke,* saying: "Chikugo, you are partial to the Dutch!" and that after Coijett's departure Inoue had not dared visit the Castle for seventy-one days, and had not been summoned by Iemitsu either.[42]

On Coijett's return to Nagasaki, the whole story of the help given to the Portuguese was raised again, this time by the Nagasaki *bugyō.* Coijett as well as his successor Dirck Snoucq were forced to keep on explaining it away, each time sinking deeper into the swamp of their own lies. This, of course, helped to pass the time with seemingly important problems until the required ambassador would arrive. This much is clear from a revealing entry in the journal kept by Coijett. He reports a visit of Sawano Chū'an, the apostate, spy *(meakashi)*, and collaborator in Inoue's interrogations of the Jesuits. Chū'an, who lived in Nagasaki, had come to Deshima to see Coijett and the company surgeon in order to get some information on the medicinal properties of a few herbs. But then: "Having switched to another topic, he told us that the dissatisfaction of the emperor with the Dutch was solely caused by the delay in showing our gratitude for the release of the prisoners. If that were to happen this year, the state of the company's affairs would undoubtedly improve. This man should be believed on this point because he daily visits Chikugo dono's house where (we may be sure) the conversation often turns to this topic."[43]

Important here is not what is being said but what is implied: that the present troubles resulting from the alleged help given to the Portuguese were nothing more than an excuse to make the Dutch feel uncertain about their situation in Japan. We can see that Chū'an repaid the Dutch factor for his kindness in letting him talk to the company's doctor by providing Coijett with some information the apostate believed to be true. And we may also agree with Coijett's assessment of the apostate (which was self-serving, of course, because the information proved that Coijett was not to be blamed for the failure of his mission in Edo).

~

Unknown to Coijett, two days after Chū'an's visit the new governor general, Cornelis van der Lijn, and his council penned the following letter to the Deshima factory:

> To our great surprise we have learned of the desire and the serious recommendation of the Commissioner Chikugodonne to send a special ambassador [to thank] for the release of the prisoners from Nambu, according to the promises made by the Senior Merchant Jan van Elserack, who, without a doubt, must have been going overboard, as was his habit. However, he has not reported nor informed us in the least of this, and therefore we are unsure, for now, what we have to do about this. Moreover, our present situation does not permit us to perform such a task properly and fittingly, for we have no rarities at hand to prepare an appropriate gift. It really is a shame that the company is being forced into unnecessary trouble, damage, and costs by the imprudence of its employees.[44]

Again, we may conclude that nobody in Batavia had heard of Elserack's promise either. The poor man was being falsely accused behind his back from all sides. No wonder that, after his return to Holland, he was never employed by the Dutch East India Company again. Van der Lijn's letter continued with the following promise:

> Because we cannot improve the past, we will have to make the best of this affair, and the [Japanese] request should be answered in such a manner that they do not take offense. If they do not insist, you had better refrain from mentioning it in the least. However, if they continue to press for it, you should answer politely that you have informed us and that you have also received an answer now, i.e., that we are very surprised, not from unwillingness and lack of inclination to show our gratitude, but because we have never been informed by anybody in the least, and that, therefore, we thought their request very strange. In spite of that, we are planning to write to Holland with the next fleet to propose the matter to our Lords, and we do not doubt that the wishes of the Japanese authorities and the required gratitude will be granted by a special envoy from Holland.[45]

Unknown to the governor general, the matter was already becoming urgent in Japan, and it would not do to play for time too long. Chief Factor Snoucq, who arrived in the summer of 1648, was denied permission even to travel to Edo. The thumbscrews, then, were being tightened on the Dutch.

Not long afterwards, when Coijett returned to Batavia in the spring of 1649, the Dutch seem to have given in and to have begun making preparations for an embassy. If the Dutch were to send an ambassador all the way from Holland, this would be a victory for bakufu foreign policy, proving beyond doubt that "the shogun's grace extended beyond the seas."[46] And not just anywhere beyond the seas, one might add, but as far away as Europe.

Of course, such an embassy would have involved an upgrading of the Japanese relationship with the Dutch from trading partners to diplomatic partners, and it was exactly this upgrading of the relationship that must have come under discussion in the meetings of the rōjū with Iemitsu during the *Breskens* affair.[47] The only problem was to make the Dutch accept the Japanese version of what had happened. Iemitsu, as shogun, could not imagine that that would be difficult. For the shogun not only had the power to make and unmake the laws according to his whim, he also clearly had a monopoly over the truth in Japan.

The shogun's truth had two versions, one for domestic use, and one for negotiations with the Dutch. After "gracefully" releasing the prisoners acquired by foul play, it was decided that these men had not really been prisoners, but rescued castaways. It is a fact that, as we have seen, the men had never been incarcerated in a true jail. The Japanese sources close to the bakufu consistently refer to the men after their release as castaways.[48] The expression used for the ship's movement is "*hyōchaku shita,*" that is, she "drifted ashore," clearly implying an emergency situation.[49] Interestingly enough, the local documents I found in Yamada do not adhere to this version of the truth, as we have seen. In those texts, the ship is simply said to have "*nyūshin shita,*" or "entered the bay."[50] One source is more precise and describes the powerful impression the ship made as she sailed before the wind into the bay.[51] Even on the official map of the Nambu domain, dating from around 1644, referring to the *Breskens'* arrival in Yamada we find the neutral expression "*chakugan suru,*" or "reach the shore."[52] These sources, unlike those related to the bakufu, do not pretend that the Dutch were helpless castaways. It is the bakufu sources that, by describing the men as "castaways," gloss over the fact that they were tricked ashore.

It is true, of course, that the prisoners themselves had stressed the fact that they had come ashore to acquire water and fresh vegetables, and to explain their presence so far north they had said, during their first interrogations, that they had been blown off course by violent storms. The true purpose of the voyage had been explained to the bakufu by Elserack, who had said that the ship's real destination had been Tartary. In its own records, however, the bakufu adhered to the first version, that is, that the shogun had shown compassion to foreign castaways because they were Dutch.

In their negotiations with the Dutch, on the other hand, the Japanese side held up the fiction of criminality on the part of the prisoners. That was the reason why they had been so roughly treated in Japan. In this second version the shogun also showed his magnanimity by releasing them, but because of their presumed criminal behavior, which "merited" the death penalty, the Dutch owed the shogun far more than if the men had been simply helpless castaways, as in the version meant for domestic consumption.

From these two versions of the "truth," one for domestic and one for

for foreign consumption, found in the Japanese and Dutch sources relating to the *Breskens* affair, we can see that there was profound unease in the highest circles of the bakufu. Because too many things required explanation, the bakufu ended up supplying two different explanations.

It may have been Iemitsu's prerogative to determine the contents of Japan's laws as well as those of the truth, but to convince the Dutch was quite another matter altogether. The most important step in the process was to pretend that Elserack had promised to come back as an ambassador. As we have seen before, there is absolutely nothing in Elserack's account that hints of any such promise.

The best proof, however, that the whole story of this promise of an ambassador was made up by the Japanese side, and in my opinion by Iemitsu himself, is that when the Dutch in Batavia finally saw the necessity of playing the game that Iemitsu had started (and that Inoue was continuing to play for his master by making the Dutch more and more uncomfortable) and they sent a *bogus* ambassador, under the pretense he had been sent directly from Holland, the ambassador was accepted by the bakufu in the full knowledge that the man was a fake! If the promise of an ambassador had been genuine, then surely the bakufu would have refused to have anything to do with an embassy that thumbed its nose at Japan.

Chapter 8

A Memorable Embassy

After Coijett's return to Batavia in the spring of 1649, preparations for an embassy began there in earnest. A response from the Gentlemen XVII in Amsterdam turned out to be unnecessary, for an "ambassador from Holland" could be sent without Holland's cooperation. The governor general at Batavia was, after all, the representative of the Dutch East India Company, and the company itself had been empowered in its charter, issued by the Estates General of the Dutch Republic, to represent Holland in Asia.[1] In fact, permission to send such an "ambassador" was given in a letter addressed to the governor general and his councilors dated 26 April 1650, but it would not have been received in Batavia before the fall of that year, at which time the "ambassador" had already left Japan and was on his way back to Batavia. This letter is interesting for it confirms, in its sarcastic phrasing, that sending a real ambassador from Holland was out of the question:

> Having seen from your most recent general as well as private communications concerning the company's trade with Japan,[2] that this arrogant nation wants to be recognized and thanked for the so-called great favor done for our nation by releasing the prisoners, who had gone ashore in Nambu from the yacht *Breskens,* a matter [i.e., the embassy] you have never raised to this body [the Gentlemen XVII] before your last general letter . . ., we understand from the said private letters that this affair is being taken extremely seriously by the highest officials around the Emperor, and we do not doubt therefore that you will have sent someone there from Batavia

with an [appropriate] title and rank. We are awaiting the news of
the success of this mission with the arrival of the next home-bound
fleet.[3]

From the assumption expressed in this letter—that Batavia had already sent the ambassador—we may conclude that Governor General
Van der Lijn and his council had not even requested a real ambassador
from Holland, knowing full well the outraged reaction such a request
would have met there.[4]

Because of the Japanese insistence that the ambassador should
come from Holland itself, it was decided to send the new principal of
the Latin school in Batavia, who had been hired at sixty guilders a
month and had just arrived from Amsterdam.[5] The man, Blokhof
by name (which he had latinized to Blockhovius), was ill to the point
of dying, but he was given no choice and had to board the yacht
Robijn bound for Japan. In the *Instructions* for the embassy, drawn
up by Inoue's counterpart at Batavia, Van der Lijn's right-hand man
François Caron, the so-called ambassador's death was foreseen, even
hoped for.[6]

With great callousness, Caron spelt out how Blockhovius' body
would have to be embalmed at sea so that the Japanese might be
convinced of the exalted status of this man, sacrificed to satisfy the
bakufu's craving for international recognition and its continual need
to legitimize the Tokugawa regime. Thinking of everything, they
had even supplied wood for a coffin. This latter point brings to mind
Ta-tuan Ch'en's story of how the Chinese investiture envoys to the
Ryukyu Islands would also take along their own coffins, bearing
the inscription "Coffin of the envoy from the Celestial Empire."[7] It is
possible that those who put this embassy together at Batavia, that
is, Van der Lijn and Caron, had sought the advice of Chinese traders
familiar with the complicated charades performed between the Ryukyu
Islands and China.

Blockhovius was, in fact, worth more dead than alive because
once dead he would be unable to tell the Japanese anything about the
true nature of his mission—or that he had known nothing about his
ambassadorial status when he left Holland, a situation reflected in
his low pay (not more than that of a simple merchant). A poignant
passage in the journal kept by his secretary, Andries Frisius, during
the trip from Batavia to Japan reads as follows: "There is no more
hope for the person of the Hon. Blockhovius. He resists being treated

with ointments. Towards the evening, the Master [i.e., the physician] asked if he could apply the oils as usual. And because he did not get an answer, he kept insisting until his Hon. aggressively told him: 'Why apply the oils, it won't help anyway. Apply them when I'm dead.' And then he started to laugh with all his heart, even though he was [already] so weakened that he could not lift a limb anymore (to eat something or to relieve himself)."[8]

One wonders how much Blockhovius knew. He certainly must have been aware of the provisions in the *Instructions* regarding his own embalmment, as he encouraged the doctor to apply the ointments after his death. Did he realize that Caron had wanted him to arrive dead in Japan? Was that what made him laugh so hard? We will never know.

Two days later, Frisius wrote:

> I have had the Master Surgeon open the corpse (in accordance with the *Instructions* of the governor general and the councilors of the Indies), and take out the entrails as well as the brain (among which, on close inspection by the Master, the liver and lungs were found to be completely rotten). These we put into a small box, especially made for the purpose, with some weights, and buried it at sea (while his Honor's bodyguard shot three musket salvos). The [rest of the] body was washed in a vinegar-based extract of herbs, and well salted afterwards. The cavity was filled with drugs and spices and sown back together. The outside was wiped with oils and put into a coffin with spices . . . which was then filled up with [dried] moss in order to preserve the rump as much as possible from rotting away and [to be able to] bring it to Japan to be shown—if necessary.[9]

So the honorable ambassador was not even deemed worthy of a salute with the ship's guns, but he had to make do with three salvos of a few muskets. His secretary Frisius, appointed in the *Instructions* to be the ambassador's successor in case of his death, recorded what he told the Japanese officials who had boarded the ship for its initial inspection on 19 September 1649, the day the *Robijn* sailed into the bay of Nagasaki: "I announced that the ambassador had been sent from Holland by the Gentlemen XVII to the Emperor of Japan to pay respect and show their gratitude for the pardon granted by His Majesty in the year 1644 [*sic*] to the chiefs and sailors of the yacht *Breskens,* but that the ambassador had died while on his way to Japan from Batavia. Thereupon I showed them the coffin in which the embalmed body lay. The coffin stood in the cabin's bunk and was decorated with [the ambassador's] chain of office and covered by a piece of black flannel cloth."[10]

When questions were asked about the ambassador's profession, standing, and age, Frisius first consulted with Dirck Snoucq, the acting chief factor, and Anthonie van Brouckhorst, his replacement, who were also present in the cabin of the *Robijn*. He then answered as follows: "The ambassador had been a Doctor of Law, and had been dispatched directly from Holland by the Supreme Authorities and because of his advanced studies had been charged with this important commission. He had not been longer than fifteen or sixteen days at Batavia, having been around fifty years old."[11]

Chief Factor Snoucq's own journal is a little more candid: "We were sharply questioned about the rank and standing of the deceased. We answered these questions in order to avoid further obstacles (knowing their loathing of merchants performing such functions as that of an ambassador) that the deceased had been a Doctor of Law who had been dispatched directly from Holland and [given] this honorable charge, because of his great learning."[12]

But the most clear is a resolution drawn up after the fact:

> Considering further how we should entitle and qualify the deceased upon inquiry [by the Japanese] (which we expect to be most rigorous), we have not been able to approve the title His Honor [the governor general] had proposed in his Instructions (for the Japanese authorities hold merchants in low esteem, and previous rumors and discussions on this topic [had promised someone of higher status]). So [we decided] to call him a scholar in the Faculty of Law and [to affirm] that he had been chosen [to head] this important embassy for his eminent qualities, the more so because, the man being dead, this assertion could not be disproved by some learned Jesuit still living here. And, if pressed, we could explain, if necessary, that scholars of law and noblemen were ranked equally in our country.[13]

Obviously, the simple schoolmaster had been conferred a posthumous Doctorate of Law by unanimous decision of the Deshima Merchant Council, meeting in emergency session on the *Robijn* before the Japanese officials arrived. The sound of their whispered consultations in the low-ceilinged cabin over the coffin of His Excellency (who had already started to smell) must have been deafening on this occasion. So far, in previous publications about this embassy, nobody seems to have realized that this so-called Doctor of Law was a post-humous alumnus of Deshima University![14]

Again, we can see the possibility that the Dutch had drawn on the diplomatic contacts of the Ryukyu Islands with the Chinese court as a model for this embassy. Envoys from the Ryukyu Islands usually were Confucian scholars of high attainment, and so were the investiture envoys to Ryukyu from China.[15] There is, furthermore, supreme irony in the designation of Blockhovius as a scholar of law. Such a scholar, it might be expected, could have lectured the Japanese on international law in detail, and in particular those finer points in which they needed instruction, such as those concerning attacks on ships of friendly nations. Had this academic specialty been a suggestion of the libertine Van Brouckhorst?[16] He was the only one present here who had spoken to the captives after their release in the summer of 1644, when the legality of the seizure of the men from the *Breskens* must still have been the prime topic of discussion among the Dutch on Deshima.

Our bogus ambassador did not even have the proper credentials, that is, letters postmarked and dated in Holland, as well as signed and sealed by the Prince of Orange, or the Estates General, or at least by the Gentlemen XVII in charge of the Dutch East India Company. This is where the Dutch at Batavia showed their naïveté in East Asian diplomacy, for, if there were no genuine letters from Holland available, the occasion clearly called for a forgery.[17] It is a thorny question, and one that is avoided everywhere in the Dutch records. There seems to have been a private letter from Caron to Inoue, but it has not been preserved for it was not accepted by Inoue who probably guessed its contents.[18] The only other document alluding to the problem is a letter from Governor General Van der Lijn (but probably drafted by Caron as well) to the Nagasaki *bugyō*, which arrived on the same ship as Frisius:

> More than five years ago, some Dutchmen were caught at Nambu and were in mortal danger. They were pardoned by His Majesty's unusual and very great magnanimity and were sent home in liberty. The Gentlemen our Lords, having heard about this, are extremely grateful and have decided in council to send a special envoy, which is being done now. They would have been willing to add their own letters of gratitude, but fearing their writing style might offend His

Majesty's dignity and uncertain whether documents in Dutch might not please in Japan, their Honors have ordered me to write such letters as best I know how. For which reason, I reverently request both of you to favor and assist the ambassador at His Majesty's court so that he may obtain the results wished for.[19]

A weak excuse is presented here for not supplying the ambassador with the proper credentials. It must have been obvious to the Nagasaki *bugyō*, and later to the *ōmetsuke* as well, that this "embassy" did not come from Holland at all, but had been organized at Batavia *for appearances' sake only*, and that François Caron was the mastermind behind the whole scheme.[20] He, with twenty-two years of experience in Japan, was the only one in Batavia who knew that all that really counted in Japan was a procession of an unusual number of Dutchmen in colorful uniforms, flying the Dutch colors, trumpeting Dutch sounds to announce the coming of a special envoy from Holland.[21] It was going to be a spectacle designed to impress the whole population of Japan.

An envoy accompanied by a chief factor was all that was required. Caron knew it, and Inoue knew it. And Caron knew that Inoue knew it and that he could get away with it if the outward pomp was impressive enough. Japan could bully its own smaller neighbors, Korea and Ryukyu, into behaving as true vassals. But Holland was too far away, and all in all the Japan trade was considered too unimportant to become a matter of state in The Hague or Amsterdam, just because of the illegal seizure of a few men. Even though the *rōjū* and Inoue must have realized that the Dutch were putting up a show, they chose to accept the charade as a real embassy.

This would probably have been impossible if Doi Toshikatsu had still been alive (he had died in 1644). In Hidetada's time, when Toshikatsu was in charge of such matters, the *rōjū* had insisted that the letters carried in 1627 by another Dutch envoy, Pieter Nuyts, did not sufficiently establish his status as an envoy from Holland. Then, the lack of credentials dated and signed in Holland had been a major stumbling block.[22] The fact that now, in 1649, the matter of the credentials was not even raised, clearly shows the guilty conscience of the bakufu. For in its eagerness to force the Dutch into sending an embassy, it passed over all matters of precedent and proper established form, which at other times had always been of supreme importance in Japan,[23] and indeed represented the ground rules for the country's own basic conception of law. Elserack's "promise" had been a self-fulfilling one, and no one was more aware of that than those in charge of Japanese foreign policy.

Preparations for the embassy, however, had been thorough and were designed to make the Japanese eager to accept it. Once the preliminaries were over, as soon as Frisius had been allowed to disembark and take up his lodgings (in the house normally reserved for the new chief factor but completely redone this year "out of respect for the envoy"), he immediately announced that one of the men in his suite was the long-awaited artillery specialist.[24] This was the Swede Johan Schedler, whose name had been "dutchified" to Juriaen Schedel. Later he became an artillery major in Stockholm.[25] Schedler was the embassy's trump card (although I doubt he was aware of it himself), for the Japanese had been waiting for the arrival of a man like him for the past ten years.

In 1639, Caron had had cast at Hirado the first mortars "made in Japan," and they had been presented to the shogun. These cannon, which are very short in proportion to the diameter of their bore, throw large shells at high angles and are, therefore, ideal for siege and mountain warfare. However, their accuracy depends exclusively on the skill in calculating the curved trajectory of the missile in relation to its weight and the composition and amount of the gun powder used. None of the regular gunners sailing on the Dutch ships to Japan had been able to instruct the Japanese in a satisfactory manner, and all Caron's mortars had done was whet the Japanese appetite for more precise information on this new technology.

On the advice of Overtwater (who did not think the Japanese should be taught how to use these modern weapons), the authorities in Batavia had so far sabotaged all Japanese requests to send someone who could show them how to operate the mortars.[26] Caron knew, of course, how eager the Japanese (but especially their warrior shogun) were to be instructed in this technology, so, in the mere presence of the Swedish major, we can again discern his deft touch in dealing with the bakufu. Towards the evening of the same day, the Nagasaki *bugyō* sent the interpreters to tell the envoy that he had read the letters addressed to him and that he was happy with the arrival of the artillery expert.

The next day, 20 September 1649, the interpreters came back in the company of the chief factors to ask the envoy if "he had no other letters for his Majesty, or if he had anything to say to His Excellency [the Nagasaki *bugyō*] apart from what was written in the letter addressed to him."[27] Frisius had to deny he had any other letters or messages. In the afternoon, the interpreters came back with their summary of the information noted down that morning to make sure they had gotten everything right. They informed the envoy that the *bugyō* would send a letter to Edo to notify the authorities of his arrival.[28]

At that point, the acting chief factor, Dirck Snoucq, cut in with the question if the envoy would not be allowed to travel to Edo, or at least to Osaka, before an answer was received.[29] The interpreters doubted that this would be permitted, but promised to transmit the request. That evening, two interpreters came back to say that the envoy would not be able to start on his trip to Edo before a reply was received from the Court. They estimated that the mail to and from the shogun's capital would take a little less than a month, so the Dutch were to prepare themselves for a lengthy stay. How lengthy the stay was to become, the envoy and the chief factors had no idea as yet. But the Japanese, even though they had been checkmated on the matter of the embassy, fought back in the manner they knew best: official procrastination of the most extreme kind and exasperating pettiness were to be the envoy's punishment for not having the proper credentials.

On 21 September, Snoucq and Van Brouckhorst went on board the *Robijn* to muster the crew and read aloud the usual orders they would have to obey while the ship was anchored in the bay of Nagasaki. While they were busy doing this, three different delegations of Japanese boarded the yacht as well. They were the representatives of the two governors of Nagasaki and the *daimyō* of Ōmura in charge of the city's defense, who had come to make a thorough search of the ship.

When the officials reached the coffin, they lifted the cloth with which it was covered and checked how it was closed.[30] Notwithstanding that the coffin was sturdily made and its lid screwed on tightly, a strong, nauseating smell was coming out of it, which made the officials decide not to push their investigation any further.[31] The Dutch were relieved and served as much liquor as the Japanese officials were willing to drink. Two days later, a new and larger coffin was ordered made, in which the first coffin was enclosed in a bed of 420 *cattij* of camphor at a cost of forty-five *taels*.[32]* However long the *Robijn* might

---

* *Cattij* was a unit of weight; one *cattij* equaled 600 grams. The *tael* as a unit of currency equaled 285 Dutch cents.

have to stay at Nagasaki, the coffin would have to remain where it was and could only be dumped safely into the sea after the ship's departure and out of sight of the Japanese coast.[33]

Meanwhile, the merchandise brought along on the *Robijn* was unloaded also, and Snoucq noted in his journal: "The Japanese showed their contempt that the envoy had come in a ship loaded with merchandise, for this nation despises us [for being traders]. They want to be honored by us, but we do not get the least kind of respect from them."[34]

If, as suggested above, tribute missions to China had been used as models for the embassy sent by the Dutch to Japan on this occasion, there should have been nothing for the Japanese to get worked up over. Clearly, many embassies in the East Asian world order served as opportunities for trade, and often trade may have been the main reason for the constant travel by the diplomats, genuine or fake, as circumstances dictated.[35] This was true especially in the case of the Ryukyu Islands, which sent tribute ships to the Chinese mainland every two years, and another ship "to come and get the envoy" in the off-year that no tribute vessels left Naha.[36] Obviously the Japanese were being a little overly punctilious in this case with the Dutch, one of many signs that they were worried about the lack of credentials of the "ambassador."

The Dutch seem to have borne the petty harassment with stoic endurance. Frisius had been forewarned, of course. As secretary to the first council of justice at Batavia, he would have outranked Blockhovius in "real life," but his job as a local company manager prevented him from being eligible for the main post of the embassy. He may have been privy to Caron's innermost reasoning. Possibly, his function as secretary to the ambassador was a disguise, meant to conceal the fact that he would have been the embassy's key person even if Blockhovius had lived. He clearly realized that all he needed to do was to be patient. Frisius' ordeal was to last over a year: he was finally able to leave Japan to return to Batavia on the *Robijn* on 12 October 1650.

～

Chief Factor Snoucq, who had not been allowed to travel to Edo during his tenure, left with the fluyt *Het Witte Paert*, on 5 November 1649. This was ten days later than the twentieth day of the ninth month, which had been designated by shogunal decree as the ultimate departure date for the Dutch ships every year. He was not allowed to offer the usual departure presents to the Nagasaki *bugyō*. It was another sign to the Dutch that all was not well, and they were getting nervous. The answer from Edo had still not arrived, or so it was said, and thus it was impossible for Snoucq to take news of the success or failure of the embassy back to Batavia. He was allowed to remain at anchor off the Japanese coast for another two days in order to "organize his personal affairs." The fluyt must have finally left on 8 November. As if by accident, two days later, on 10 November, news from Edo "arrived," and Frisius and Van Brouckhorst were given permission to travel to the shogun's capital later that month.

On 16 November, the envoy and chief factor were received by the Nagasaki *bugyō*. The men of Frisius' guard had to accompany him unarmed—only the envoy himself was allowed to wear his pistol. On the morning of his visit, Nishi Kichibei, the oldest interpreter in Nagasaki, instructed him on the proceedings at the *bugyōsho* (official residence of the governor), located on the bluff next to the island of Deshima. The envoy would be allowed to enter the reception room a third of the way in, but the chief factor was instructed to kneel down on the tatami mats just inside the sliding doors giving access to the room. In contrast to the chief factor, however, Frisius was not allowed to offer any presents to the *bugyō* before he had been received by the shogun.[37] An hour later, other interpreters came to Frisius' apartment and asked him a crucial question.

On his arrival, they said, Frisius had told them that the envoy had been sent "to his Majesty by our superiors." They wanted to know what was meant by the word "superiors," for they did not know whether it meant the prince, the Gentlemen XVII, or the governor general. Frisius notes: "To this I answered frankly: that it meant the Honorable High and Mighty Gentlemen of the Estates General of the United Netherlands, who had sent the deceased directly from Holland to His Japanese Majesty (having been requested to do so in view of his great learning) so that he might pay his respects and transmit their gratitude for the pardon granted mercifully to the ten Dutchmen who had gone ashore in Nambu in the year 1643."[38]

Here, although the historian can observe our substitute fake envoy "frankly" telling an outright lie, it was not possible at the moment for the Japanese to prove this. All the interpreters could do was to ask for confirmation that the envoy had not been sent by merchants "for these cannot send ambassadors," and to ask if Frisius meant that the

envoy had been sent by the prince of Holland. Frisius answered that
he had meant the "High Authorities and the regents of Holland" and
that the prince was the supreme commander of the Dutch armies at
sea as well as at land, but that he was not the "Lord of Holland."[39]
This confused the interpreters so much that they left again to go and
report the envoy's answers.

An hour later, the interpreter Denbei finally came to get Frisius,
and they crossed the island together towards the land gate. There,
Frisius found all the other interpreters waiting for him and he was
told that two police officers had been sent by the *bugyō* to accompany him. Frisius, followed by his servants, crossed the bridge con-
necting the island with the city proper, turned left through Edomachi
towards the Ōhato pier, and from there climbed up the stairs towards
the *bugyōsho*. He was allowed to enter through the main gate, and
was successively received by the principal secretaries of both *bugyō*
and brought into their respective audience halls. There he introduced
himself twice in an identical manner:

> The High Authorities of the Dutch government had heard from
> their vassals the regents of the Dutch East India Company about
> the pardon granted mercifully by His Imperial Majesty of Japan to
> ten Dutchmen who had gone ashore in Nambu in the year 1643.
> For that reason, they had decided in council, by request of the
> regents, to send an envoy to His Majesty as a token of their grati-
> tude, and had ordered and qualified a famous scholar to do so.
> However, as the envoy had died an untimely death between Batavia
> and Japan (for nothing is as certain in this life as death, and nothing
> as uncertain as the time we die), I had been empowered to execute
> this embassy by the Governor General Cornelis van der Lijn repre-
> senting the said High Authorities [at Batavia]. In this capacity, then,
> I came to bring greetings in the name [of my superiors], wish [the
> governors] a happy tenure of office and request their help and favor
> to obtain the same from the Great Commissioner Chikugodono so
> that I might make a short and successful visit to the Court.[40]

Once more, we catch Frisius in the act of telling lies. Neither the
Estates General in The Hague nor the supreme management council
of the company in Amsterdam had had anything to do with sending
this embassy, let alone the prince of Holland who "was not the Lord
of Holland." But the *bugyō* told the interpreters to tell Frisius that
they thanked him for taking the trouble of making such a long, dangerous, and difficult journey, that they wished for his success in Edo,

and that they promised to do everything possible to assure the same. Fruits were served and Frisius was accompanied back to the main gate.

~

The Dutch entourage, when it was finally ready to leave Nagasaki, consisted of twenty-four Dutchmen, the largest number ever to travel to Edo during the Tokugawa period.[41] There were actually two trains, a large one of sixteen Dutchmen headed by Frisius, and a smaller one of eight headed by Van Brouckhorst.[42] Officially, then, two trains traveled to Edo, one after the other, sleeping in inns of different quality along the way. Twelve of the men in Frisius' train were in uniform. They had been provided with three different liveries. One in blue serge for daily use, one in dark brown wool for use along the Tōkaidō road, and a third, the most precious, made especially for the occasion of the audience with the shogun, in red and white stripes. All men had been provided with silver rapiers.[43]

The day of departure was 25 November 1649, for it had been divined that this day was more propitious than the day before, which had initially been designated as the day the Dutch would have to leave Nagasaki. Three large cargo barks had been rented at a cost of 715 *taels*. One bark carried two large cannon, culverins, their carriages, and other accouterments that had been included by Caron among the gifts for the shogun. The second carried the twenty-four Dutchmen, three police officers sent from Edo, and the three interpreters Nishi Kichibei, Ishibashi Shōsuke, and Inomata Denbei. The third bark carried twenty-four other Japanese, such as cooks, fish cutters, and washermen. A total of sixty-four Japanese left Nagasaki with the Dutch train. After all the well-wishers had been treated to sake at the company's expense, the barks were towed out of Nagasaki Bay. Then, the wind turned and the boats were forced to wait idly in the offing for three days. From the Dutch perspective, 25 November had turned out to be an inauspicious day after all. Worse delays were still to come.

After reaching Osaka on 13 December, the Dutch were ready to leave for Edo again one week later. The luggage was sent first on eighty-two horses, accompanied by about 150 Japanese men. An hour later, the three palanquins of Frisius, Van Brouckhorst, and Kichibei (who had been allowed one in view of his age) followed, each of them accompanied by ten carriers in brand new outfits. The other

Dutchmen all went on horseback, as did the guards, interpreters, and secretaries (all together forty-six horses), and another hundred carriers transported the gifts for the shogun, the envoy's "wine cellar," the medicine chests, and so on.

On 31 December, the entourage reached Edo, where all the Dutchmen were lodged together in the Nagasakiya. There they found that some rooms had been added, but even so their number was so much larger than usual that they were still forced to sleep "almost on top of each other," for none of the Dutchmen wanted to sleep downstairs with the Japanese where there would have been sufficient room. Frisius notes that twenty-four Dutchmen and seventy-three Japanese stayed in the inn at the expense of the Dutch East India Company.[44]

That evening after dinner, the police officer Ichirōbei, who had been sent from Edo to Nagasaki to fetch the envoy, reported that he had gone to inform Inoue Masashige of Frisius' safe arrival in Edo. When he had gone to do the same at the residence of Baba Saburōzaemon, he had found the latter in an unusually good mood. Just that day Saburōzaemon had been received in audience by the shogun, who had especially asked if the artillery expert had also come and if he was in good health. When answered affirmatively, this particular information had pleased Iemitsu most. The envoy, then, may have been allowed to travel to Edo primarily because of Schedler's presence in his following.

I will abbreviate the depressing and boring story of the lengthy wait for an audience with Iemitsu in Edo, with its extensive preparations, repeated deceptions, and disappointments.[45] The problem was that the longer the audience was postponed, the more difficult it would be for Frisius to return to Batavia with the monsoon. If the *Robijn* did not set out before the second moon of the Japanese new year, that is, before March 1650, it would become impossible to sail south and the ship would have to remain idle until the next season. For traders, this was a horror to be avoided at all costs. The Japanese, however, could not have cared less about the financial considerations of the Dutch merchants, and the delays were designed, partly at least, to make the Dutch squirm with regret about the lost cargo space.

The excuse given for the delays in Edo was that the shogun's health did not allow him to receive the envoy. The latter, however, having traveled so far, could not possibly leave without having had the opportunity to "gaze upon His Majesty's countenance." So Frisius' patience was being tested between the rock of the shogun's "weak condition" and the hard place of his "high consideration" for the envoy.

Apart from the two diaries kept by Frisius and Van Brouckhorst, which abound in rumors and silly details (for the authors had little else to do but chronicle their frustrations),[46] we have two Japanese sources for the time period when the embassy was in Edo. They are the *Keian nikki*, or the official Castle record,[47] and the *Hitomi shiki*, or Private Record of the Hitomi. The latter family functioned as shogunal court physicians, so we should expect some extra details on the shogun's health.

As is clear from the Japanese records, the shogun spent the month of January mainly hunting. However, according to the *Hitomi shiki*, on 26 January Iemitsu seems to have had abdominal pains.[48] On 31 January (the date for which the audience with the Dutch envoy had been scheduled) he was coughing.[49] The bellyache returned the next day, and one week later the shogun had "the chills" *(okan)*.[50] On 10 February the shogun reappeared in public and the next day, according to the *Keian nikki*, the daimyo residing in Edo came to the Castle to celebrate his recovery.[51] The *Keian nikki* reports that the shogun was ill again on 14 February,[52] but the *Hitomi shiki* has him up and consulting with the *rōjū* on the nineteenth.[53]

There are no entries about the shogun's illness in the *Hitomi shiki* for March, which might indicate that the physician of this family had not been consulted during that month. On 19 March, the *Keian nikki* intimates that the shogun was sick but gives no details,[54] while on the first and the third of April both records agree on another sick spell.[55] The shogun appeared again in public on 7 April, according to the *Hitomi shiki*,[56] but the *Keian nikki* intimates that he was still sick.[57] This was the exact day that the Dutch envoy was finally received in the Castle by the *rōjū*, representing the shogun, and Ietsuna, his heir. Four days later, while the Dutch were still in town, the shogun went out to hunt.[58]

It is difficult to decipher what exactly was going on. The Dutch accounts up to 30 January reflect certainty that the audience would take place on the thirty-first, as scheduled on their arrival. Horses and manpower to carry the gifts to the Castle had been engaged. On the morning of 31 January everything was ready. But the shogun did not appear. Although they had not been used, the horses and carriers

had to be paid for anyway.[59] There can be no doubt that, at that end
of January and in the first week of February, the shogun really was
sick. Hunting out in the cold weather may have been the cause.[60] Psy-
chological triggers may also have played a part, given the coincidence
of the timing of his illness exactly when the audience with the Dutch
had been firmly scheduled.

There is, on the other hand, no hard evidence in the Japanese
sources that the shogun was really ill in March, and although the two
Japanese sources quoted above agree on a short indisposition in the
beginning of April, it cannot have been sufficient reason not to receive the Dutch envoy. This is confirmed by the fact that the shogun
was suddenly well enough to go hunting on 11 April, while the Dutch
were still in town.

The fact is, of course, that Iemitsu felt cheated. He had refused to
see Coijett in 1648, and had not even allowed the latter's successor,
Snoucq, to travel to Edo. The bogus ambassador who had been sent
from Batavia had not been refused permission to travel to the shogun's
capital, for he had brought someone along who could teach the
ballistics of mortars and culverins to the Japanese. But to receive the
substitute fake envoy himself must have been too much for the
shogun's stomach. I cannot be completely sure, but the three months'
delay in Edo likely indicates that the shogun was resisting pressure
from his advisers to receive the Dutch.

If we now turn to the Japanese sources dealing with the embassy of
1649–1650 itself, we find that they are, not surprisingly, very brief,
contrasting sharply with the records about the embassies from Korea
and the Ryukyu Islands. What is more, the main source we have, the
Edo bakufu nikki (Daily records of the Edo bakufu) is exasperatingly
vague on the most important point, namely, where this so-called ambassador had come from: "For the first time, the Lord of Holland
sent an envoy to both their Highnesses [the shogun and his heir] offering various gifts. Today, this envoy and the *kapitan* paid their respects,
coming to the Castle where they were seated in the *denjō no ma* (antechamber). Although the shogun should have appeared, he did not
because of his illness."[61]

The Japanese text has *"Oranda yakata"* for what I translate here
as "the Lord of Holland." This, of course, does not specify which
"lord" was meant, or even where he was supposed to reside, in Hol-

land or in Batavia. The text suggests (but does no more) that because the chief factor was sent every year as a representative of the governor general and his status was clearly assessed to be lower than that of the envoy, the envoy had to have been dispatched by the governor general's superior, that is, the "Lord of Holland."[62]

Thus, on the morning of 7 April, at nine o'clock, the envoy and the chief factor received orders to leave for the Castle. Later Frisius noted in his journal that all along the way, the streets were lined with masses of people. The sight must have been one to behold. Twenty-one white and one black Dutchmen followed on horseback behind two palanquins with the emblem of the Dutch East India Company on their doors. Among the men of lower status, dressed identically in red and white striped uniforms, were two trumpeters. Banners hung from their trumpets, which they blew "in the Dutch manner." The men of higher rank all wore long dark blue capes. Their curly "red" hair hung loose to their shoulders, and around their necks they wore jabots of exquisite lace. Their long noses resembled those of *tengu* (devils). Truly, it must have appeared a little uncanny to the Japanese throngs.

Frisius was conducted along the same route Elserack and the other representatives of the Dutch East India Company had been taken in the years before. The antechamber had been upgraded, though, for the Dutchmen were seated in the *denjō no ma*. There, Inoue Masashige welcomed Frisius with the words that it was a "superb day, on which they [i.e., the Dutchmen of the embassy] would be given satisfaction for their superiors," whatever that latter word may have meant.[63] The *ōmetsuke* was happy about this, he said, and he congratulated the men, who thanked him for his kind words. They waited for a little less than an hour, and then Inoue and Baba Saburōzaemon (the latter leading the way) took the envoy along the outer verandah *(ochien)* to the *ōhiroma*. The gifts for the shogun had been displayed in the wooden corridor by guards dressed in *nagabakama* (long pants) formal clothing.[64]

The *Keian nikki* lists the following gifts: one large mirror, one carpet with flowers, one golden telescope, three pieces of Indian cloth, six pieces of colored woolen cloth, thirty pieces of Indian cloth, thirty pieces of striped cotton cloth, and, presented "in one piece," one hundred *momme** of mummy[65] (a tarlike substance used as medicine,

---

*Here *momme* is a unit of weight equal to 3.75 grams.

much in demand by the highest levels of *bushi* society in Japan, and imported by the Dutch from Persia).[66] Iemitsu's toys, the two huge culverins, are not mentioned, for it would not do to have the Dutch arm the supreme warrior of Japan in front of all his vassals. A barrel of Spanish wine that had also been offered by the Dutch is similarly missing from this list. Who knows why.

The Dutch envoy was led opposite the "Imperial councilors," Sakai Tadakatsu, Matsudaira Nobutsuna, Abe Tadaaki, and Abe Shigetsugu,[67] who "greeted him and invited him to sit on the mats just inside the room where they sat themselves [*gedan no ma*], and reaching out for the telescope they were extremely pleased. Chikugo no kami and Saburōzaemon spoke to Sanuki to kami [Tadakatsu] to show and explain the gifts. Both men then spoke to the interpreter [Inomata Denbei] who translated for the said envoy. Then the [latter] knelt down and retired along the same outer corridor. After this, the gifts were taken away."[68]

This procedure was repeated with Van Brouckhorst, and then again, a quarter of an hour later, twice in front of the shogun's heir Ietsuna, who was dressed for the occasion in a blue jacket (*haori*) and baggy pants (*hakama*), and took his seat in the *jōdan no ma*,[69] on a "gilded throne" raised a couple of inches from the floor and with gilded animals on its four corners. His face was long and handsome.[70]

Apart from the usual precious fabrics, the envoy presented Ietsuna with a miniature landscape in coral, and two telescopes, one of gold and one of silver. The chief factor had brought him the silver replica of a Dutch ship and two parrots.[71] This time, it was Mizuno Bingo no kami who showed the future shogun his gifts from the wooden corridor. "When this was done, all the sliding doors were opened, and the future shogun withdrew into the interior of the Castle under the eyes of all the *fudai daimyō*."[72]

The next day, both Frisius and Van Brouckhorst had to return to the Castle once more to receive the shogun's counter-gifts and his permission to travel back to Nagasaki. This time the formalities took place in the eastern room of the *ōhiroma*. Frisius was allowed to sit on the first tatami mat inside the room. The interpreter Kichibei, however, had to stay in the outer corridor.[73] The rooms around the reception room were filled "with the shogun's relatives as well as other lords."[74] For "his master," the envoy from the "Lord of Holland" received five hundred bars of white silver which had been put on display in the room.[75] Again, the *rōjū* were sitting in order, facing the Dutchman, and instructed Inoue Masashige and Baba Saburōzaemon to transmit the shogun's message to the Dutch envoy. The foreign affairs officials, in their turn, informed the interpreter, who then translated their words. This was the content of the shogun's message:

> Years ago, when a Dutch ship drifted ashore in a bay of Nambu, ten men from that country were caught and brought to Edo, where they were closely examined. These ten Dutchmen were then ordered to be released into the hands of the Dutch *kapitan* so that they might sail home. That the Dutch had reflected on this and sent an ambassador had pleased the shogun.[76]

This message was the shogun's official communication to the "Lord of Holland." It indicated his superior status over the Dutch through the expression that the Dutch "had reflected on this," implying Dutch penitence had caused the embassy to be sent (instead of Japanese pushiness). After hearing this message, the envoy was allowed to retire to the antechamber, and a little later he was called again, this time to receive two hundred bars of silver and ten sets of cotton clothing for himself. When Frisius, after having bowed his head to the mats in gratitude, indicated that he wanted to get up, he was ordered to remain seated. The interpreter Kichibei was called, and he then translated what Inoue Masashige read from a document handed to him by the rōjū. Frisius' journal records:

> For two years in a row, there has no been audience given [by the shogun] to the Dutch *kapitan* because of some problems created by the Portuguese ambassador who had been to Batavia as well as elsewhere. His Majesty has now completely forgiven this matter. Concerning the ten-year truce between the Dutch and the Portuguese, I was told to inform His Excellency the Governor General at Jacatra that this should not happen again, if we wanted to continue to come to Japan.[77]

This is the shogun's unofficial communication to the governor general, for officially the hierarchical distance between them was too great for communication to be possible. Once more, we have evidence that the whole episode over the supposed help given by the Dutch to the Portuguese ambassador had been nothing but a diversionary tactic. For here we see that the shogun was still of the opinion that the Portuguese ambassador had been to Batavia before coming to Japan (which was indeed true but which had been denied by all chief factors and the envoy since Coijett), but even so he "completely forgave" the Dutch. Iemitsu could have his cake and eat it too. The warning not to conclude any more truces without Japanese consent rings rather hollow, if we consider that the Dutch envoy was, after all, treated as a real envoy, with valuable gifts and honorable seating arrangements in the reception hall inside the Castle itself.

The message, therefore, was contradictory. On the one hand, the very real honors prove that the Japanese desperately wanted the Dutch to keep on coming to Japan. On the other hand, the non-appearance of the shogun himself, his illogical message, and pathetic warning give the impression that Iemitsu himself was losing touch with reality, and that his advisers had a hard time reconciling the needs of the country with the needs of this xenophobic shogun who imagined that he was at war with the Iberian nations and the rest of the Roman Catholic world.

Seen in this light, we may understand better why the Dutch envoy had been made to wait so long. When the envoy had arrived in Edo, on 31 December 1649, the *rōjū* had initially scheduled the audience with the shogun for 31 January, one month later. This would have been a quite appropriate time, allowing all preparations on both sides to be made without undue haste. It must have been Iemitsu himself, however, who balked at the idea of receiving the bogus ambassador he himself had wanted so badly, and he refused in a manner least likely to offend anyone: by becoming sick. During the months of February and March, the shogun's advisers may have tried to change his mind, and only when it became obvious that Iemitsu was not going to do that, was a new date for a reception of the envoy by the *rōjū* set, with, as icing on the cake, another reception by the shogun's heir.

Frisius thanked the *rōjū* for the shogun's message, and assured them that the Dutch would never undertake anything against Japan's interests. When Inoue Masashige had transmitted these words, the councilors "laughed a bit."[78] They may have been thinking of the fact that the Dutch had just sent a bogus ambassador, but if they did, this was no longer the time to bring it up. They warned the envoy that he should "request the Gentlemen XVII in Holland and the governor general in Batavia, if they ever heard of Portuguese designs on Japan, to write to the governors of Nagasaki and inform them at the earliest opportunity, which would be of service to Japan."[79] This time, the "Lord of Holland" seems to have gotten lost somewhere in the translation.

~

By order of the bakufu, four men stayed behind in Edo when the Dutch train left for Nagasaki on 16 April 1650.[80] They were our old friend Wilhem Bijlvelt, by now promoted to full Merchant; Juriaen Schedler, the artillerist; Caspar Schamberger, the surgeon; and Jan Schmidt, a corporal.[81] A truly European company, for Bijlvelt, who was put in charge, was the only Dutchman among them. Schedler, as we have seen, came from Sweden, Schamberger from Leipzig in Germany, and Schmidt was a Swiss silversmith who knew how to give military signals on the bugle. All three men, then, had a special skill the Japanese were eager to learn.

The delegation was warned to be careful not to give information about the embassy itself, the 1648 peace treaty with Spain, or the rank and quality of the ambassador, and to repeat only what they had heard the envoy say himself. For their reference, they were given an extract from the *Daghregister*, so that none of them would ever be caught saying something different from what had been said before.[82]

For five months this cultural delegation stayed in the shogun's capital, answering questions by bakufu retainers concerning their specialties.[83] Schedler explained the operation of mortars, their methods of loading, aiming, and firing. Inoue himself seems to have been interested in the art of surveying, which used many of the techniques for calculating the distances between the mortar and its target. Schedler showed him how to measure long distances with an astrolabe, and taught the secrets of the calculus to some of his retainers who knew Portuguese.[84] Twice a trip was made to the plain of Mure in Musashi to fire the mortars and other guns in the presence of all the men in charge of the Iemitsu's arsenal.[85]

The principal reason why Frisius' embassy is remembered at all in Japan, however, is that this cultural mission provided an opportunity for a more detailed study of Western medicine than had been possible before.[86] While Schedler made the shogun's guns boom in the Kanto, Schamberger was quietly visiting influential patients of the *bushi* upper class, accompanied by the interpreter Inomata Denbei. Without realizing it, Schamberger was ensuring his own immortality. It seems that Denbei and other interpreters kept notes on Schamberger's diagnoses and cures, for there still exist some twenty different

Japanese manuscripts today that bear the good doctor's name.[87] These form the tradition of the *Kasuparu-ryū,* or Caspar-style medicine, the techniques of which were transmitted until well into the nineteenth century.[88]

It may be that the success of this cultural mission was its own undoing. Shortly after the last successful firing of the mortars on 23 September 1650, the Dutchmen were suddenly ordered to leave the city, although the *ōmetsuke* had previously announced they were to stay until the next year when the chief factor would come back to Edo once more on his annual visit. The Dutchmen guessed that the shogun had been convinced by the anti-foreign faction in the Castle that the Dutch presence in the shogun's capital had lasted long enough.[89] Others may have been of the opinion that the esoteric knowledge of firing mortars was misplaced in the hands of Inoue's retainers.

Conclusion: Was Japan Isolated during the Edo Period?

In the Chinese world order, envoys served to confirm and entertain the links between the Son of Heaven and his vassals. The envoys themselves were of minor import, and frequently their reception by the Chinese was such that the diplomats had good reason to complain about maltreatment. If envoys were dispensable commodities, it was their credentials that counted. Envoys were supposed to present documents addressed in the proper phraseology and dated in the Chinese calendar, thus making explicit the vassal's recognition of the Chinese emperor as the center of the cosmos. Because of this great emphasis on proper documentation, conforming to certain well-established standards and serving as the sole determinants for the acceptability of foreign envoys, the whole East Asian tradition of diplomatic correspondence reveals a fascinating undergrowth of "lost" documents, forgeries, and other deceptions.

A famous instance of an envoy "losing" his documents is reported in Japan's earliest work of history, the *Nihongi*, for the year 608, when a Japanese envoy Imoko no Ōmi returned home from a visit to the Chinese court and reported: "When I was leaving, the Chinese emperor gave me a letter. But while passing through the Land of Paekche, the men from Paekche searched me and took it from me. Therefore I am unable to present it."[1]

From the account of this embassy in the *Sui shu* (History of the Sui Dynasty), we understand that a phrase used by the Japanese court in its communication with the Chinese emperor had given offense: "The Son of Heaven in the land where the sun rises addresses a letter to the Son Heaven in the land where the sun sets."[2] "When the [Chinese] Emperor saw this letter, he was displeased and told the chief official of foreign affairs that this letter from the barbarians was discourteous, and that such a letter should not again be brought to his attention."[3]

Of course, there could not be two Sons of Heaven, as the Japanese address had suggested, for the Chinese universe did not allow for the possibility of two centers. The letter Imoko no Ōmi received from the Chinese emperor must have made this abundantly clear. Here, then, we have an instance of an envoy who knew that the letter from the Chinese court would, in turn, disappoint and displease his superiors at home. Rather than be the bringer of such an inauspicious document, he chose to run the risk of being punished for losing the letter. The point here, obviously, is the clash between the interests of two separate "centers" in East Asia, which made the envoy "lose" his documents.

Forgeries of diplomatic correspondence also abound, although the study of these, from their very nature, is still in its infancy and only slowly becoming possible through a comparison of the records of the different countries involved. A famous forgery was composed by Konishi Yukinaga (1555–1600), one of Hideyoshi's new men, who in 1594 wrote a letter of apology in the name of his lord to the emperor of China for the invasion of Korea.[4] As we have seen, another forgery case came to light during the years 1631–1635, when the daimyo of Tsushima, Sō Yoshinari, was forced to submit a disagreement with one of his senior retainers for arbitration by the rōjū. At that time it was revealed that the whole process of reconciliation between Japan and Korea, which had been pursued since the time of Ieyasu, had been based on documents falsified in Tsushima.[5]

Even though the Tsushima daimyo was a vassal of the Tokugawa shoguns, the status of the islands itself was disputed by the Koreans, so that a well-known Japanese scholar of Korean-Japanese relations could write not too long ago: "Korea *stubbornly* regarded Tsushima as a tributary state" (emphasis mine).[6] It is likely that the recent discovery of a number of false seals in the Tsushima archives will help considerably to advance our knowledge of Korean-Japanese relations and the function of previous forgeries.[7]

The field of bogus ambassadors in East Asia is also wide and varied, ranging from envoys from completely fictitious countries in 1478–1482,[8] through Japanese embassies competing for the same credentials in China in 1523,[9] to the fundamentally deceptive embassies sent by the Ryukyuan kings. The latter case is especially illustrative, wedged, as it was in early Tokugawa times, between the different centers of Ming loyalists, Qing conquerors, Satsuma overlords, and the Tokugawa bakufu. This constantly called for "situational weighing,"[10] and an occasional outright lie, combined with false documents. In Fairbank's edited 1968 volume on the Chinese world order, Ta-tuan Ch'en details the lengths to which Satsuma officials went in collaborating with the Ryukyuan court to keep its administrative control over the islands hidden from the Chinese of the Ming and Qing dynasties. Ta-tuan Ch'en concludes: "As time wore on, a spirit of deception naturally prevailed in the tribute relationship [between Ryukyu and China] and also in historiography."[11]

Also well known is the case of the Confucian scholar Sai Kokki, who, on a mission to China in 1677, took the precaution of having his "government" prepare two sets of documents, "one congratulating the anti-Qing rebels on their glorious victory, the other satisfying the requirements of diplomatic relations with the Qing."[12] Sai burned the first set when he learned on his arrival in Fuzhou that the Ming loyalists had been decisively defeated. When questioned about Ryukyuan support for the rebel cause, Sai blandly denied everything and produced the second set of documents as proof of the good faith of the Ryukyu king.

Deception, then, was part and parcel of the contest between different centers. It is, of course, the typical defense of the weak against the strong. The long-standing Japanese desire to form an independent center in East Asia should therefore be examined in the light of its own inner contradictions. Derivative from the Chinese diplomatic tradition and unable to shake free of the principal premises on which that tradition was based,[13] the Japanese were forced to either ignore the existence of China, or to conquer it.

When Japan emerged, under Hideyoshi, from the era of inner turmoil known as *sengoku* (warring states), it tried the latter option first. But Hideyoshi's successors, the Tokugawa shoguns, no longer considered the conquest of the Chinese center a reasonable alternative to Japanese diplomacy. In order to create a center independent of China, therefore, Japan was forced to ignore the existence of the Chinese center and engage in diplomatic relations only with those countries that could somehow be forced to recognize Japan as the center of the world.

This is the fundamental contradiction that characterized Japan's foreign relations from the 1630s until the mid-nineteenth century. On the one hand, the country conducted diplomacy according to Chinese philosophical ideas, but on the other it was too proud to entertain diplomatic relations with the Middle Kingdom itself. Japanese efforts to create an alternative view of the cosmos and replace China as the center continued to borrow elements of Chinese cosmology, which had long ago been appropriated by the Asuka, Nara, and Heian courts.

These elements were rediscovered in the late 1970s and early 1980s by Arano Yoshinori and Ronald Toby, building on ideas first formulated by Asao Naohiro and Tanaka Takeo.[14] Toby beat Arano to the publication in book form of their common ideas, and in 1984 published his *State and Diplomacy in Early Modern Japan,* in which he sought to demonstrate that, contrary to conventional wisdom, the Tokugawa bakufu had a clear agenda and goals that organized its foreign relations, meaning to replace China as the center of East Asia.

For this reason, Toby argued, the concept of *sakoku* (closed country) was outdated and should be replaced by his own description of a Japan-centered world order. In fact, what he went on to describe was a rather pathetic attempt on the part of early Tokugawa Japan to bully its weaker neighbors into the use of diplomatic language and behavior that would suffice as proof of Japan's centrality. Such paper realities, of course, should not be taken at their face value.[15] Toby's contribution to the field of Tokugawa studies does not lie in his revision of Japan's foreign relations but rather in his analysis of the domestic perception of such "foreign relations" and their importance as instruments of legitimization of Tokugawa rule.[16]

As has been shown in this study, the bakufu also tried to bully the Dutch, and the fact that Toby (and everybody else participating in the discussion) overlooked the resulting Dutch embassy of 1649 is in itself significant, for it testifies to the fact that the embassy left only the faintest trace in the Japanese record—*because* it did not sufficiently confirm Japan's centrality. The company managers in Batavia had tried to pass off an envoy without official papers. Inexperienced in the East Asian diplomatic tradition (and perhaps unwilling to commit themselves on paper), the organizers of the embassy do not seem to have realized that, if the embassy was to be taken seriously in Japan, the occasion obviously called for forgeries.

It may be more useful to concentrate on the practical meaning of the diplomatic contacts the bakufu preserved with mainland East

Asia, through its links via Tsushima and Ryukyu, rather than view them as proofs of a vibrant reorganization of the East Asian world order. For example, we could consider these island groups as *buffers* that allowed Japan to officially ignore China while at the same time enabling it to keep an eye on developments on the continent, that is, in Korea, Manchuria, and China itself.[17]

Complete isolation was, of course, undesirable and unpractical, for if the bakufu wanted to preserve Japan's independence from the outside world it needed to preserve and cultivate channels through which essential intelligence could be obtained, as Toby himself has convincingly argued.[18] A *degree* of isolation, however, was rational and probably a necessary prerequisite for a Japan ruled by warriors who were already technologically behind the times, and, as this study has shown for the case of mortar technology, *knew* themselves to be so.

The Dutch trade was preserved because of the usefulness of a European buffer, which could provide necessary intelligence about the new and unpredictable element in the East Asian world order, represented by the sea power of the Portuguese, Spanish, English, Dutch, and even the Danish, and possibly that of other nationalities of which the Japanese had not yet heard. In order to make them function smoothly, the buffers were given a measure of independence and respect (or, as in the case of the Dutch, hard cash). It is in the rewards to the buffers that we see the creativity of the bakufu most clearly, for each of them was treated in a different manner.

The Ryukyu Islands were allowed to play out their tragicomedy of national independence for the benefit of their Chinese contacts. Tsushima was given control over the trade with Korea in exchange for its help in smoothing a potentially awkward relationship with the Korean king and his court. The Dutch, at least during the seventeenth century, were paid handsomely for their services in providing the news from Southeast Asia, the Philippines, and Europe.

Moreover, the bakufu managed to have its isolationist cake and eat it too, for Korea and the nominally independent Ryukyuan kingdom agreed to send occasional envoys to Edo. It is important to keep in mind that the Japanese domestic "consumption" of these spectacles was more important than their actual content, as we have seen with the Dutch embassy of 1649–1650. The great crowds that turned out to see the foreign embassies validate the concept of isolation, rather than prove its opposite, as Toby has tried to convince us. Since the "opening" of Japan in the nineteenth century, foreigners no longer excite the Japanese quite as much as during the Edo period when everyone, even ex-emperors, came to watch to pass them by: "There was no one in any of the shops; they simply left their goods [untended]. . . . Along the route were male and female, young and old, both commoners and samurai. The lines of people were endless, and never gave out, all the way to Ueno. . . . The people were as blades of grass on a mountainside in spring; so many heads they were as grains of sand on a beach. . . . It was as if the dikes had burst and the water had begun to gush forth from the beach."[19]

Descriptions such as these can only apply to a country isolated to a high degree from the rest of the world. Even if it be admitted that Toby accomplished a corrective of the simplistic Western view of Tokugawa Japan, as a country *without* foreign relations,[20] the concept of *sakoku*—standing for Japan's isolation—still has considerable vitality, especially seen from the point of view of the Japanese themselves who, with the exception of certain residents of Tsushima and Satsuma, were forbidden to travel overseas.[21]

At their most basic level, then, the foreign embassies to Japan were charades performed to stave off trouble. Japan, ruled by warriors and therefore essentially different from the Confucian bureaucracy in charge in other East Asian countries (most notably China, Korea, and Ryukyu), never shed its threatening image as a potential invader.[22] It could, however, be easily and cheaply pacified with foreign envoys. Viewed in this light, we are not surprised to see that the bakufu also tried to strong-arm the Dutch into performing like the Koreans and Ryukyuans. The difference was that the Dutch were new at the diplomatic game being played between the different centers of the East Asian universe.

In spite of the success of the cultural mission that had followed the embassy, the whole affair of the bogus ambassador left a profound bad taste in bakufu circles. Never again were the Dutch either required or forced to send an ambassador, and the records of Frisius' visit were kept as brief as was possible without admitting that this very serious matter had turned into an obvious farce.

The embassy of 1649–1650, then, set the precedent for all subsequent Japanese-Dutch interactions during the rest of the Edo period. It is doubtful, however, that if the envoy had been supplied with the credentials the Japanese wanted, the relationship between the two countries would have developed in an essentially different manner. For, just as Tsushima with Korea and the Ryukyu Islands with China, the main function of the Dutch in the larger context of Japan's foreign relations was to provide a buffer between Japan and Europe.

We can speculate that if the Japanese had not insisted on linking the Dutch embassy with the *Breskens* affair, but had, instead, offered more freedom for the Dutch traders in Japan, the likelihood that a real ambassador with the proper credentials might have been sent from Holland during the 1640s would have been much greater. Given Iemitsu's xenophobia and megalomania, however, this was out of the question. In the end, then, Japanese arbitrariness prevented Dutch compliance, and we have to conclude that the Dutch, through their charade, expressed their refusal to adhere to the fiction of a Japan-centered diplomatic world order.

But even if a full-blown diplomatic relationship was not to be, Japanese enthusiasm for continuing trade with the Dutch after the *Breskens* affair was unmistakable. Apart from the immediate necessity of gaining information about the intentions of Spain and Portugal, the Japanese continued to be eager to learn from the West. A large part of the attraction of Christianity in Japan had always been the vistas of new Western learning it had opened to the Japanese.

After the 1640s Christianity was no longer visible in Japan. The case of the last Jesuits in Japan has been described in this study. About 25,000 other Christians died as a consequence of the bakufu's anti-Christian policy.[23] Whether this number qualifies the policy as genocide,[24] or whether the shogun was simply engaged in assuring "Japanese security,"[25] I leave for the reader to decide. It is significant, however, that the vast majority of the victims died during the reign of Tokugawa Iemitsu. The shogun himself, therefore, must be held chiefly responsible, and I argue that the intensity of the persecutions reflects principally Iemitsu's state of mind.

The shogun's power, however, was only nominally absolute, as I have shown. Despotism, in the case of Iemitsu, was a very mixed blessing. Behind the scenes, his advisers and other close associates had to work hard at damage control, playing elaborate games to limit the effect of Iemitsu's obsession with Japan's foreign relations. While the senior councilors went along with the shogun's decision to expel the Portuguese, the consensus was that the Dutch could serve a useful function and needed to be treated fairly.

The latter were forced to step into the shoes left empty by the Jesuits, and, almost in spite of themselves, provided Japan with an opportunity to learn about Western weaponry, fortifications, military drills, and medicine. Clearly these branches of knowledge were closely related to current fears about the intentions of Portugal and Spain, and when those fears ebbed away so did the bakufu-sponsored eagerness to learn from Holland, at least for awhile.

But it never completely disappeared. Slowly the Nagasaki interpreters switched from Portuguese to Dutch, following the precedent set by the *Breskens* affair. Then they started to read Dutch books and teach other scholars until, in the eighteenth century, "Hollandology" *(rangaku)* was born, a discipline unique to Japan, the practitioners of which studied the West through books in Dutch.

When viewed from the outside, especially from Europe but also from China, Japan was indeed highly isolated, but from the inside one might, with Toby and Arano, get the impression of thriving diplomatic activity. The truth, of course, lies somewhere in between. Only because Japan kept its relationship with Holland and made the Deshima-Batavia connection its buffer with Europe, was it able to ignore the rest of the European powers until the end of the eighteenth century.[26]

But Japan was never as isolated during the Tokugawa period as some Europeans thought it was. The Dutch presence and the fashionable status acquired by Dutch studies is proof of that.[27] Furthermore, we have to distinguish between the bakufu and its policy of seclusion, protected by buffers, and Japanese civilization itself. Curiosity about the outside world never abated in Japan, and scholarship in both Dutch and Chinese studies flourished during the Tokugawa period. If anything, the men making up the bakufu may themselves have been more isolated than those they intended to insulate from disruptive foreign thought.

Notes

ABBREVIATIONS

ARA	Algemeen Rijksarchief (Dutch National Archives) at The Hague
BSDR	*Bijlvelt/Schaep Debriefing Report* (ARA VOC 1148, tols. 355–392)
BTLV	*Bijdragen tot de Taal-, Land-, en Volkenkunde van Nederlands Indië*
GG	Gouverneur Generaal (Governor General of the Dutch East Indies)
HJAS	*Harvard Journal of Asiatic Studies*
HSDJ	*Hanshu daijiten* (Encyclopedia of Domains and Daimyo during the Edo Period)
JAS	*Journal of Asian Studies*
JJS	*Journal of Japanese Studies*
KCSF	*Kansei chōshū shoka fu* (Genealogies of the Various Warrior Houses Augmented and Improved during the Kansei Era)
LV	*Linschoten Vereniging*
MGOA	*Mitteilungen der deutschen Gesellschaft für Natur- und Völkerkunde Ostasiens*
MKMK	Morioka Kōminkan (Morioka Municipal Archive, Iwate Prefecture)
MN	*Monumenta Nipponica*
NB	Naikaku Bunko (Japanese National Archives) in Tokyo
NFJ	Nederlandse Factorij Japan (Deshima Archive) at ARA
NSSK	*Nambu-han sankō keizu* (Genealogies of the Various Families Related to the Nambu Fief)
RGP	*Rijks Geschiedkundige Publicatiën* (Historical Publications of the Kingdom of the Netherlands)
RR	Raden van India (Councilors of the Indies)
SHJ	Shiryōhensanjo (Historiographical Institute of Tokyo University)
TASJ	*Transactions of the Asiatic Society of Japan*
TJ	*Tokugawa jikki* (Veritable Records of the Tokugawa)
TSTK	Tōno Shiritsu Toshokan (Tōno Municipal Library)

VOC   Vereenigde Oost-Indische Compagnie (Dutch East India Company Archive) at ARA

YKMK   Yamada Kōminkan (Yamada Municipal Archive)

INTRODUCTION

1. The following explanation of what is known as the "Chinese World Order" draws heavily on John K. Fairbank, ed., *The Chinese World Order* (Cambridge, Mass.: Harvard University Press, 1968). Although I am aware that Fairbank has come under attack from different directions for the past thirty years, for our purposes here his classical model of the Chinese World Order during the Ming dynasty is supremely relevant for Japanese diplomacy during the Edo period.

2. See Charles R. Boxer, *The Dutch Seaborne Empire* (New York: Knopf, 1966); and by the same author, *The Portuguese Seaborne Empire* (New York: Knopf, 1969); see also Holden Furber, *Rival Empires of Trade* (Minneapolis: University of Minnesota Press, 1976).

3. Charles R. Boxer, *The Great Ship from Amacon* (Lisboa: Centro de Estudos Historicos Ultramarinos, 1959).

4. Margaretha van Opstall, *De reis van de vloot van Pieter Willemsz Verhoeff* (The Hague: Nijhoff, 1972); and Derek Massarella, *A World Elsewhere* (New Haven and London: Yale University Press, 1990).

5. Pieter van Dam, *Beschryvinge van de Oostindische Compagnie,* ed. F. W. Stapel and W. Th. van Boetzelaer (The Hague: Nijhoff, 1927–1954); Femme S. Gaastra, *De geschiedenis van de VOC* (Haarlem: Fibula-Van Dishoek; Antwerpen: Standaard Uitgeverij, 1982).

6. Mary E. Berry, *Hideyoshi* (Cambridge, Mass.: Harvard University Press, 1982).

7. Conrad Totman, *Politics in the Tokugawa Bakufu 1600–1843* (Cambridge, Mass.: Harvard University Press, 1967); and by the same author, *Early Modern Japan* (Berkeley and London: University of California Press, 1993).

8. Harold Bolitho, *Treasures among Men* (New Haven: Yale University Press, 1974).

9. Like the notion of the Chinese World Order, the concept of *sakoku* has been under attack for the last two decades; see Ronald P. Toby, "Reopening the Question of Sakoku: Diplomacy in the Legitimation of the Tokugawa Bakufu," *JJS* 3, no. 2 (1977): 323–363; Ronald P. Toby, *State and Diplomacy in Early Modern Japan* (Princeton, N.J.: Princeton University Press, 1984); Arano Yoshinori, "Bakuhansei kokka to gaikō," *Rekishigaku kenkyū 1978 nendo taikai hōkoku tokushūgō* (November 1978): 95–105; and Tashiro Kazui, "Foreign Relations during the Edo Period: Sakoku Reexamined," *JJS* 8, no. 2 (1982): 283–306.

10. Charles R. Boxer, *The Christian Century in Japan 1549–1650* (Berkeley and London: University of California Press, 1967); Michael Cooper, *They Came to Japan* (Berkeley and Los Angeles: University of California Press, 1965).

11. For the deification, see Willem Jan Boot, "The Death of Shōgun: Deification in Early Modern Japan," in John Breen and Mark Teeuwen, eds., *Shinto in History: Ways of the Kami* (London: Curzon, 2000), 144–166.

12. For this and the following, see Yamamoto Hirofumi, *Sakoku to kaikin no jidai* (Tokyo: Azekura Shobō, 1995), 26–90; and Matsui Yōko and Reinier Hesselink, "Sakoku," in *Nichiran kōryū yonhyaku nen no rekishi to tenbō,* ed. Leonard Blusse, Willem Remmelink, and Ivo Smits (Tokyo: Nichiran Gakkai [The Japan-Netherlands Institute], 2000), 41–42.

13. A. J. C. Geerts, "The Arima Rebellion and the Conduct of Koecke-backer," *TASJ* 11, no. 1 (1883): 51–116.

14. Charles R. Boxer, "Embaixada de Macau ao Japão em 1640," *Anais do Club Militar Naval 57,* nos. 9, 10 (1933); *The Great Ship from Amacon* (1959), 163–165; *The Christian Century* (1967), 384–385.

15. *Daghregister,* 9 November 1640.

16. Tashiro Kazui, *Kakikaerareta kokusho* (Tokyo: Chūō Kōronsha, 1983).

17. Robert K. Sakai, "The Satsuma-Ryukyu Trade and the Tokugawa Seclusion Policy," *JAS* 23 (1964): 391–403; and "The Ryukyu Islands as a Fief of Satsuma," in *The Chinese World Order,* ed. John K. Fairbank, 112–134.

18. Ta-tuan Ch'en, "Investiture of Liu-ch'iu Kings in the Ch'ing Period," in *The Chinese World Order,* ed. John K. Fairbank, 163.

19. James Hevia, *Cherishing Men from Afar* (Durham and London: Duke University Press, 1995), 232–239.

20. In China, the Dutch took the same attitude; see John E. Wills, "Ch'ing Relations with the Dutch, 1662–1690," in *The Chinese World Order,* ed. John K. Fairbank, 225–256; and John E. Wills, *Pepper, Guns, and Parleys* (Cambridge, Mass.: Harvard University Press, 1974).

Chapter 1 FLYING DUTCHMEN

1. For the seating arrangements in Chiyoda Castle, see Ōno Kiyoshi, *Tokugawa seido shiryō* (Tokyo: the author, 1927).

2. For help with identifying the fifteen different Matsudaira present on this occasion, I am grateful to Professor Yamamoto Hirofumi of SHJ.

3. Totman, *Politics,* 155.

4. *KCSF,* 13:8.

5. NB ms *Kan'ei nikki, Ryūeiroku* copy. The printed version in *Tsūkō Ichiran,* ed. Hayashi Akira and Miyazaki Shigemi (Osaka: Seibundō, 1967), 6:325, has several editorial mistakes.

6. Kimura Naoki, "17 seiki nakaba bakuhansei kokka to ikokusen taisaku," *Shigaku zasshi* 29, no. 2 (2000): 61–62.

7. NB ms *Tenkan nikki,* Kan'ei 20/5/11 (26 June 1643).

8. Ibid., 5th month, 3rd day (18 June 1643).

9. J. E. Heeres, ed., *Abel Janszoon Tasman's Journal* (Amsterdam: F. Muller, 1898); and R. Posthumus Meyes, *De reizen van Abel Janszoon Tasman en Franchoys Jacobszoon Visscher* (The Hague: Nijhoff, 1919).

10. *BSDR,* title page.

11. Heeres, *Tasman's Journal,* 15–38; Oskar Nachod, "Ein unentdecktes Goldland," *MGOA* (1900): 372–385; J. Verseput, *De reis van Matthijs Quast en Abel Jansz Tasman* (The Hague: Nijhoff, 1954).

12. W. Ph. Coolhaas, "Gegeevens over Antonio van Diemen," *BTLV* 103: 469–546.

13. Femme S. Gaastra, *Bewind en beleid bij de VOC 1672–1702* (Zutphen: De Walburgpers, 1989), tables on pp. 284–285.

14. W. Ph. Coolhaas, "De Oud-Gouverneur-Generaal Hendrick Brouwer en de Oud-Gouverneur-Generaal Pieter Nuyts over in het oosten te onderneemen ontdekkingstochten," *Bijdragen en Mededeelingen van het Historisch Genootschap* 70 (1955): 166–179.

15. P. A. Leupe, *Reize van Maerten Gerritsz Vries* (Amsterdam: Muller, 1858), 35–40.

16. Gentlemen XVII to GG and RR: 11 September 1640 (ARA VOC 316, fol. 296r).

17. Quoted in Heeres, *Tasman's Journal,* 34.

18. The *Instructions* were first published by Philip Franz Von Siebold, "Chrônique," in *Le Moniteur des Indes Orientales et Occidentales* (The Hague: Belinfante, 1849), 390–407; and later in Dutch by Leupe, *Reize,* 11–31.

19. Leupe, *Reize,* 30.

20. Ibid., 16.

21. Ibid., 17.

22. Ibid., 19.

23. Ibid., 23.

24. Ibid., 60–61.

25. Ibid., 68–69.

26. Ibid., 69.

27. Ibid., 71–72.

28. Ibid., 73.

29. Ibid., 80.

30. Hendrick Brouwer, *Journael ende historisch verhael van de reyse gedaen by oosten de Straet le Maire* (Amsterdam: Broer Jansz, 1646), 95–104.

31. C. A. Davids, *Zeewezen en wetenschap* (Dieren: De Bataafsche Leeuw, 1986), 69–85.

32. J. R. de Bruijn, F. S. Gaastra, and I. Schöffer, eds., *Dutch-Asiatic Shipping* (The Hague, Nijhoff, 1987), 2:88–89.

33. His signature is found on the sentence issued on the fluyt *De Rijp* anchored off Hirado: see NFJ 5: *Resolutien* 1641.

34. For Schaep's wife, see VOC 5274 (*Grootboeck fluijt De Roch,* fol. 1).

35. TSTK ms *Nambu Hō'iki Shiroku, Suibu ge, Kōkai hen.* I am indebted to Mr. Kawabata Hiroyuki of Yamada for drawing my attention to this manuscript.

36. Ibid., section on *Ōura.*

37. YKMK ms *Satōke monjo.* At the Yamada Municipal Archive are preserved three documents *(komonjo)* directly related to the *Breskens* affair. They are the *Satōke monjo,* the *Minatoke monjo,* and the *Uezawake monjo.* Of these, the *Minatoke monjo* is the oldest, and dates (according to the brush style used) from the first half of the eighteenth century. Next oldest is the *Satōke monjo,* dating from the late eighteenth century or early nineteenth century. The *Uezawake monjo* displays the characteristics of a brush from the Meiji period. The date of the *Breskens'* visit to Yamada is different on each document, proving that

the information in these three documents was transmitted independently from each other as well as from the documents preserved in the domain capital of Morioka. I am grateful to Mr. Satō Hitoshi of Yamada for introducing me to these documents, and to Prof. Katō Hideyuki, formerly of the Shiryōhensanjo, for his expert help in determining the different time periods of these documents.

38. YKMK ms *Satōke monjo*. The term for the knives is *"yamanata"* (lit., mountain hatchet).

39. *BSDR,* 8 November 1643.

40. YKMK ms *Uezawake monjo.*

41. Nicolaes Witsen, *Noord en Oost Tartarije* (Amsterdam: Halma, 1692). I have used the second and revised edition of 1705, 138–139.

42. Ibid., 139.

43. Hayashi and Miyazaki, eds., *Tsūkō Ichiran,* 6:325.

44. MKMK ms map *Kan'ei Morioka no zu* (Morioka during the Kan'ei Era).

45. Yoshida Yoshiaki and Oyokawa Kazuya, eds., *Morioka Yonhyakunen* (Morioka: Kyōdo bunka kenkyūkai, 1985), 1:49.

46. *NSSK,* 4:66.

47. Sawauchi Kenji, *Zoku Hanawa Tono Sama* (Miyako: the author, 1996), 21–25.

48. YKMK ms *Uezawake monjo.*

49. Ibid.

50. YKMK ms *Satōke monjo* and *Minatoke monjo.*

51. YKMK ms *Uezawake monjo.*

52. Iwate Kenritsu toshokan (Iwate Prefectural Library), ed., *Naishiryaku* (Morioka: Iwate-ken bunkazai aigo kyōkai, 1973), 1:511.

Chapter 2   GANJI GARAME

1. *Naishiryaku,* 1:511

2. *BSDR,* 29 July 1643.

3. NB ms *Kan'ei nikki:* Kan'ei 20/06/23. Quoting the diary of the Ki family: "The retainers of Yamashiro no kami had disguised themselves as fishermen and boarded the huge ship." From here, it found its way into *TJ.*

4. *Naishiryaku,* 1:511.

5. *BSDR,* 10 October 1643.

6. *Naishiryaku,* 1:512.

7. SHJ ms copy: *Ishimoda monjo.*

8. Ibid.

9. *Naishiryaku,* 1:511.

10. According to YKMK ms *Uezawake monjo:* Cape Densaku; according to Satō Rokuzō, *Ōsawa mura sonshi gaiyō* (Morioka: Ōsawa Shōgakkō, 1936), 42: off Ōsawa.

11. YKMK ms *Minatoke monjo.*

12. YKMK ms *Satōke monjo.*

13. *Naishiryaku,* 1:512.

14. *BSDR,* 29 July 1643.

15. In *Nambu hyōchakuki* (Tokyo: Kirishitan bunka kenkyūkai, 1974), 18, Nagazumi Yōko confuses "een groot edelman" (an important nobleman) with "een grote edelman" (a tall nobleman). This elementary mistake in the first sentence of the debriefing report (along with five other glaring errors in the same sentence) shows that the translator of the report was obviously not ready to tackle such a difficult text on her own.

16. *BSDR*, 29 July 1643.

17. Ibid.

18. Ibid.

19. *Naishiryaku*, 1:512.

20. J. I. Israel, "A Conflict of Empires: Spain and the Netherlands 1618–1648," *Past and Present* 76 (1977): 46.

21. Leupe, *Reize*, 19.

22. *BSDR*, 29 July 1643.

23. *Naishiryaku*, 1:512.

24. *BSDR*, 29 July 1643.

25. Ibid.

26. Ibid.

27. YKMK ms *Satōke monjo.*

28. For another example of foreign sailors as divine, see Marshall Sahlins, "The Apotheosis of Captain Cook," in *Between Belief and Transgression*, ed. Michel Izard and Pierre Smith (Chicago: University of Chicago Press, 1982); and by the same author, "Captain James Cook; or The Dying God," in his *Islands of History* (Chicago: University of Chicago Press, 1985). I am indebted to Herman Ooms for these references.

29. YKMK ms *Uezawake monjo.*

30. On *muen*, see Amino Yoshihiko, *Muen kugai raku* (Tokyo: Heibonsha, 1978), passim.

31. Amino Yoshihiko, *Shokunin uta'awase* (Tokyo: Iwanami shoten, 1992), 97–99.

32. Sahlins, "Apotheosis," 91.

33. Yamadachōshi hensan iinkai, ed., *Yamadachōshi* (Yamada: Yamadachō Kyōiku iinkai, 1986), 1:357.

34. YKMK ms *Uezawake monjo.*

35. *BSDR*, 30 July 1643.

36. 2 May 1644: GG and RR aan Jan van Elserack. Per 't schip *De Swaen* (VOC 868, fol. 215).

37. YKMK ms *Satōke monjo.*

38. In the *Satōke monjo* the date of the capture corresponds with 20 April 1631 and has to be rejected completely. If we assume that, by the time this document was copied in the early nineteenth century, worms had eaten away the horizontal stroke of the number twenty (for the correct year was Kan'ei 20) and much of the rest of the date, the two remaining vertical strokes might have resembled the character for "eight"; the copyist therefore would have substituted Kan'ei 8 (=1631) for Kan'ei 20. Pointing to this explanation is the fact that the other dates inside the document itself, which do not repeat the year, are correct if we take them as dates for Kan'ei 20, but incorrect if we take them as dates of Kan'ei 8.

39. Engelbert Kaempfer, *The History of Japan* (Glasgow: John MacLehose, 1906), 2:340–341.

40. Ibid., 341.

41. *BSDR,* 29 July 1643.

42. Vladimir M. Golovnin, *Narrative of My Captivity in Japan during the Years 1811–1813* (London: Colburn, 1818), 87.

43. *BSDR,* 29 July 1643.

44. Representative is Nagazumi's 1974 publication, *Nambu hyōchakuki* (Record of the Castaways from Nambu), but also Katō Ei'ichi's "Buresukensugō no Nambu hyōchaku to Nihongawa no tai'ō," *Nichiran gakkai kaishi* 14, no. 1 (1989): 1–20.

Chapter 3   INCOMPATIBLE JAILBIRDS

1. Regarding long noses, see SHJ ms copy of *Nabeshima Katsushige fukōho,* Kan'ei 20/05/12 (27 June 1643).

2. Quoted from SHJ ms copy *Kaibara Kuroda kafu,* Kan'ei 20/05/12 (27 June 1643).

3. The story is mainly based on the SHJ ms copy of *Kaibara Kuroda kafu,* Kan'ei 20/05/12. A similar story is told by the Dutch factor, *Daghregister,* 4 July 1643.

4. *Kaibara Kuroda kafu,* Kan'ei 20/05/12.

5. *Nabeshima Katsushige fukōho,* Kan'ei 20/05/12.

6. NB ms *Okachikata mannenki,* Kan'ei 20/05/27 (12 July 1643).

7. *TJ,* Kan'ei 20/05/27 (12 July 1643), has: "Because it was reported that, before they could land, a patrol boat had closed in on them and arrested them all, the shogun's countenance was pleased."

8. SHJ ms copy *Ōmurake oboegaki,* Kan'ei 20/05/29 (14 July 1643); SHJ ms copy *Nabeshima Katsushige fukōho,* Kan'ei 20/05/29.

9. SHJ ms copy *Kuroda Fukuoka kafu,* Kan'ei 20/05/12 (27 June 1643).

10. For the second Rubino group, see Léon Pagès, *Histoire de la religion chrétienne au Japon* (Paris: Douniol, 1869), 1:873–879; Herbert Thurston, "Japan and Christianity. IV The Mystery of the Last Five Jesuits in Japan," *The Month* (May 1905): 505–525; Anesaki Masaharu, *Kirishitan dendō no kōhai* (Tokyo: Dōbunkan, 1930), 726–736; and by the same author, "Prosecution of Christians after the Shimabara Insurrection," *MN* 1 (1938): 296–300; Gustav Voss and Hubert Cieslik, *Kirishitoki und Sayo-yōroku* (Tokyo: Sophia University, 1940), 166–189; Boxer, *The Christian Century,* 393, 395; George Elison, *Deus Destroyed* (Cambridge, Mass.: Harvard University Press, 1973), 201–203.

11. The phrase is Elison's, from *Deus Destroyed,* 185.

12. For Christovão Ferreira/Sawano Chū'an, see Elison, *Deus Destroyed,* chapter 7; and Hubert Cieslik, "The Case of Christovão Ferreira" *MN* 29, 1 (1974): 1–54.

13. Anesaki Masaharu, "A Refutation of Christianity Attributed to Christovão Ferreira, the Apostate Padre," *Proceedings of the Imperial Academy* 6, no. 2 (1930): 2.

14. *Daghregister,* 17 November 1646.

15. *Daghregister,* 17 March 1643.

16. Ibid.

17. Pagès, *Histoire,* 1:873.

18. J. F. Schütte, *Introductio ad historiam societatis Jesu in Japonia, 1549–1650* (Rome [Roma]: Institutus Historicus Societatis Jesu, 1968), 373: "P. Pedro Marques, Portugues, qui hia com patente de Provincial."

19. SHJ ms copy *Tadatoshi Sukune nikki,* Kan'ei 20/05/12.

20. *Daghregister,* 4 July 1643.

21. *Kuroda Fukuoka kafu,* Kan'ei 20/05/12.

22. *Daghregister,* 27 July 1643.

23. Boxer, *The Christian Century,* 351.

24. SHJ ms copy *Ōmurake oboegaki,* Kan'ei 20/05/12.

25. Arrival of the second Rubino group in Edo: NB ms *Kan'ei nikki,* Kan'ei 20/07/10 (24 August 1643); see also *TJ,* same day. Arrival of the men from the *Breskens, TJ,* Kan'ei 20/07/11 (25 August 1643); see also *BSDR,* 25 August 1643.

26. For a more detailed description of the adventures of the prisoners between 30 July and 25 August 1643, see my *Orandajin hobaku kara saguru kinseishi* (Yamada: Yamadachō Kyōiku iinkai, 1998), 45–83.

27. *Daghregister,* 14 January 1642.

28. Tamai Tetsuo, *Edo* (Tokyo: Heibonsha, 1986), 115.

29. Okada Hajime, ed., *Haifū Yanagidaru zenshū* (Tokyo, Sanseidō, 1977), 6:263, no. 83:60.

30. *BSDR,* 25 August 1643.

31. Ibid.

32. *KCSF,* 4:305.

33. Ibid.

34. *Daghregister,* 8–9 March 1654.

35. *KCSF,* 4:305; and Hubert Cieslik, "Das Schicksal der letzten Japanmissionare im 17. Jahrhundert," *Neue Zeitschrift für Missionswissenschaft,* 13 (1957): 129.

36. *KCSF,* 4:305.

37. *Daghregister,* 24 February 1655.

38. *Daghregister,* 2 March 1654.

39. *Tōkyō shishi kō,* ed. Tōkyō shiyakusho (Tokyo: Hakubunkan, 1912); see map of Edo, dated Shōhō 1 (1644).

40. *BSDR,* 25 August 1643.

41. On the office of the Nagasaki *bugyō,* see Lane Earns, The Development of Bureaucratic Rule (Ph.D. dissertation, University of Hawai'i, 1987).

42. *KCSF,* 2:394–395.

43. VOC 1148, fol. 409v.

44. Nagazumi Yōko, "Inoue Chikugo no kami Masashige to rangaku," *Rangaku shiryō kenkyūkai kenkyū hōkoku.* 292A (15 March 1975): 7–9.

45. Nagazumi Yōko, "Orandajin no hogosha to shite no Inoue Chikugo no kami Masashige," *Nihon rekishi.* 327 (Aug. 1975): 1–16.

46. *BSDR,* 25 August 1643.

47. He appears in *BSDR,* 12–13 August 1643.

48. *BSDR,* 26 August 1643.

49. Ibid.

50. The scene was purged, for example, from the only contemporary account of the *Breskens* affair by Arnoldus Montanus, *Gedenkwaerdige Gesantschappen* (Amsterdam: Jacob Meurs, 1669), 304. So far all Western authors dealing with the second Rubino group have based their analyses on this adulterated and biased (because violently anti-Jesuit) version.

51. *BSDR*, 5 September 1643.

52. Adachi Shirokichi, *Edo meishoki.* (Series:) *Edo sōsho* 2. (Tokyo: Edo Sōsho Kankōkai, 1917), vol. 2.

53. *BSDR*, 5 September 1643.

54. I am indebted to Hotta Masahisa (mayor of Sakura City from 1959 to 1975) for information on the Hotta family. Sakura City is the present location of the former Hotta domain of Sakura.

55. See Mitamura Engyo, *Zenshū* (Tokyo: Chūō Kōronsha, 1976), 1:53–58; Koike Tōgorō, *Kōshoku monogatari* (Tokyo: Kamakura Insatsu, 1963), 265–267; Kaionji Chōgorō, "Tokugawa Iemitsu," in *Shōgun to daimyō*, ed. Shinjo Yoshimoto (Tokyo: Sekai Bunkasha, 1967), 65.

56. *TJ*, Kan'ei 19 intercalary 09/09 (1 November 1642). A similar entry can be found in *TJ*, Kan'ei 10/05/13.

57. *KCSF*, 4:402; see also Kuroda Hideo, *Ō no shintai, ō no shōzō* (Tokyo: Heibonsha, 1993), 56–107.

58. *KCSF*, 10:412.

59. Anesaki, *Kirishitan dendō*, 726–736.

60. *BSDR*, 5 September 1643.

61. *BSDR*, 15 October 1643.

62. Anesaki, "Prosecution of Christians," 296.

63. Ichizaemon (Martin Shikimi) and Shōhaku (P. Porro) had hung in the pit together with Pedro Kasui who had defied Inoue to the end. Only when Kasui had been killed did both of the former apostatize. Afterwards, they served the bakufu for about ten years. See Hubert Cieslik, "P. Pedro Kasui (1587–1639): Der letzte japanische Jesuit der Tokugawa Zeit," *MN* 15, nos. 1/2 (1959): 81–85.

64. The shogun himself had visited his dying wet nurse, Kasuga no Tsubone, on his way to Hotta's mansion at Asakusa on 9 October 1643; see *TJ*, Kan'ei 20/08/27.

65. *BSDR*, 5 September 1643.

66. Ibid.

67. Testimony of the Franciscan Diego de Francisco Pardo, translated in Michael Cooper, *They Came to Japan*, 391–393, quoted with permission of the translator.

68. Montanus, *Gedenkwaerdige Gesantschappen*, 242b.

69. *BSDR*, 23 September 1643.

Chapter 4   A STRICT INVESTIGATION

1.See Katō Ei'ichi, "The Japanese-Dutch Trade in the Formative Period of the Seclusion Policy," *Acta Asiatica* 30 (1976): 34–84; Nagazumi Yōko, *Kinsei shoki no gaikō* (Tokyo: Sōbunsha, 1990).

2. Notes of Mrs. N. Zadoks-Josephus Jitta at ARA, *Aanwinsten 1965,* I-2, "Biographical sketch of P. A. Overtwater."

3. VOC 1148, fol. 396r.

4. *Daghregister,* 10 September 1643.

5. *Daghregister,* 7 September 1643.

6. *Daghregister,* 10 September 1643.

7. Ibid.

8. Ibid.

9. *BSDR,* 19 October 1643. For a more detailed description of this visit see my dissertation, The Prisoners from Nambu: The Breskens Affair in Historical and Historiographical Perspective (University of Hawai'i, 1992), 224–228.

10. *BSDR,* 28 September 1643.

11. Ibid.

12. Ibid.

13. Katō Ei'ichi, "Hirado Oranda shōkan no Nihonjin koyōsha ni tsuite," in *Nihon kinseishi ronsō* (Tokyo: Yoshikawa Kōbunkan, 1984), 1:230, 242–243.

14. Katagiri Kazuo, *Oranda tsūji no kenkyū* (Tokyo: Yoshikawa Kōbunkan, 1985).

15. *BSDR,* 1 October 1643.

16. Ibid.

17. *BSDR,* 9 October 1643.

18. *TJ,* Kan'ei 20/08/27 (9 October 1643).

19. *Daghregister,* 23 November 1643.

20. *BSDR,* 9 October 1643.

21. Ibid. See also Leupe, *Reize,* "Instructies," 16.

22. *BSDR,* 9 October 1643.

23. Furber, *Rival Empires,* 54.

24. *BSDR,* 9 October 1643.

25. Ibid.

26. Ibid.

27. Ibid.

28. Ibid.

29. Ibid.

30. *BSDR,* 14 October 1643.

31. SHJ ms copy *Nagasaki kokin shūran.*

32. Cape Espirito Santo: the easternmost point of the Philippines on the island of Samar.

33. *Daghregister,* 3 December 1643.

34. *BSDR,* 9 October 1643.

35. P. W. Klein, "The Trip Family in the 17th Century," *Acta Historiae Neerlandica* 1 (1966): 187–211; D. G. Nijman, "Louis de Geer (1587–1652), vader van de Zweedse industrie?" *Tijdschrift voor Geschiedenis* 104 (1991): 213–232.

36. *BSDR,* 10 October 1643.

37. Ibid.

38. *BSDR,* 20 November 1643.

39. *BSDR,* 10 October 1643.

40. The Dutch text has *pofferken* (little banger).

41. *BSDR,* 10 October 1643.

42. Elison, *Deus Destroyed,* 208.

43. Supposedly the "Japanese September" meant the ninth month of the lunar calendar. However, the twenty-eighth day of the ninth month of that year corresponds to 9 November 1643, whereas the twenty-eighth day of the eighth month would be 10 October 1643.

44. *BSDR,* 10 October 1643.

Chapter 5   UNWITTING WITNESSES

1. *BSDR,* 20 October 1643.

2. Ibid.

3. Ibid.

4. *TJ,* Kan'ei 20/09/10.

5. *BSDR,* 22 October 1643.

6. *TJ,* Kan'ei 20/08/29 (11 October 1643): "Ten bags of rice were allotted to the Nagasaki apostate Chū'an."

7. *BSDR,* 20 October 1643.

8. Ibid.

9. Ibid.

10. Most recently, Elison, *Deus Destroyed,* 201–202; and Cieslik, "The Case of Christovão Ferreira," 34–35; but both are based on the adulterated Montanus' version of the *Gedenkwaerdige Gesantschappen.*

11. Catholic historians have tried to deny or conceal the apostasy of the second Rubino group until well into this century: D. Bartoli, *Dell'Istoria della Compagnia de Giesu* (Rome [Roma]: Varese, 1660), 507–508; Cornelis Hazart, *Sot uyt de Mauw dat is Arent Montanus* (Antwerpen: Cnobbaert, 1670); F. X. Charlevoix, *Histoire de l'établissement, des progrès et de la décadence du christianisme dans l'empire du Japon* (Rouen: Behourt, 1715), 2:430; Pagès, *Histoire,* 878; L. Delplace, *Le catholicisme au Japon* (Brussels, Albert Dewit, 1910), 2:237.

12. Totman, *Politics,* 164, 207.

13. Quoted by Fujino Tamotsu, *Tokugawa bakkaku* (Tokyo: Chūō Kōronsha, 1965), 127.

14. In English a now outdated account is given by Totman, *Politics,* 207–210. More recent accounts are Yamamoto Hirofumi, *Kan'ei jidai* (Tokyo: Yoshikawa Kōbunkan, 1989): 13–30; and by the same author, *Bakuhansei no seiritsu to kinsei no kokusei* (Tokyo: Azekura Shobō, 1990); and Fujii Jōji, *Edo bakufu rōjūsei keisei katei no kenkyū* (Tokyo: Kōsō Shobō, 1990).

15. Komiya Kiyora, "Gojikki inyō nikki no kentō: Edo bakufu kirokurui no kaimei no tame ni," *Nihon rekishi* 486 (1988): 50–70.

16. *KCSF,* 2:21.

17. *Daghregister,* 25 January 1645.

18. Quoted from Montanus, *Gedenkwaerdige Gesantschappen,* 111a. For a modern treatment of the gates, see William H. Coaldrake, "Edo Architecture and Tokugawa Law," *MN* 36, no. 3 (1981): 119–138; and by the same author,

"The Gatehouse of the Shogun's Senior Councillor," *Journal of the Society of Architectural Historians* 47, no. 4 (Dec. 1988): 397–410.

19. *KCSF,* 10:413.

20. *KCSF,* 6:49.

21. On the significance of Mt. Nikkō, see Herman Ooms, *Tokugawa Ideology* (Princeton, N.J.: Princeton University Press, 1985), 57–60.

22. Toby, *State and Diplomacy,* chapters 3 and 5.

23. Th. H. Lunsingh Scheurleer, "Koperen kronen en waskaarsen voor Japan," *Oud Holland,* 93 (1979).

24. *TJ,* Kan'ei 9/12/01; *KCSF,* 2:21.

25. Kan'ei 20/11/04 (14 December 1643): *KCSF,* 4:404.

26. *KCSF,* 2:22. For a mistaken interpretation of this entry, see Totman, *Politics,* 207–208, and 306, n. 5.

27. *BSDR,* 28 October 1643.

28. *TJ,* Kan'ei 20/09/30 (11 November 1643).

29. NB ms *Okachikata mannenki,* Kan'ei 20/09/30.

30. *BSDR,* 13 November 1643.

31. *BSDR,* 19 November 1643.

32. *Daghregister,* 9 December 1643.

33. *BSDR,* 20 November 1643.

34. Ibid.

35. *Daghregister,* 24 November 1643.

36. Ibid.

37. *Daghregister,* 2 December 1643.

38. Voss and Cieslik, *Kirishitoki,* 81.

39. *Daghregister,* 18 December 1643.

40. Ibid.

41. *Daghregister,* 14 February 1644.

42. *Daghregister,* 22 May 1644.

43. Voss and Cieslik, *Kirishitoki,* 81.

44. *Daghregister,* 14 January 1645.

45. For the *kirishitan yashiki,* see *Tōkyō shishi kō, Shigaihen,* 6:167; J. M. Dixon, "The Christian Valley," *TASJ* 16 (1888): 207–214; L. Lönholm, "Arai Hakuseki und Pater Sidotti," *MGOA* 6, pt. 54 (1893): 149–189; Kawamura Tsuneki, *Shiseki kirishitan yashiki kenkyū* (Tokyo: Kyōdo Kenkyūsha, 1930); Max von Künburg, "Kirishitan yashiki, das ehemalige Christengefängnis in Koishikawa," *MN* 1 (1938): 592–596; Voss and Cieslik, *Kirishitoki,* 191–201; Bunkyō kuyakusho, ed., *Bunkyōku-shi* (Tokyo: Bunkyōku, 1968), 395–415.

46. Miwa Zennosuke, "Chikuzen to Okamoto San'emon," *Fukuoka* 44 (1914): 28–29.

47. Mito ms *Sokkyōhen,* vol. 6, quoted in Voss and Cieslik, *Kirishitoki,* 179.

48. Toby, "Reopening the Question of Sakoku," *JJS* 3, no. 2 (1977): 359–360.

49. The position of Ii Naotaka is a case in point. Officially, he still occupied the first place among the senior councilors, but he was excluded from all informal policy meetings because he had once been under suspicion for preferring Iemitsu's younger brother as shogun. The Dutch were aware of this, for they did not honor him with presents as they did the rest of the council members.

50. The first Jesuits to honestly acknowledge and try to understand the existence of the apostates in Japan were Gustav Voss and Hubert Cieslik.

Chapter 6   A MAGNANIMOUS GESTURE

1. *BSDR*, 30 November 1643.
2. *TJ*, Kan'ei 20/10/19 (30 November 1643).
3. *KCSF*, 10: 413, 351.
4. *BSDR*, 30 November 1643.
5. Leupe, *Reize*, 175.
6. *BSDR*, 8 November 1643.
7. NB ms *Tenkan nikki*, 20/10/17 (28 November 1643); *TJ*, same date.
8. Leupe, *Reize*, 210.
9. *BSDR*, 30 November 1643.
10. Ibid.
11. Ibid.
12. Ibid.
13. Ibid.
14. Ibid.
15. For example, SHJ ms copy *Hosokawakeki*: Shōhō 1/05/17 (21 June 1644).
16. *BSDR*, 1 December 1643.
17. *BSDR*, 27 November 1643.
18. *BSDR*, 2 December 1643.
19. *Daghregister*, 10 September 1643.
20. *BSDR*, 2 December 1643.
21. *Daghregister*, 2 December 1643.
22. *Daghregister*, 3 December 1643.
23. Ibid.
24. *KCSF*, 6:284.
25. *Daghregister*, 3 December 1643.
26. The fourteenth day of the twelfth month of Kan'ei 19 corresponds with 2 February 1643.
27. *Daghregister*, 3 December 1643.
28. See Nagazumi, *Kinsei shoki no gaikō*, 183.
29. *Daghregister*, 5 December 1643.
30. Ibid.
31. Ibid.
32. *BSDR*, 5 December 1643.
33. *Daghregister*, 6 December 1643.
34. Ibid.
35. Ibid.
36. François Valentijn, *Oud en Nieuw Oost-Indiën* (Dordrecht: Joannes van Braam; Amsterdam: Gerard onder de Linden, 1726), 9:103a; N. MacLeod, *De Oostindische Compagnie als zeemogendheid in Azië (1602–1650)* (Rijswijk: Blankwaardt & Schoonhoven, 1927), 306; Marius P. H. Roessingh, "The Prisoners of Nambu," *Supplement to the Bulletin of the European Association for Japanese*

Studies. History Papers Hague Conference, ed. Ian Nish, 23 (1985): 25. I am indebted to Ian Nish for providing me with a copy of this article.

37. *TJ,* Kan'ei 20/10/25 (6 December 1643).

38. NB ms *Kan'ei nikki,* Kan'ei 20/10/25.

39. *Daghregister,* 6 December 1643.

40. *BSDR,* 8 December 1643.

41. Ibid.

42. NB ms *Hitomi shiki,* Kan'ei 20/10/27. On the layout of the *ōhiroma,* see Naitō Akira, *Edozu byōbu* (Tokyo: Heibonsha, 1972), 64.

43. *Daghregister,* 8 December 1643.

44. *BSDR,* 8 December 1643.

45. *Daghregister,* 8 December 1643.

46. NB ms *Hitomi shiki,* Kan'ei 20/10/27 (8 December 1643).

Chapter 7   ELSERACK'S PROMISE

1. On the lantern, see *Daghregister* for 9, 21, 29, and 30 August 1643; 1 and 9 September 1643; 6 November 1643; 4, 6, 9, 10, 13, and 14 December 1643. See also ARA VOC 1148, fol. 73; and Lunsingh Scheurleer, "Koperen kronen," 80–85.

2. Miao-ling Tjoa, "Sakoku: The Full Range of Tokugawa Foreign Relations?" in *As the Twig is Bent,* ed. Erica de Poorter (Amsterdam: Gieben, 1990), 209–236; Toby, *State and Diplomacy,* 103.

3. *Daghregister,* 10 December 1643.

4. Asao Nobuhiro, *Sakoku* (Tokyo: Shōgakkan, 1975), 259.

5. *Daghregister,* 11 December 1643.

6. *Daghregister,* 6 January 1647.

7. *Daghregister,* 11 December 1643.

8. The Castle diaries as they have been transmitted to us today have a rather complicated and partly unknown copying history. It is possible, therefore, that the editing noticed here was done, for the same reasons, at a later time.

9. Although Tadakatsu was away in Kyoto, the *TJ* records another visit to the Sakai country mansion in Ushigome on this day: *TJ,* Kan'ei 20/10/29 (10 December 1643).

10. *Daghregister,* 17 December 1643. The Dutch translation of this document is printed in *Corpus Diplomaticum Neerlando-Indicum,* ed. J. E. Heeres (The Hague: Nijhoff, 1907), 1:419–422. The Dutch were also given a copy in Japanese (VOC 1156), printed in Kanai Madoka, *Nichiran kōshōshi no kenkyū* (Kyoto: Shibunkaku, 1986), 432–433.

11. *Daghregister,* 17 December 1643.

12. *Daghregister,* 23 December 1643.

13. NFJ 1162, fol. 4v.

14. Elserack to GG Van Diemen, 15 October 1644 (VOC 1148). Elserack was not present at the debriefing of the men from the *Breskens.* He arrived in Batavia from Taiwan on 16 January 1645; cf. VOC 1158, fol. 88v.

15. Quoted from Shiryōhensanjo, ed., *Diaries Kept by the Heads of the Dutch Factory in Japan* (Tokyo: The University Tokyo Press, 1990), 6:207.

16. Oskar Nachod, *Die Beziehungen der Niederländischen Ostindischen Kompagnie zu Japan* (Leipzig: Friese, 1897), 303.

17. Elserack to GG Van Diemen, 15 October 1644 (VOC 1148).

18. Nachod, *Beziehungen*, 305. For a thorough criticism of Nachod's understanding of the Dutch Company's bookkeeping system, see Yukutake Kazuhiro, "Deshima Oranda shōkan no kaikeichōbo," *Shakai keizai shigaku* 517, no. 6 (1992): 59–98.

19. NB ms *Hitomi shiki*, Kan'ei 20/10/27. *Daghregister*, 16 January 1648.

20. Kanai, *Nichiran kōshōshi no kenkyū*, 31, 81, 94, 334, 366.

21. *Daghregister*, 8 March 1646.

22. Later Overtwater would get the reputation of someone who "as usual is going overboard with proposals which one usually calls building castles in the sky." (GG and RR to Overtwater in Taiwan, 9 May 1647 [VOC 871, 181r].)

23. *Daghregister*, 8 January 1645.

24. *Daghregister*, 9 February 1646.

25. *Daghregister*, 12 February 1646.

26. Nagazumi, *Kinsei shoki no gaikō*, 194.

27. *KCSF*, 8:11.

28. *Daghregister*, 13 February 1646.

29. Ibid.

30. P. H. Pott, "Willem Versteegen, een extra ordinaris Raad van Indië als avonturier in India in 1659," *BTLV* 112 (1956): 367.

31. *Daghregister*, 3 December 1643.

32. *Daghregister*, 8 January 1647.

33. Ibid.

34. *Daghregister*, 22 January 1647.

35. Ibid.

36. Translated by Elison, *Deus Destroyed*, 206.

37. The ambassador had come to see if Japan would not revise its prohibition on trade with the Portuguese from Macao, now that the Portuguese crown had gained its independence from Spain. On this embassy, see Charles R. Boxer, "The Embassy of Captain Gonçalo de Siquiera de Souza," *MN* 2 (1939): 40–73.

38. *Daghregister*, 24 December 1648.

39. W. Ph. Coolhaas, *Generale Missiven van Gouverneurs Generaal en Raden aan de Heren XVII der Verenigde Oostindische Compagnie*. *RGP* no. 112 (The Hague: Nijhoff, 1964): 245.

40. *Daghregister*, 2 January 1648.

41. *Daghregister*, 16 January 1648.

42. *Daghregister*, 13 January 1650.

43. *Daghregister*, 12 July 1648.

44. GG and RR to Frederick Coijett, 14 July 1648 (VOC 872: 170).

45. Ibid.

46. Asao, *Sakoku*, 259, quoted by Toby, *State and Diplomacy*, 72.

47. On the difference between *tsūshō* and *tsūshin*, see Toby, *State and Diplomacy*, 239, 241.

48. NB ms *Kan'ei nikki*; SHJ ms copy *Kajōryaku*; SHJ ms copy *Hosokawakeki*.

49. For example, NB ms *Keian nikki*, Keian 3/03/08.

50. YKMK *Satōke monjo.*

51. YKMK *Uezawake monjo.*

52. MKMK *Namburyō sō ezu;* see also Katō Ei'ichi, "Buresukensugō no Nambu hyōchaku," 13–18. See also the cover of this book.

Chapter 8   A MEMORABLE EMBASSY

1. For the organization of the Dutch East India Company (VOC), see Pieter van Dam, *Beschryvinge, RGP* no. 63 (1927); J. K. J. de Jonge, *De opkomst van het Nederlandsch gezag in Oost Indië (1595–1610)* (The Hague: Nijhoff; Amsterdam: Muller, 1865); J. K. J. Klerk de Reus, *Geschichtlicher Überblick* (Batavia and The Hague: Nijhoff, 1894); modern accounts are in Gaastra, *De geschiedenis van de VOC;* and Noor Oosterhof, "De politieke en bestuurlijke struktuur van Vereenigde Oost-Indische Compagnie," in *De Verenigde Oostindische Compagnie in Amsterdam,* ed. F. M. Wieringa (Amsterdam: Universiteit van Amsterdam, 1982), 155–188.

2. Each year GG and RR informed the VOC management and the shareholders about the state of affairs of the Dutch East India Company in lengthy *generale missiven,* which have been published by Prof. W. Ph. Coolhaas (1960, 1964). These letters were accompanied by *particuliere missiven,* containing confidential information for use only by the Gentlemen XVII.

3. VOC 317, fol. 161v.

4. This is confirmed by the *generale missive* dated 18 January 1649 (VOC 1167), published in Coolhaas, *Generale Missiven, RGP* no. 112: 366–367.

5. Pieter van Dam, *Beschryvinge, RGP* no. 74: 380.

6. VOC 873, fols. 60–69. These *Instructies* were published, in abridged form, by Montanus, *Gedenkwaerdige Gesantschappen,* 364–368. This abridgment was translated by Nachod, *Beziehungen,* clxxiii–clxxx.

7. Ta-tuan Ch'en, "Investiture of Liu-ch'iu Kings in the Ch'ing Period," 141.

8. VOC 1176, *Journal Frisius,* 16 August 1649.

9. Ibid., 18 August 1649.

10. Ibid., 19 September 1649.

11. Ibid.

12. *Daghregister,* 19 September 1649.

13. *Resolutienboeck* NFJ 5.

14. Naturally, this famous scholar had no publications to his name. Cf. David Levyssohn, "Levensbijzonderheden van den legaat Pieter Blockhovius," *Themis* 14 (1853): 587.

15. Ta-tuan Ch'en, "Investiture of Liu-ch'iu Kings," 138–139.

16. C. C. van der Plas, "Tonkin 1644/45. Journaal van de reis van Antonio Brouckhorst," *Mededeling no. 51 van het Koninklijk Instituut voor de Tropen* (Amsterdam, 1955), 16, has remarked on Van Brouckhorst's irony.

17. Forgeries abound in the East-Asian world order, although recognition of this fact has, from its very nature, been slow in coming. For the case of Japan, see Tashiro Kazui, *Kakikaerareta kokusho;* Tashiro Kazui and Yonetani Hiroshi, "Sōke kyūzō 'tosho' to mokuin," *Chōsen gakuhō* 156 (1995): 13–96; and Yone-

tani Hiroshi, "Kinsei shoki Nitchō kankei ni okeru gaikō monjo no gisaku to kaizan," *Waseda daigaku daigaku'in bungaku kenkyūka kiyō* 41, no. 4 (1996): 1–33.

18. Coolhaas, *Generale Missiven, RGP* no. 112: 422.

19. VOC 873, fol. 76v.

20. On Caron, see F. W. Stapel, "François Caron," *De Indische Gids* 55 (1933): 385–403; Charles R. Boxer, *A True Description of Japan* (London: Argonaut Press, 1935), xv–cxx.

21. For a description of similar Korean processions throughout Japan, see Ronald P. Toby, "Carnival of the Aliens, Korean Embassies in Edo Period Art and Popular Culture," *MN* 41, no. 4 (1986): 415–456.

22. Katō Ei'ichi, "Sakoku to bakuhansei kokka," in *Sakoku,* ed. Katō Ei'ichi and Yamada Tadao (Tokyo: Yūhikaku, 1981): 86–87, and note 44 on pp. 113–114 where the author cites the Japanese reasoning as noted by Sūden in his *Ikoku nikki.*

23. Nagazumi, *Kinsei shoki no gaikō,* 114–125.

24. *Daghregister,* 20 September 1649.

25. Oloff Erichszon Willman, "Reesa till Ostindien," in *Een kort Beskriffning uppa Trenne Reesor* (Witsindzborg: Hans Hoeg, 1674), 181.

26. See for example GG and RR to Frederick Coijett, 14 July 1648 (VOC 872, fol. 170–171).

27. *Journal Frisius,* 20 September 1649.

28. *Daghregister,* 20 September 1649.

29. *Journal Frisius,* 20 September 1649.

30. *Daghregister,* 21 September 1649.

31. Ibid.

32. NFJ 1168.

33. In contrast to Montanus' imaginary (no source given) funeral of the ambassador in Japan, cf. Montanus, *Gedenkwaerdige Gesantschappen,* 44b.

34. *Daghregister,* 26 September 1649.

35. For the Western literature on these embassies-for-trade in East Asia, see Matteo Ricci, *China in the Sixteenth Century,* trans. from the Latin by Louis J. Gallagher (New York, Random House, 1953), 515; Henry Serruys, *Sino-Mongol Relations during the Ming II: The Tribute System and Diplomatic Missions (1400–1600)* (Brussels: Institut Belge des Hautes Études Chinoises, 1967), 117–118; Fairbank, *The Chinese World Order,* 83.

36. Sakai, "The Satsuma-Ryukyu Trade," 393.

37. *Journal Frisius,* 16 November 1649.

38. Ibid.

39. Ibid.

40. Ibid.

41. *Journal Frisius,* 25 November 1649.

42. I have not been able to trace the names of all the men participating in this embassy. Future research may expand the following list: Andries Frisius, Anthonie van Brouckhorst, Wilhem Bijlvelt, Willem Thijmonsz, Johan Oetgens, Cornelis May, Johan Bocheljon, Dirck Meulenaar, Johan Schedler, Caspar Schamberger, Johan Schmidt, Jacob Jansz Blauduijff, Jan Hakkius.

43. Cf. *Instructies* (VOC 873, fol. 66).

44. *Journal Frisius,* 31 December 1649.

45. Wolfgang Michel, "Caspar Schambergers Reisen nach Edo," *Dokufutsu bungaku kenkyū* 42 (1992): 34–47.

46. There is a third diary that was used by Montanus, *Gedenkwaerdige Gesantschappen;* see my "Memorable Embassies," forthcoming a.

47. Part of the *Edo bakufu nikki* series: NB ms *Keian nikki, Ryūeiroku* copy.

48. NB ms *Hitomi shiki,* Keian 2/12/24.

49. Ibid., Keian 2/12/29.

50. NB ms *Keian nikki, Ryūeiroku* copy, Keian 3/01/08; NB ms *Hitomi shiki,* same date.

51. NB ms *Keian nikki, Ryūeiroku* copy, Keian 3/01/11.

52. NB ms *Koian nikki, Ryūeiroku* copy, Keian 3/01/14.

53. NB ms *Hitomi shiki,* Keian 3/01/19.

54. NB ms *Keian nikki, Ryūeiroku* copy, Keian 3/02/17.

55. NB ms *Keian nikki, Ryūeiroku* copy, Keian 3/03/03; NB ms *Hitomi shiki,* Keian 3/03/01 and 3/03/03.

56. NB ms *Hitomi shiki,* Keian 3/03/07.

57. *Journal Frisius,* 2 February 1650.

58. NB ms *Keian nikki, Ryūeiroku* copy, Keian 3/03/11; NB ms *Hitomi shiki,* same date.

59. *Journal Frisius,* 31 January 1650.

60. *Journal Frisius,* 2 February 1650.

61. NB ms *Keian nikki,* Keian 3/03/07.

62. In the nineteenth century when *Tsūkō Ichiran* (Japanese Diplomacy at a Glance) was compiled, editors Hayashi and Miyazaki took the liberty of substituting *Oranda koku'ō* (King of Holland) for *Oranda yakata. Koku'ō,* of course, was the proper term for a "vassal king" (Hayashi Akira and Miyazaki Shigemi, eds., *Tsūkō Ichiran* [Osaka: Seibundō, 1967], 6:328.

63. *Journal Frisius,* 7 April 1650.

64. NB ms *Keian nikki,* Keian 3/03/07.

65. *TJ,* Keian 3/03/07.

66. See the chapter, "Mumia nativa," in Engelbert Kaempfer, *Amoenitatum exoticarum politico-physico-medicarum fasciculi V.* (Lemgo: Heinrich Wilhelm Meyer, 1712).

67. *Journal Frisius,* 7 April 1650.

68. NB ms *Keian nikki,* Keian 3/03/07.

69. NB ms *Keian nikki,* Keian 3/03/07. Dressed in blue: *Daghregister,* 7 April 1650.

70. *Journal Frisius,* 7 April 1650.

71. NB ms *Keian nikki,* Keian 3/03/07.

72. Ibid.

73. NB ms *Keian nikki,* Keian 3/03/08.

74. *Journal Frisius,* 8 April 1650.

75. NB ms *Keian nikki,* Keian 3/03/08.

76. Ibid.

77. *Journal Frisius,* 8 April 1650.

78. Ibid.

79. Ibid.

80. *Daghregister,* 22 January 1650.

81. *Daghregister,* 26 January 1650.

82. VOC 1183, fols. 413–414.

83. For a more detailed description of this cultural mission, see my *Oranda-jin hobaku kara saguru kinseishi,* 286–298.

84. NFJ 283, 7 June 1650.

85. SHJ ms copy *Keian nikki,* Keian 3/08/06 (1 September 1650). SHJ ms copy *Shichō nichiroku,* same date.

86. Wolfgang Michel, "Deshima rankan'i Kasuparu Shamuberugeru no shōgai ni tsuite," *Nihon Ishigaku zasshi* 36, no. 3 (1990): 201–210; Frits Vos, "From God to Apostate: Medicine in Japan before the Caspar School," in *Red-Hair Medicine,* ed. H. Beukers, A. M. Luyendijk-Elshout, M. D. van Opstall, and F. Vos (Amsterdam: Rodopi, 1991), 9–26.

87. Cf. *Kokusho Sōmokuroku* (Tokyo: Iwanami shoten, 1972), under *Kasuparu* and *Oranda Kasuparu.*

88. Sōda Hajime, "Rankan'i Kasuparu saikō," *Rangaku shiryō kenkyū hōkoku* 188 (1966): 193–199; 196 (1967): 183–185; and by the same author, *Zusetsu Nihon iryō bunkashi* (Kyoto: Shibunkaku, 1989).

89. *Daghregister,* 14 November 1650.

CONCLUSION

1. Quoted (with some adaptations) from W. G. Aston, *Nihongi* (Rutland, Vt., and Tokyo: Tuttle, 1972), 2:137.

2. Ryūsaku Tsunoda and L. Carrington Goodrich, *Japan in the Chinese Dynastic Histories* (South Pasadena: Perkins, 1951), 32.

3. Ibid.

4. Jurgis Elisonas, "The Inseparable Trinity: Japan's Relations with China and Korea" *Cambridge History of Japan,* 4:283.

5. Tashiro, *Kakikaerareta kokusho.*

6. Tashiro, "Foreign Relations," 306.

7. Tashiro and Yonetani, "Sōke kyūzō 'tosho' to mokuin."

8. Kenneth Robinson, "The Jiubian and Ezogachishima Embassies to Choson, 1478–1482," *Chōsenshi kenkyūkai ronbunshū* 35 (1997): 55–86.

9. Embassies from the Ō'uchi and the Hosokawa fought at Ningpo in 1523; see Wang Yi-t'ung, *Official Relations between China and Japan* (Cambridge, Mass.: Harvard University Press, 1953), 76–77.

10. The phrase is from Gregory Smits, "The Sages' Scale: Nakae Tōjū and Situational Weighing," *TASJ,* 4th series, 6 (1991): 4.

11. Ta-tuan Ch'en, "Investiture of Liu-ch'iu Kings," 159.

12. Gregory Smits, "The Intersection of Politics and Thought in Ryukyuan Confucianism: Sai On's Uses of Quan," *HJAS* 56 no. 2 (1996): 454–455.

13. In *Cherishing Men from Afar* (29–41), James Hevia has presented the latest elaboration of the Chinese diplomatic tradition as it was practiced under

the Qing. Hevia goes out of his way to give the Manchu point of view, which (he asserts, but does not make entirely clear how) differs from the Chinese.

14. Arano Yoshinori, "Taikun gaikō taisei no kakuritsu," in *Sakoku*, ed. Katō Ei'ichi and Yamada Tadao (Tokyo: Yūhikaku, 1981), 117–221.

15. This point was already made forcefully by Tashiro Kazui when she reviewed Toby's book in *JJS* (13, no. 1 [1987]: 196): "his argument frequently tends to be that of *tatemae,* or principle, and not of substance," and again on page 199: "When one engages in analysis relying on *tatemae,* as Toby does, one is apt to neglect all that occurred outside formal channels and laws, and to conclude that all was determined by the will of the state and that all actions were taken as indicated by the evidence gathered examining the *tatemae.* One should at no time forget that in the Tokugawa period, *tatemae* and *honne* (i. e., true motive) were used skillfully in adroit juxtaposition." The handling of the *Breskens* affair is an excellent example of such skillful use and adroit juxtaposition of reality and make-believe.

16. Tsuruta Kei, "Kinsei Nihon no yotsu no 'kuchi'," in *Ajia no naka no Nihonshi,* vol. 2, *Gaikō to sensō,* ed. Arano Yoshinori, Ishii Masatoshi, and Murai Shōsuke (Tokyo: Tōkyō Daigaku Shuppankai, 1992), 300.

17. The idea of Tsushima as a *buffer* between the bakufu and Korea is also found in Tashiro's review of Toby's book (*JJS* 13, no. 1: 197).

18. Toby, *State and Diplomacy,* 161–166.

19. Matsura Seizan, quoted in Toby, "Carnival of the Aliens," 416.

20. Toby neglects, however, to give references to any serious study advocating this point of view, which is repeatedly attacked throughout his book.

21. One sometimes gets the impression that the whole discussion is about nothing more substantial than the use of the term *sakoku.* As has long been known, this word (written with the characters for "chains" and "country," suggesting the idea of being "behind lock and key") was a neologism coined in the early nineteenth century by the interpreter Shizuki Tadao, who needed it to translate the title of a Dutch version of Kaempfer's essay, known in English as "An Enquiry, whether it be conducive for the good of the Japanese *empire, to keep it shut up,* as it now is, and not suffer its inhabitants to have any Commerce with foreign nations, either at home or abroad" (Kaempfer, 1906, 3:301–336; italics mine). It was the historiographers of the Meiji period, wanting to stress the accomplishment of their contemporaries in having successfully changed the country's policy of isolation and "opened" it to foreign intercourse, who felt the need to rewrite the whole history of Japan up to 1868. They started to use *sakoku* for the seventeenth and eighteenth centuries as a counterpart to *kaikoku* (the "open country") for their own time. *Sakoku* then became part of a neat and easily remembered periodization, which fitted it in between *sengoku* (the "country at war") of the fifteenth and sixteenth centuries and *kaikoku* of the nineteenth century. Following Toby, some Japanese historians now want to abandon *sakoku* together with the idea that Japan was isolated (see Nagazumi Yōko, '*Sakoku' wo minaosu* [Tokyo: Yamakawa Shuppansha, 1999]). Others, such as Arano, want to replace it with the term *kaikin* (i.e., "prohibition on overseas travel"). For Western historians, there is no need to be strict in following these fashions of Japanese historiography.

22. This is called *"bui"* (martial splendor) by Japanese historians of the recently emerging neo-nationalist type, i.e., Arano Yoshinori (*Kinsei Nihon to Higashi Ajia* [Tokyo, Tōkyō Daigaku Shuppankai, 1988], 57); Yamamoto (*Sakoku to kaikin no jidai,* 178–212); and other graduates of the history department of Tokyo University.

23. The true toll of the Christian persecutions is extremely hard to measure. Clearly, Boxer's figure of 2,128 martyrs is too low (*The Christian Century,* 448). Elison quotes Laures' figure of 4,045 ("Die Zahl der Christen und Martyrer im alten Japan," *MN* 7, no. 1/2 [1951]: 84–101), and then comments that "Laures' scrupulous calculations . . . do not yet exhaust the sources" (*Deus Destroyed,* 397). I follow here Juan Ruiz-de-Medina (*El martirologio del Japon 1558–1873* [Roma: Institutum Historicum S. I., 1999], 253, 740), who counts 20,000 of the 37,000 executed after the fall of Hara castle (Shimabara) in April 1638 as Christian martyrs.

24. Elison, *Deus Destroyed,* 208, compares Inoue Chikugo no kami Masashige with Adolf Eichman.

25. Toby, "Reopening the Question of Sakoku," 359.

26. Donald Keene, *The Japanese Discovery of Europe, 1720–1830* (Stanford: Stanford University Press, 1969), 31–58.

27. Timon Screech, *The Western Scientific Gaze* (New York: Cambridge University Press, 1996).

Bibliography

MANUSCRIPTS IN DUTCH

Archief van de Nederlandse Factorij Japan (Archive of the Dutch Factory in
Japan) at ARA and at SHJ

Archief van het Provenhuis van Geertruid Bijlevelt (Archive of the Poorhouse
Established by Geertruid Bijlevelt, 1664) preserved at the Alkmaar Municipal Archive

*Journael of te Dach Register Geannoteert, ende Beschreven door den Opper-
stierman Cornelis Jansz Coen, Varende op't Fluijtschip Castricom* [. . . .] at
Leiden University Library *Westerse handschriften* BPL 2251

Overgekomen Brieven en Papieren (Letters and Documents Received from the
Indies) at ARA VOC and at SHJ

The records of the VOC at ARA I have quoted as follows:

1. All documents from the Deshima archive as NFJ + number, in which the
   numbers correspond with those in Marius Roessingh's *The Archive of
   the Dutch Factory in Japan* (The Hague: ARA, 1964). The one exception to this rule is the factory diary or *Daghregister* of which I give only
   the date of the entry quoted.
2. All documents from the section *Overgekomen brieven en papieren*, as
   well as other sections of the VOC archive at ARA, as VOC + number,
   where the numbers are those currently in use at ARA. There are copies
   of the *Daghregister* in this section as well. The exception here is Bijlvelt's
   debriefing report (VOC 1148) of which I give the date of the entry
   quoted.

MANUSCRIPTS IN JAPANESE

Edo bakufu nikki (Daily records of the Edo bakufu):

Kan'ei nikki (Daily records of the Kan'ei period) at NB
Keian nikki (Daily records of the Keian period) at NB
Keian nikki zōbu (Daily records of the Keian period, enlarged) at NB
Keian nikki, Ryūeiroku (Daily Records of the Keian period, *Ryūeiroku*
  copy) at NB
Shōhō jitsuroku (Veritable records of the Shōhō period) at SHJ
Tenkan nikki (Daily records of the Tenna and Kan'ei periods) at NB

Hitomi shiki (Private records of the Hitomi family) at NB
Hokkaitō hakki (A record of ships near the islands of the Northern Sea, by
  Matsumoto Tanechika) at Tokyo University Library
Hosokawakeki (Records of the Hosokawa family) at SHJ
Ishimoda monjo (Documents preserved in the Ishimoda family) at SHJ
Kaibara Kuroda kafu (A genealogy of the Kaibara Kuroda family) at SHJ
Kajōryaku (Compilation of the Mito domain) at SHJ
Kokuto dainenpu (Great Annals of Country Government) at MKMK
Kuroda Fukuoka kafu (A genealogy of the Kuroda family) at SHJ
Minatoke monjo (Document preserved in the Minato family) at YKMK
Nabeshima Katsushige fukōho (Revised Annals of Nabeshima Katsushige)
  at SHJ
Nagasaki kokinshūran (Old and New Collected and Seen in Nagasaki) at SHJ
Nambu hō'iki shiroku (Historical documents relating to the Nambu fief) at
  Tōno Municipal Library
Nambuke kiroku (Records of the Nambu family, also called: *Gotōke Gokiroku*)
  at MKMK
Okachikata mannenki (Eternal records of the Castle Police) at NB
Ōmurake oboegaki (Memorandum preserved in the Ōmura family) at SHJ
Satōke monjo (Document preserved in the Satō family) at YKMK
Shichō nichiroku (Daily record of Things Seen and Heard) at SHJ
Tadatoshi Sukune nikki (Diary of Ozuki Tadatoshi) at SHJ
Tokuen kakun (House Precepts by Master Tokuen) at MKMK
Uezawake monjo (Document preserved in the Uezawa family) at YKMK

PUBLISHED SOURCES

Adachi Shirokichi. *Edo meishoki*. [Series:] *Edo sōsho 2*. Tokyo: Edo Sōsho Kan-
  kōkai, 1917.
Akkeshi chōshi hensan iinkai, eds. *Akkeshi chōshi*. Sapporo: Toppan Insatsu,
  1975.
Amino Yoshihiko. *Muen, kugai, raku: Nihon chūsei no jiyū to heiwa*. Tokyo:
  Heibonsha sensho 58, 1978.
———. *Shokunin uta'awase*. Tokyo: Iwanami shoten, 1992.
Anesaki Masaharu. *Kirishitan dendō no kōhai*. Tokyo: Dōbunkan, 1930.

———. "A Refutation of Christianity Attributed to Christovão Ferreira, the Apostate Padre." *Proceedings of the Imperial Academy* [of Japan] 6, no. 2 (1930a): 2.

———. "Prosecution of Kirishitans after the Shimabara Insurrection." *Monumenta Nipponica* 1 (1938): 293–300.

Arano Yoshinori. "Bakuhansei kokka to gaikō." *Rekishigaku kenkyū 1978 nendo taikai hōkoku tokushūgō* (November 1978): 95–105.

———. "Taikun gaikō taisei no kakuritsu." In *Sakoku*, edited by Katō Ei'ichi and Yamada Tadao, 117–221. Tokyo: Yūhikaku, 1981.

———. *Kinsei Nihon to Higashi Ajia.* Tokyo: Tōkyō Daigaku Shuppankai, 1988.

———. "Kaikin to sakoku." In *Ajia no naka no Nihonshi*, vol. 2, *Gaikō to sensō*, edited by Arano Yoshinori, Ishii Masatoshi, and Murai Shōsuke, 191–222. Tokyo: Tōkyō Daigaku Shuppankai, 1992.

Asao Nobuhiro. *Sakoku.* Tokyo: Shōgakkan, 1975.

Aston, William G. *Nihongi: Chronicles of Japan from the Earliest Times until AD 697.* Rutland, Vt., and Tokyo: Tuttle, 1972.

Bartoli, D. *Dell'Istoria della Compagnia de Giesu. Il Giappone Seconda Parte dell'Asia.* Rome (Roma): Varese, 1660.

Berry, Mary E. *Hideyoshi.* Cambridge, Mass.: Harvard University Press, 1982.

Bolitho, Harold. *Treasures among Men: The Fudai Daimyo in Tokugawa Japan.* New Haven: Yale University Press, 1974.

Boot, Willem Jan. "The Death of a Shogun: Deification in Early Modern Japan." In *Shinto in History: Ways of the Kami*, edited by John Breen and Mark Teeuwen, 144–166. London: Curzon, 2000.

Boxer, Charles Ralph: "Embaixada de Macau ao Japão em 1640." *Anais do Club Militar Naval* 57, nos. 9 and 10 (1933).

———. *A True Description of Japan by François Caron and Joost Schouten.* London: Argonaut Press, 1935.

———. "The Embassy of Captain Gonçalo de Siquiera de Souza to Japan in 1644–1647." *Monumenta Nipponica* 2 (1939): 40–73.

———. *Jan Compagnie in Japan, 1600–1850.* The Hague: Nijhoff, 1950.

———. *The Great Ship from Amacon. Annals of Macao and the Old Japan Trade 1550–1640.* Lisboa: Centro de Estudos Historicos Ultramarinos, 1959.

———. *The Dutch Seaborne Empire.* New York: Knopf, 1965.

———. *The Christian Century in Japan 1549–1650.* Berkeley and London: University of California Press, 1967.

———. *The Portuguese Seaborne Empire.* New York: Knopf, 1969.

Brouwer, Hendrick. *Journael ende historisch verhael van de reyse gedaen by oosten de Straet le Maire naer de custen van Chili onder het beleyt van den heer generael Hendrick Brouwer in den jare 1643 voorgevallen. . . . Alsmede een beschryvinghe van het Eylandt Eso, ghelegen ontrent dertigh Mylen van het machtigh Rijcke van Japan, op de hooghte van 39 graden, 49 minuten, Noorder breete; soo als eerst in't selvige jaer door het schip Castricom bezeylt is.* Amsterdam: Broer Jansz, 1646.

Brownlee, John S. *Political Thought in Japanese Historical Writing. From Kojiki (712) to Tokushi Yoron.* Waterloo, Ontario: Wilfrid Laurier University Press, 1991.

Bunkyō kuyakusho, ed. *Bunkyōku-shi*. Tokyo: Bunkyō kuyakusho, 1968.

Bruijn, J. R., F. S. Gaastra, and I. Schöffer. *Dutch-Asiatic Shipping in the 17th and 18th centuries*. Rijks Geschiedkundige Publicatiën nos. 165–167, 3 vols. The Hague: Nijhoff, 1987.

Cardim, A. F. *Batalhas da Companhia de Jesus na sua gloriosa Provincia do Japão*. Lisboa: Imprensa Nacional, 1849.

Charlevoix, F. X. *Histoire de l'établissement, des progrès et de la décadence du christianisme dans l'empire du Japon*. Rouen: Behourt, 1715.

Chassigneux, Edmond. "Rica de Oro et Rica de Plata." *T'oung Pao* 30 (1930): 37–84.

Ch'en, Ta-tuan. "Investiture of Liu-ch'iu Kings in the Ch'ing Period." In *The Chinese World Order*, edited by John K. Fairbank, 135–164. Cambridge, Mass.: Harvard University Press, 1968.

Cieslik, Hubert. "Das Schicksal der letzten Japanmissionare im 17. Jahrhundert." *Neue Zeitschrift für Missionswissenschaft* 13 (1957): 119–138.

———. "P. Pedro Kasui (1587–1639). Der letzte japanische Jesuit der Tokugawa Zeit." *Monumenta Nipponica* 15, no. 1.2 (1959): 35–66.

———. "The Case of Christovão Ferreira." *Monumenta Nipponica* 29, no. 1 (1974): 1–54.

Coaldrake, William H. "Edo Architecture and Tokugawa Law." *Monumenta Nipponica* 36, no. 3 (1981): 119–138.

———. "The Gatehouse of the Shogun's Senior Councillor: Building Design and Status Symbolism in Japanese Architecture of the Late Edo Period." *Journal of the Society of Architectural Historians* 47, no. 4 (1988): 397–410.

Colenbrander, H. T, ed. *Dagh-Register gehouden int Casteel Batavia vant passerende daer ter plaetse als over geheel Nederlandts-India. Anno 1643–1644*. The Hague: Nijhoff, 1902.

Coolhaas, W. Ph. "Gegeevens over Antonio van Diemen." *Bijdragen tot de Taal-, Land-, en Volkenkunde van Nederlands Indië* 103 (1946): 469–546.

———. "De Oud-Gouverneur-Generaal Hendrick Brouwer en de Oud-Gouverneur-Generaal Pieter Nuyts over in het oosten te onderneemen ontdekkingstochten." *Bijdragen en Mededelingen van het Historisch Genootschap* [Utrecht] 70 (1955): 166–179.

———. *Generale Missiven van Gouverneurs Generaal en Raden aan de Heren XVII der Verenigde Oostindische Compagnie*. Rijks Geschiedkundige Publicatiën nos. 104, 112. The Hague: Nijhoff, 1960, 1964.

Cooper, Michael. *They Came to Japan: An Anthology of European Reports on Japan 1543–1640*. Berkeley and Los Angeles: University of California Press, 1965.

Dam, Pieter van. *Beschryvinge van de Oostindische Compagnie*. Edited by F. W. Stapel and W. Th. van Boetzelaer. Rijks Geschiedkundige Publicatiën nos. 63, 68, 74, 76, 83, 87, and 96. The Hague: Nijhoff, 1927–1954.

Davids, C. A. *Zeewezen en wetenschap: de wetenschap en de ontwikkeling van de navigatie techniek in Nederland tussen 1585 en 1815*. Dieren: De Bataafsche Leeuw, 1986.

Delplace, L. *Le catholicisme au Japon. L'ère des martyrs 1593–1660*. Brussels: Albert Dewit, 1910.

Dixon, J. M. "The Christian Valley." *Transactions of the Asiatic Society of Japan* 16 (1888): 207–214.

Duyvendak, J. J. L. "The Last Dutch Embassy to the Chinese Court (1794–1795)." *T'oung Pao* 34, 1–2 (1939): 1–116.

Earns, Lane R. *The Development of Bureaucratic Rule in Early Modern Japan: The Nagasaki Bugyō in the Seventeenth Century.* Ph.D. dissertation, University of Hawai'i at Mānoa, 1987.

Elison, George. *Deus Destroyed: The Image of Christianity in Early Modern Japan.* Cambridge, Mass.: Harvard University Press, 1973.

Elisonas, Jurgis. "The Inseparable Trinity: Japan's Relations with China and Korea." In *The Cambridge History of Japan*, vol. 4, edited by John W. Hall, 235–300. Cambridge: Cambridge University Press, 1991.

Fairbank, John K., ed. *The Chinese World Order: Traditional China's Foreign Relations.* Cambridge, Mass.: Harvard University Press, 1968.

Fairbank, John K., and S. Y. Teng. "On the Ch'ing Tributary System." *Harvard Journal of Asiatic Studies* 6 (1941): 135–246.

Fu Lo-shu. *A Documentary Chronicle of Sino-Western Relations (1644–1820).* 2 vols. Tucson: University of Arizona Press, 1966.

Fujii Jōji. *Edo bakufu rōjūsei keisei katei no kenkyū.* Tokyo: Kōsō Shobō, 1990.

———. *Tokugawa Iemitsu.* Jinbutsu Sōsho, no. 213. Tokyo: Yoshikawa Kōbunkan, 1997.

———, ed. *Nihon no kinsei*, vol. 3: *Shihai no shikumi.* Tokyo: Chūō Kōronsha, 1991.

Fujino Tamotsu. *Tokugawa bakkaku.* Tokyo: Chū'ō Kōronsha, 1965.

Furber, Holden. *Rival Empires of Trade in the Orient 1600–1800.* Minneapolis: University of Minnesota Press, 1976.

Gaastra, Femme S. *De geschiedenis van de VOC.* Haarlem: Fibula-Van Dishoek; Antwerpen: Standaard Uitgeverij, 1982.

———. *Bewind en beleid bij de VOC 1672–1702.* [Zutphen]: De Walburgpers, 1989.

Geerts, A. J. C. "The Arima Rebellion and the Conduct of Koeckebacker." *Transactions of the Asiatic Society of Japan* 11, no. 1 (1883): 51–116.

Gerhart, Karen M. *The Eyes of Power: Art and Early Tokugawa Authority.* Honolulu: University of Hawai'i Press, 1999.

Golovnin, Vladimir M. *Narrative of My Captivity in Japan during the Years 1811–1813.* London: Colburn, 1818.

Hayashi Akira and Miyazaki Shigemi, eds. *Tsūkō Ichiran.* Edited by Kokusho Kankōkai. 8 vols. Osaka: Seibundō, 1967.

Hazart, Cornelis. *Sot uyt de Mauw dat is Arent Montanus.* Antwerpen: Michiel Cnobbaert, 1670.

Heeres, J. E., ed. *Abel Janszoon Tasman's Journal of His Discovery of Van Diemen's Land and New Zealand in 1642.* Amsterdam: F. Muller, 1898.

———. *Corpus Diplomaticum Neerlando-Indicum.* The Hague: Nijhoff, 1907.

Hesselink, Reinier H. "333 Years of Dutch Publications on Japan." In *Nihon yōgakushi no kenkyū*, vol. 9, edited by Arisaka Takamichi, 1–40. Osaka: Sōgensha, 1989.

————. "Karuwanshugi shisōka: Arunorudosu Montanusu to sono gyōseki" (A Calvinist Ideologist: Arnoldus Montanus and His Work). In *Nihon yōgakushi no kenkyū,* vol. 10, edited by T. Arisaka, 1–23. Osaka: Sōgensha, 1991.

————. The Prisoners from Nambu: The Breskens Affair in Historical and Historiographical Perspective. Ph.D. dissertation, University of Hawai'i at Mānoa, 1992.

————. "Eruserakku no yakusoku." *Nihon rekishi 547* (1993): 41–58.

————. *Orandajin hobaku kara saguru kinseishi.* Yamada (Iwate Prefecture): Kyōiku iinkai, 1998.

————. "Memorable Embassies: The Secret History of Arnoldus Montanus' *Atlas Japannensis.*" Zutphen: Walburgpers, 2000.

————. *De gevangenen uit Nambu: een waar geschiedverhaal over de VOC in Japan.* Forthcoming b.

Hesselink, Reinier H., and Matsui Yōko. "Sakoku or Japan 'Closed off' from the Outside World. A New Stage: The Second Half of the Seventeenth Century." In *Bridging the Divide: 400 Years The Netherlands—Japan,* edited by Leonard Blussé, Willem Remmelink, and Ivo Smits, 33–53. Hotei Publishing and Teleac, 2000.

Hevia, James L. *Cherishing Men from Afar: Qing Guest Ritual and the Macartney Embassy of 1793.* Durham and London: Duke University Press, 1995.

Hirano Saburō. *Tokugawa Iemitsu kōden.* Nikkō: Tōshōgū, 1961.

Hullu, J. de, ed. *Dagh-Register gehouden int Casteel Batavia vant passerende daer ter plaetse als over geheel Nederlandts-India Anno 1644–1645.* The Hague: Nijhoff, 1903.

Israel, J. I. "A Conflict of Empires: Spain and the Netherlands 1618–1648." *Past and Present 76* (1977): 34–74.

Itazawa Takeo. "Ransen Buresukensugō no Nambu nyūkō." *Nihon rekishi 68* (1954): 27–29.

Iwao Seiichi. *Sakoku.* Tokyo: Chūō Kōronsha, 1966.

Iwate Kenritsu toshokan (Iwate Prefectural Library), ed. *Naishiryaku.* Morioka: Iwate-ken bunkazai aigo kyōkai, 1973.

Jonge, J. K. J. de. *De opkomst van het Nederlandsch gezag in Oost-indië (1595–1610).* The Hague: Nijhoff; Amsterdam: Muller, 1865.

Kaempfer, Engelbert. *Amoenitatum exoticarum politico-physico-medicarum fasciculi V.* Lemgo: Heinrich Wilhelm Meyer, 1712.

————. *The History of Japan.* Translated by J. G. Scheuchzer. 3 vols. Glasgow: James MacLehose, 1906.

————. *Kaempfer's Japan: Tokugawa Culture Observed.* Translated by Beatrice Bodart-Bailey. Honolulu: University of Hawai'i Press, 1999.

Kaionji Chōgorō. "Tokugawa Iemitsu." In *Shōgun to daimyō,* edited by Yoshimoto Shinjo, 61–73. Nihon rekishi shiriizu 12. Tokyo: Sekai Bunkasha, 1967.

Kanai Madoka. *Nichiran kōshōshi no kenkyū.* Kyoto: Shibunkaku, 1986.

Katagiri Kazuo. *Oranda tsūji no kenkyū.* Tokyo: Yoshikawa Kōbunkan, 1985.

Katō Ei'ichi. "The Japanese-Dutch Trade in the Formative Period of the Seclusion Policy: Particularly on the Raw Silk Trade by the Dutch Factory at Hirado 1620–1640." *Acta Asiatica 30* (1976): 34–84.

———. "Sakoku to bakuhansei kokka." In *Sakoku,* edited by Katō Ei'ichi and Yamada Tadao, 54–115. Tokyo: Yūhikaku, 1981.

———. "Hirado Oranda shōkan no Nihonjin koyōsha ni tsuite." *Nihon kinseishi ronsō* 1: 215–264. Tokyo: Yoshikawa Kōbunkan, 1984.

———. "Buresukensugō no Nambu hyōchaku to Nihongawa no tai'ō." *Nichiran gakkai kaishi* 14, no. 1 (1989): 1–20.

———. *Bakuhansei kokka no keisei to gaikoku bō'eki.* Tokyo: Azekura Shobō, 1993.

Kawamura Tsuneki. *Shiseki kirishitan yashiki kenkyū.* Tokyo: Kyōdo Kenkyūsha, 1930.

Keene, Donald. *The Japanese Discovery of Europe, 1720–1830.* Stanford: Stanford University Press, 1969.

Kimura Naoki. "17 seiki nakaba bakuhansei kokka to ikokusen taisaku." *Shigaku zasshi* 29, no. 2 (2000): 55–77.

Klein, P. W. "The Trip Family in the 17th Century: A Study of the Behavior of the Entrepreneur on the Dutch Staple Market." *Acta Historiae Neerlandica* 1 (1966): 187–211.

Klerk de Reus, J. K. J. *Geschichtlicher Überblick der administrativen, rechtlichen, und finanziellen Entwicklung der Niederländisch-Ostindischen Compagnie.* Batavia and The Hague: Nijhoff, 1894.

Koike Tōgorō. *Kōshoku monogatari.* Tokyo: Kamakura Insatsu, 1963.

Kokusho Sōmokuroku. Tokyo: Iwanami shoten, 1972.

Komiya Kiyora. "Gojikki inyō nikki no kentō: Edo bakufu kirokurui no kaimei no tame ni." *Nihon rekishi* 486 (1988): 50–70.

Künburg, Max von. "Kirishitan yashiki, das ehemalige Christengefängnis in Koishikawa." *Monumenta Nipponica* 1 (1938): 592–596.

Kuroda Hideo. *Ō no shintai, ō no shōzō.* Tokyo: Heibonsha, 1993.

Kuroita Katsumi, ed. *Tokugawa jikki.* Kokushi taikei, vols. 38–41. Tokyo: Yoshikawa Kōbunkan, 1964.

Lach, Donald F., and Edwin J. Van Kley. *Asia in the Making of Europe,* vol. III, *A Century of Advance,* book 4, *East Asia.* Chicago: University of Chicago Press, 1993.

Laures, Johannes. "Die Zahl der Christen und Martyrer im alten Japan." *Monumenta Nipponica* 7, no. 1–2 (1951): 84–101.

Ledyard, Gari. *The Dutch Come to Korea.* Seoul: Royal Asiatic Society, Korea Branch, 1971.

Leupe, P. A. *Reize van Maarten Gerritsz Vries in 1643 naar het Noorden en Oosten van Japan, volgens het journaal gehouden door C. J. Coen op het schip* Castricum. Amsterdam: Muller, 1858.

Levyssohn, David H. "Levensbijzonderheden van den legaat Pieter Blockhovius, met verzoek om nadere berigten omtrent deze rechtsgeleerde." *Themis* 14 (1853): 587.

Lönholm, L. "Arai Hakuseki und Pater Sidotti." *Mitteilungen der deutschen Gesellschaft für Natur- und Völkerkunde Ostasiens* 6, pt. 54 (1893): 149–189.

Lunsingh Scheurleer, Th. H. "Koperen kronen en waskaarsen voor Japan." *Oud Holland* 93 (1979): 69–95. A Japanese translation of this article by Dazai Takashi appeared under the title "Nikkō Tōshōgū no Oranda Tōrō—Nihon ni okurareta dōsei tōka to rōsoku" in *Nichiran gakkai kaishi* 5, no. 1 (1980): 3–32.

MacLeod, N. *De Oost-Indische Compagnie als zeemogendheid in Azië (1602–1650)*. Rijswijk: Blankwaardt & Schoonhoven, 1927.

Massarella, Derek. *A World Elsewhere: Europe's Encounter with Japan in the Sixteenth and Seventeenth Centuries*. New Haven and London: Yale University Press, 1990.

Matsui Yōko, and Reinier H. Hesselink. "Sakoku." In *Nichiran kōryū yonhyaku nen no rekishi to tenbō*, edited by Leonard Blussé, Willem Remmelink, and Ivo Smits, 39–71. Tokyo: Nichiran Gakkai (The Japan-Netherlands Institute), 2000.

Merklein, Johann Jacob. *Ost-Indianische Reise, welche er im Jahr 1644 löblich angonommen und im Jahr 1653 glücklich vollendet*. Printed as addition to the translation into German of Fr. Caron and Jod. Schouten, *Wahrhaftige Beschreibungen zweyer mächtigen Königreiche, Jappan und Siam*. Nürnberg: Michael und Joh. Friederich Endters, 1663.

Michel, Wolfgang. "Deshima rankan'i Kasuparu Shamuberugeru no shōgai ni tsuite." *Nihon ishigaku zasshi* 36, no. 3 (1990): 201–210.

———. "Caspar Schambergers Reisen nach Edo." *Dokufutsu bungaku kenkyū* 42 (1992): 1–85.

———. "Willem Bijlevelt no kinsen suitōbo." *Yōgakushi kenkyū* 10 (1993): 38–81.

Mitamura Engyo. *Zenshū*. Tokyo: Chūō Kōronsha, 1976.

Miwa Zennosuke. "Chikuzen to Okamoto San'emon." *Fukuoka* 44 (1914): 28–29.

Montanus, Arnoldus. *Gedenkwaerdige Gesantschappen der Oost-Indische Maatschappy in't Vereenigde Nederland aan de Keisaren van Japan*. Amsterdam: Jacob Van Meurs, 1669.

Murakami Naojirō. *Nagasaki Oranda shōkan no nikki*. 3 vols. Tokyo: Iwanami shoten, 1956–1958.

Nachod, Oskar. *Die Beziehungen der Niederländischen Ostindischen Kompagnie zu Japan im siebzehnten Jahrhundert*. Leipzig: Friese, 1897.

———. "Ein unentdecktes Goldland." *Mitteilungen der deutschen Gesellschaft für Natur- und Völkerkunde Ostasiens* (1900): 372–385.

Nagazumi Yōko. *Nambu Hyōchakuki*. Tokyo: Kirishitan Bunka Kenkyūkai, 1974.

———. "Inoue Chikugo no kami Masashige to rangaku." *Rangaku shiryō kenkyūkai kenkyū hōkoku* 292A (15 March 1975): 7–9.

———. "Orandajin no hogosha to shite no Inoue Chikugo no kami Masashige." *Nihon rekishi* 327 (Aug. 1975): 1–16.

———. *Kinsei shoki no gaikō*. Tokyo: Sōbunsha, 1990.

———. *'Sakoku' wo minaosu*. Tokyo: Yamakawa Shuppansha, 1999.

Naitō Akira. *Edozu byōbu*. Tokyo: Heibonsha, 1972.

Nijman, D. G "Louis de Geer (1587–1652), vader van de Zweedse industrie?" *Tijdschrift voor Geschiedenis* 104 (1991): 213–232.

Okada Hajime. *Haifū Yanagidaru zenshū*. Tokyo: Sanseidō, 1977.

Omaru Isamu. *Byōsekigaku kara mita Matsudaira Tadanao, Tokugawa Iemitsu, Tokugawa Tsunayoshi*. Tokyo: Rekishi Toshosha, 1970.

Ōno Kiyoshi. *Tokugawa seido shiryō*. Tokyo: the author, 1927.

Ooms, Herman. *Tokugawa Ideology: Early Constructs 1560–1680.* Princeton, N.J.: Princeton University Press, 1985.

Oosterhof, Noor. "De politieke en bestuurlijke struktuur van de Vereenigde Oost-Indische Compagnie." In *De Verenigde Oostindische Compagnie in Amsterdam,* edited by F. M. Wieringa, 155–188. Amsterdam: Universiteit van Amsterdam, 1982.

Opstall, Margaretha van. *De reis van de vloot van Pieter Willemsz Verhoeff naar Azië 1607–1614.* The Hague: Nijhoff, 1972.

Ōta Kōtarō. *Nambu sōsho.* Morioka: Nambusōsho kankōkai, 1927.

Pagès, Léon. *Histoire de la religion chrétienne au Japon.* 2 vols. Paris: Douniol, 1869.

Pflugfelder, Gregory M. *Cartographies of Desire: Male-male Sexuality in Japanese Discourse 1600–1950.* Berkeley, Los Angeles, and London: University of California Press, 1999.

Plas, C. C. van der. "Tonkin 1644/45. Journaal van de reis van Antonio Brouckhorst." *Mededeling no. 51 van het Koninklijk Instituut voor de Tropen.* Amsterdam, 1955.

Pott, P. H. "Willem Versteegen, een extra ordinaris Raad van Indië als avonturier in India in 1659." *Bijdragen tot de Taal-, Land-, en Volkenkunde van Nederlands Indië* 112 (1956): 355–382.

Posthumus Meyes, R. *De reizen van Abel Janszoon Tasman en Franchoys Jacobszoon Visscher ter nadere ontdekking van het Zuidland in 1642–3 en 1644.* Linschoten Vereniging 17. The Hague: Nijhoff, 1919.

Ricci, Matteo. *China in the Sixteenth Century: The Journals of Matteo Ricci: 1583–1610.* Translated from the Latin by Louis J. Gallagher. New York: Random House, 1953.

Robinson, Kenneth R. "The Jiubian and Ezogachishima Embassies to Choson, 1478–1482." *Chōsenshi kenkyūkai ronbunshū* 35 (1997): 55–86.

Roessingh, Marius P. H. *The Archive of the Dutch Factory in Japan 1609–1860.* The Hague: Algemeen Rijksarchief (Dutch National Archives), 1964.

———. "The Prisoners of Nambu." In History Papers Hague Conference, edited by Ian Nish. *Supplement to the Bulletin of the European Association for Japanese Studies* 23 (1985): 18–26.

Ruiz-de-Medina, Juan. *El martirologio del Japon 1558–1873.* Rome (Roma): Institutum Historicum S. I., 1999.

Sahlins, Marshall. "The Apotheosis of Captain Cook." In *Between Belief and Transgression. Structuralist Essays in Religion, History, and Myth,* edited by Michel Izard and Pierre Smith, 73–102. Translated by John Leavitt. Chicago: University of Chicago Press, 1982.

———. "Captain James Cook; or The Dying God." In *Islands of History,* 104–135. Chicago: University of Chicago Press, 1985.

Sakai, Robert K. "The Satsuma-Ryukyu Trade and the Tokugawa Seclusion Policy." *Journal of Asian Studies* 23 (1964): 391–403.

———. "The Ryukyu Islands as a Fief of Satsuma." In *The Chinese World Order,* edited by John K. Fairbank, 112–134. Cambridge, Mass.: Harvard University Press, 1968.

Satō Hitoshi. *Yamada ura Orandasen nyūshin no tsuiseki.* Miyako: the author, 1986.

Satō Rokuzō. *Ōsawa mura sonshi gaiyō*. Morioka: Ōsawa Shōgakkō, 1936.

Sawauchi Kenji. *Zoku Hanawa Tono Sama: Nambu Nijūkyūdai Shigenobu no shūhen*. Miyako: the author, 1996.

Schlegel, G. "De betrekkingen tusschen Nederland en China volgens Chineesche bronnen." *Tijdschrift van het Koninklijk Instituut voor de Taal-, Land-, en Volkenkunde van Nederlandsch Indië*, 5th series, 8 (1893): 1–32.

Schütte, J. F. *Introductio ad historiam societatis Jesu in Japonia, 1549–1650*. Rome (Roma): Institutus Historicus Societatis Jesu, 1968.

Screech, Timon. *The Western Scientific Gaze and Popular Imagery in Later Edo Japan: The Lens within the Heart*. New York: Cambridge University Press, 1996.

Serruys, Henry. *Sino-Mongol Relations during the Ming II: The Tribute System and Diplomatic Missions (1400–1600)*. Brussels: Institut Belge des Hautes Études Chinoises, 1967.

Shiryōhensanjo, ed. *Nihon kankei kaigai shiryō: Historical Documents in Foreign Languages Relating to Japan (Original Texts), Selection 1: Diaries Kept by the Heads of the Dutch Factory in Japan*. 9 vols. Tokyo: The University Tokyo Press, 1974–1999.

Siebold, Philip Franz von. "Chrônique." In *Le Moniteur des Indes Orientales et Occidentales*, 390–408. The Hague: Belinfante, 1849.

———. *Geschichte der Entdeckungen im Seegebiete von Japan*. Leiden: the author, 1852.

———. *Geographical and Ethnographical Elucidations to the Discoveries of Maerten Gerritsz Vries, Commander of the Flute Castricum A.D. 1643 in the East and North of Japan*. Translated from the Dutch by F. M. Cowan. Amsterdam: Muller, 1859.

Smits, Gregory. "The Sages' Scale in Japan: Nakae Tōju (1608–1648) and Situational Weighing." *Transactions of the Asiatic Society of Japan*, 4th series, 6 (1991): 1–26.

———. "The Intersection of Politics and Thought in Ryukyuan Confucianism: Sai On's Uses of *Quan*." *Harvard Journal of Asiatic Studies* 56, no. 2 (1996): 443–477.

———. *Visions of Ryukyu: Identity and Ideology in Early Modern Thought and Politics*. Honolulu: University of Hawai'i Press, 1999.

Sōda Hajime. "Rankan'i Kasuparu saikō." *Rangaku shiryō kenkyū hōkoku* 188 (1966): 193–199; 196 (1967): 183–185.

———. *Zusetsu Nihon iryō bunkashi*. Kyoto: Shibunkaku, 1989.

Stapel, F. W. "François Caron." *De Indische Gids* 55 (1933): 385–403.

———. "De historie van Japan en de verhouding met Nederlandsch-Indië." In *Van vriend tot vijand. De betrekkingen tusschen Nederlandsch-Indië en Japan*, edited by A. C. D. de Graeff, 1–68. Amsterdam: Elsevier, 1945.

Tamai Tetsuo. *Edo: ushinawareta toshi kūkan wo yomu*. Tokyo: Heibonsha, 1986.

Tashiro Kazui. "Foreign Relations during the Edo Period: Sakoku Reexamined." *Journal of Japanese Studies* 8, no. 2 (1982): 283–306.

———. *Kakikaerareta kokusho: Tokugawa Chōsen gaikō no butai ura*. Tokyo: Chūō Kōronsha, 1983.

———. Review of *State and Diplomacy in Early Modern Japan*. *Journal of Japanese Studies* 13, no. 1 (1987): 195–200.

Tashiro Kazui, and Yonetani Hiroshi. "Sōke kyūzō 'tosho' to mokuin." *Chōsen gakuhō* 156 (July 1995): 13–96.

Thurston, Herbert. "Japan and Christianity. IV The Mystery of the Five Last Jesuits in Japan." *The Month* (May 1905): 505–525.

Tjoa, Miao-ling. "Sakoku: The Full Range of Tokugawa Foreign Relations?" In *As the Twig Is Bent... Essays in Honour of Frits Vos*, edited by Erica de Poorter, 209–236. Amsterdam: Gieben, 1990.

Toby, Ronald P. "Reopening the Question of *Sakoku*: Diplomacy in the Legitimation of the Tokugawa Bakufu." *Journal of Japanese Studies* 3, no. 2 (1977): 323–363.

———. *State and Diplomacy in Early Modern Japan: Asia in the Development of the Tokugawa Bakufu*. Princeton, N.J.: Princeton University Press, 1984.

———. "Carnival of the Aliens, Korean Embassies in Edo Period Art and Popular Culture." *Monumenta Nipponica* 41, no. 4 (1986): 415–456.

Tōkyō shiyakusho, ed. *Tōkyō shishi kō*. Tokyo: Hakubunkan, 1912.

Totman, Conrad. *Politics in the Tokugawa Bakufu 1600–1843*. Cambridge, Mass.: Harvard University Press, 1967.

———. *Early Modern Japan*. Berkeley and London: University of California Press, 1993.

Tsuji Tatsuya. *Edo kaifu*. Tokyo: Chūō Kōronsha, 1966.

Tsunoda, Ryūsaku, and L. Carrington Goodrich. *Japan in the Chinese Dynastic Histories*. South Pasadena: Perkins, 1951.

Tsuruta Kei. "Kinsei Nihon no yotsu no 'kuchi'." In *Ajia no naka no Nihonshi*, vol. 2: *Gaikō to sensō*, edited by Arano Yoshinori, Ishii Masatoshi, and Murai Shōsuke, 297–316. Tokyo: Tōkyō daigaku shuppankai, 1992.

Valentijn, François. *Oud en Nieuw Oost-Indiën*. Dordrecht: Joannes van Braam; Amsterdam: Gerard onder de Linden, 1726.

Verseput, J. *De reis van Matthijs Quast en Abel Jansz Tasman ter ontdekking van de Goud- en Zilvereilanden*. Linschoten Vereniging 56. The Hague: Nijhoff, 1954.

Vixseboxse, J. *Een Hollandsch gezantschap naar China in de zeventiende eeuw (1685–1687)*. Leiden: E. J. Brill, 1946.

Vos, Frits. "From God to Apostate: Medicine in Japan before the Caspar School." In *Red-Hair Medicine. Dutch-Japanese Medical Relations*, edited by H. Beukers, A. M. Luyendijk-Elshout, M. E. van Opstall, and F. Vos, 9–26. Amsterdam: Rodopi, 1991.

Voss, Gustav, and Hubert Cieslik. *Kirishitoki und Sayo-Yōroku. Japanische Dokumente zur Missionsgeschichte des 17. Jahrhunderts*. Tokyo: Sophia University, 1940.

Wang Yi-t'ung. *Official Relations between China and Japan*. Cambridge, Mass.: Harvard University Press, 1953.

Willman, Oloff Erichszon. *Een kort Beskriffning uppa Trenne Reesor och Peregrinationer sampt Koningarijker Japan*. Witsindzborg: Hans Hoeg, 1674.

Wills, John E. "Ch'ing Relations with the Dutch, 1662–1690." In *The Chinese World Order*, edited by John K. Fairbank, 225–256. Cambridge, Mass.: Harvard University Press, 1968.

———. *Pepper, Guns, and Parleys: The Dutch East India Company and China, 1662–1681*. Cambridge, Mass.: Harvard University Press, 1974.

———. *Embassies and Illusions: Dutch and Portuguese Envoys to K'ang-hsi (1666–1687)*. Cambridge, Mass.: Council on East Asian Studies, Harvard University, 1984.

Witsen, Nicolaes. *Noord en Oost Tartarije ofte bondigh ontwerp van eenige dier landen en volken welke voormaels bekent zijn geweest*. Amsterdam: Halma, 1692, 1705.

Yamadachōshi hensan iinkai, ed. *Yamadachōshi*. Yamada (Iwate prefecture): Yamadachō Kyōiku iinkai, 1986.

Yamamoto Hirofumi. *Kan'ei jidai*. Tokyo: Yoshikawa Kōbunkan, 1989.

———. *Bakuhansei no seiritsu to kinsei no kokusei*. Tokyo: Azekura Shobō, 1990.

———. *Junshi no kōzō*. Tokyo: Kōbundō, 1994.

———. *Sakoku to kaikin no jidai*. Tokyo: Azekura Shobō, 1995.

Yonetani Hiroshi. "Kinsei shoki Nitchō kankei ni okeru gaikō monjo no gisaku to kaizan." *Waseda daigaku daigaku'in bungaku kenkyūka kiyō* 41, no. 4 (1996): 1–33.

———. "16 seiki Nitchō kankei ni okeru gishi haken no kōzō to jittai." *Rekishigaku kenkyū* 697 (1997): 1–18.

Yoshida Yoshiaki, and Oyokawa Kazuya, eds. *Morioka yonhyakunen*. Morioka: Kyōdo bunka kenkyūkai, 1985.

Yukutake Kazuhiro. "Deshima Oranda shōkan no kaikeichōbo." *Shakai keizai shigaku* 517, no. 6 (1992): 59–98.

Index